# Before the English Civil War

# Before the English Civil War

## Essays on Early Stuart Politics and Government

EDITED BY

### HOWARD TOMLINSON

MACMILLAN PRESS
LONDON

First published 1983 by
THE MACMILLAN PRESS LTD
London and Basingstoke
Companies and representatives throughout the world

ISBN 0 333 30898 0 (hc)
ISBN 0 333 30899 9 (pbk)

Printed in Hong Kong

*To All Wellingtonian*
*and Old Wellingtonian Historians*

# Contents

# Note

The year is taken to begin on 1 January, but in other respects the 'Old Style' is used. Spelling and punctuation have been modernised throughout.

# Preface

NEARLY twenty years ago my history master issued me with G. M. Trevelyan's *England Under the Stuarts* and J. R. Tanner's *Constitutional Conflicts of the Seventeenth Century* to begin my study of seventeenth-century English history. These were both excellent works in their way, and judging by the number of reprints they are still in demand, but they were outdated, even in the mid-1960s. Students now are better served than I was by way of introduction to the early Stuart period. But even to-day, the most recent and best of the textbooks to be published on the period, Robert Ashton's *The English Civil War, 1603–49* (1978) and Barry Coward's *The Stuart Age* (1980), are inadequate, such is the turnover in seventeenth-century historical scholarship. Indeed since I began teaching this period as an 'A' level special subject nearly six years ago, the booklist has had to be constantly revised by the Oxford and Cambridge Board, and the title (although not the content) of the paper changed, in the best revisionist manner, from 'The Causes of the English Civil War, 1603–42' to 'Politics, Religion and Society in England, 1603–42'. I have edited these essays, therefore, in the hope that newcomers to the period might be acquainted with the latest research on some of the major topics of early Stuart government. Having tasted these fruits it is not inconceivable that they might be tempted to look beyond them.

Schoolmasters these days do not have much leisure during term-time to devote to literary pursuits and this has put me under a greater obligation than usual to publisher and contributors alike, all of whom have had to take second place to my pupils. I am grateful for their patience in awaiting the publication of this volume. In particular, I would like to thank Sarah Mahaffy, of Macmillan, for her enthusiastic response to my initial proposal for this book and for her care in seeing it

through its final stages; and Conrad Russell and Kevin Sharpe
for their suggestions as to contributors and their helpful
criticism of the first draft of my chapter. Conrad Russell's
letters from across the Atlantic, too, were a constant source of
encouragement. Peter White of Wellington College also made
some perceptive comments about my chapter, and has been
and continues to be an inspiring colleague. Other Wellington
historians have done more than they know in making this
volume possible, and another Wellington connection, Jean
Fox, my typist, coped magnificently with my badly mutilated
manuscript. But my greatest debt is to my family: my four
children, who have been a pleasant and necessary diversion
from editorial duties; and, above all, to my wife, who during
the time this book has been in preparation not only has
continued to write and teach, but also has borne more than her
fair share of parental responsibilities. That she has found time,
as well, to read my contributions to this volume, thereby saving
me from many textual errors, is a matter of some wonder.
Although my writing has not whetted her appetite for
seventeenth-century history, she has sustained all her burdens
with characteristic cheerfulness.

*Wellington College, Berkshire*          HOWARD TOMLINSON
*September 1982*

# Introduction

In the last few years there have been a number of editions of essays published on the early Stuarts. *The Origins of the English Civil War* and *Faction and Parliament*[1] are among the most important of these. Although this collection contains chapters by the editors of these two volumes, it does not seek to rival them. We are not dealing with one particular theme and these essays are of a more general nature. *The English Civil War and After*[2] might afford a closer comparison with this volume, and not simply because both collections have been edited by schoolmasters.

The title, *Before the English Civil War*, may require some further explanation. It is not intended to suggest a Whiggish stance on behalf of the editor or any of the other authors. Indeed, it would be paradoxical, to say the least, if this was intended, as the book contains essays by Conrad Russell and Kevin Sharpe, two leading revisionists,[3] and another by Anthony Fletcher, who in his latest book[4] argues convincingly that the Civil War was by no means inevitable. The title therefore simply describes the period under review and does not carry any implication of an impending drift towards civil war: the history of the early seventeenth century is presented here, as in *Faction and Parliament* 'from the perspective of the early Stuart period itself'.

I make no claim that this is a comprehensive survey. It will not take much searching to find that there are no chapters dealing specifically with, for example, social, economic, legal or cultural matters. Nor does each author necessarily attempt to synthesise the state of current research: an impossible task in some fields as will be seen from the first chapter. What I do suggest, however, is that each chapter deals with a subject of immense importance to an understanding of the period as a whole, and involves some reassessment of early Stuart politics and government.

1

The case for a re-examination of the policies and role of James I and Charles I is made in the chapters by Patrick Collinson, Kevin Sharpe and Simon Adams.

Patrick Collinson emphasises that the Hampton Court Conference should be seen 'as a kind of round-table conference on a variety of ecclesiastical topics rather than as a debate between two sides'. There were good reasons for the king's celebrated outburst on the second day and in any case this was untypical of the nature of the rest of the proceedings. He suggests that we should not see early seventeenth-century ecclesiastical history in terms of a 'relentless struggle' and that there was essential unity in the 'substance of religion' at least until James I's death.[5] As far as James himself is concerned we are left with the impression of a king who could be shrewd in his judgement of character and who was actively concerned with the state of the English church: Gardiner's depiction of the conference revealing 'the essential littleness of the man' is hardly borne out by this examination.

James I's son hardly possessed his father's acumen, but we are led to understand through Kevin Sharpe's sympathetic account of Charles I's Personal Rule that it is of prime importance that we take into account the circumstances of his monarchy before denigrating his abilities as king: his decisions to rule without parliament in 1629 and to go to war against the Scots, for example, were at least understandable to many contemporaries of the period. Nor was Charles's Personal Rule quite so sterile as some historians have claimed. Indeed, Kevin Sharpe presents the period as one of active and, in many cases, effective government, which mirrored the king's ideals for an ordered society. That the king's schemes ultimately failed, Kevin Sharpe suggests, is no reason to depict them as being necessarily those of a utopian dreamer, cocooned in his court.

One of the major reasons for Charles's decision to dissolve parliament in 1629 was its reluctance to finance a war which it had advocated. Simon Adams, indeed, sees the crown's conduct of foreign policy throughout the period as being hampered by financial constraints which severely limited its freedom of manoeuvre. The second major influence on foreign policy, he observes, was ideological and prompted by the outbreak of the Thirty Years War in Europe. The belief that a

continental catholic league for the extermination of heresy had
been created which could only be countered by a protestant
alliance was widely shared but was not accepted by either
James or Charles. Again, Simon Adams, unlike some historians, convincingly shows that both kings had good reasons to
avoid 'confessional confrontation', but the resultant tensions
between the crown and many of its most influential subjects
produced bitter factional rivalries unknown in Elizabeth's
reign. This, together with the other constraints, prevented the
pursual of an effective and consistent foreign policy.

In the remaining chapters of this book, David Thomas,
Conrad Russell and Anthony Fletcher deal more specifically
with the structure of the early Stuart state. David Thomas
describes the elaborate balancing act required to ensure that
the crown's expenses did not exceed its receipts. At the start of
the period the scales seemed to be fairly evenly weighted: peace
meant that customs revenue would increase and defence
spending decline, and there was considerable potential for
further sources of income. That this inheritance was
squandered and the strenuous efforts made by senior crown
officials to cut spending and increase revenue failed was not
due entirely to James's extravagance and lack of royal support.
Structural weaknesses – the way in which the crown paid its
servants, the terms of their appointment and their corruption –
were also responsible for the crown's difficulties, as was
(albeit unknowingly) parliament. Attempts to alter radically
the financial system through appeals to parliament – and
here David Thomas puts the Great Contract in context –
floundered, and the numerous parliamentary subsidies
granted in the 1620s were insufficient to meet the real costs of
war. As in Kevin Sharpe's chapter, the 1630s are presented
here as a time of governmental reform and financial
innovation, but the obstacles to sound government remained.

Conrad Russell's important chapter continues his reassessment of parliament, or, more accurately, those 'irregularly
recurring events called parliaments'. For, as he observes, such
is the strength of the Whig tradition that we need to be
constantly on guard against anachronism. We need to be reminded that for this period the king was a member of parliament; there was no separation of powers between the executive

and the legislature; legislation was not necessarily a key part of government; parliaments were summoned by the king's writ and existed during his pleasure, their powers being derived from and exercised through him; the reasons for calling parliaments all had something to do with consent; MPs were aware of their own impermanence; not every gentleman wanted to be an MP; the parliamentary system was brought to the verge of extinction because it had proved so inadequate; and strongly held parliamentary convictions did not necessarily have to be opposition ones – at least until the end of 1641. Not the least of Conrad Russell's contributions in this chapter, however, is his observation that by the end of the period we are in a different world. The importance of parliaments to Englishmen, he suggests, alters in direct proportion to the state of the kingdom, so that in unsettled times, as at a time of disputed succession, royal minority or, as in Charles's case, the end of Personal Rule, 'people reach for a parliament to put things together again'. But even then, he emphasises, it is not until the passage of the Triennial Act and the Act against Dissolution that we break new ground in what it might now be legitimate to term parliamentary history.

The notion of a county community has also been the subject of some recent academic controversy. In the last chapter of this book, however, Anthony Fletcher, while not denying the reality of other kinds of community, defends the importance of the county communities because 'they were the principal unit of local government and politics'. More research will be needed before a full answer is possible to the questions of how national political awareness emerged and why it appears to have developed much more rapidly in some counties than in others, but Anthony Fletcher's survey is a more sophisticated interpretation than has been attempted hitherto. The importance of this chapter should not be underestimated. As Anthony Fletcher indicates, the energetic involvement of some localities in the political crisis of the early 1640s does not explain why a civil war broke out in 1642 but it did make it possible for both Charles and Pym to contemplate a resort to arms.

Overall, two things especially emerge from this group of essays. First, that the workings of early Stuart politics and government were much more complex than was once thought.

The simplistic judgements of the old Whig school will not do for this generation: revisionists and neo-Whigs agree about this if about nothing else. All our contributors have shown that we need to examine the mentality of the period – or in Patrick Collinson's words, 'the legal and institutional rigidities of early seventeenth-century society' – before judging the success or failure of the early Stuarts, whether in church reform, financial management or foreign policy. The second point brought out clearly by all contributors is that the early Stuarts were not doomed to failure and that the Civil War was, to quote Anthony Fletcher's last line, a 'most surprising and unintended catastrophe'. Patrick Collinson denies the existence of a 'high road to civil war' as far as Jacobean ecclesiastical affairs are concerned. Kevin Sharpe, like Clarendon, stresses that there was nothing inevitable about the collapse of Charles's Personal Rule, while Simon Adams emphasises that the foreign policy of the early Stuarts was, at worst, not without a certain logic. We see from David Thomas's survey the potential that existed from Crown revenue in 1603 – a potential that was, in part, successfully tapped in the 1630s. Finally, Conrad Russell suggests that not until late 1641 was it clear to Charles's inner circle of advisers 'that a strong and principled attachment to parliaments was incompatible with Charles's service'. Perhaps behind this phrase lies the story of the real origins of the English Civil War.

These are independent judgements; they are not presented as those of a revisionist 'school' of historians. Nor are they expected to be definitive. Indeed, if I have learnt one thing from my opening historiographical survey, it is the historian's need for humility.

# 1.  The Causes of War: A Historiographical Survey

## HOWARD TOMLINSON

It will be wondered at hereafter, that in a judging and discerning state, where men had, or seemed to have, their faculties of reason and understanding at the height; in a kingdom then unapt and generally uninclined to war .... those men who had the skill and cunning, out of froward and peevish humour and indispositions, to compound fears and jealousies and to animate and inflame those fears and jealousies into the most prodigious and the boldest rebellion that any age or country ever brought forth ....

> Clarendon, *Selections from the History of the Rebellion* ... ed. Hugh Trevor-Roper (Oxford, 1978), p. 224

And by these degrees came the House of Commons to raise that head which since hath been so high and formidable unto their princes that they have looked pale upon those assemblies. Nor was there anything now wanting unto the destruction of the throne but that the people, not apt to see their own strength, should be put to feel it, when a prince, as stiff in disputes as the nerve of monarchy was grown slack, received that unhappy encouragement from his clergy which became his utter ruin; while trusting more unto their logic than the rough philosophy of his parliament, it came unto an irreparable breach; for the house of peers, which alone had stood in this gap, now sinking down between the King and the Commons, showed that Crassus was dead and Isthmus broken. But a monarchy divested of her nobility

7

hath no refuge under heaven but an army. *Wherefore the dissolution of this government caused the war, not the war the dissolution of this government.*

> Harrington, 'The Commonwealth of Oceana' from *The Political Works of James Harrington*, ed. J. G. A. Pocock (Cambridge, 1977), p. 198

## I

CLARENDON'S *History of the Rebellion* and Harrington's *The Commonwealth of Oceana* are very different works. With the encouragement of Charles I, *The History of the Rebellion* was written deliberately – to counter the parliamentary history of Tom May – as an historical narrative 'of the grounds, circumstances and artifices of this rebellion' on the model of the great works of classical antiquity. Although it was, in part, a work of political philosophy, in that Clarendon sought to show that the misfortunes resulted 'from the same natural causes and means' as had taken place at other times and in other kingdoms, 'swollen with long plenty, pride and excess, towards some signal mortifications and castigation of heaven', its primary purpose was didactic – a warning about past mistakes and a guide to future actions. *The Commonwealth of Oceana*, on the other hand, is essentially a work of political theory. Like Clarendon's *History* it was probably composed for political purposes as a post-war defence of the Good Old Cause of 'constant successive parliaments, freely and equally chosen by the people', and in opposition to the Protectorate of Oliver Cromwell, but its form is that of a republican tract rather than of an historical narrative. *Oceana* sought to explain how England had become a commonwealth of independent free-holders and how this commonwealth should have been organised for government as a republic, but the historical content was essentially subordinate to the republican message. Unlike Clarendon, Harrington wrote teleologically: he fictionalises the history of England as that of *Oceana* 'to show the rise, progress and declination of modern prudence' in order to prove that the government's only recourse had been to form a republican commonwealth based on all its citizens.

Given the contrasting natures of the *History of the Rebellion* and *Oceana* it is not surprising to find that their interpretations of the origins of the English Civil War are fundamentally different. As the opening extract indicates, Clarendon saw the reasons for the outbreak of hostilities as having been essentially short-term. He started the narrative in 1625, but it is quite clear that he believed war was by no means inevitable from that date. To Clarendon the kingdom (in the 1630s) enjoyed 'the greatest calm and the fullest measure of felicity that any people in any age, for so long time together, have been blessed with, to the wonder and envy of all parts of Christendom'; in November 1640 'it was not imaginable' that the Long Parliament 'would have run the courses it afterwards did', and the majority of members 'consisted of men who had no mind to break the peace of the kingdom or to make any considerable alteration in the government of church or state'; and in November 1641 at the time of the Grand Remonstrance debates, the 'poor kingdom' was near 'to its deliverance'.[1] That this deliverance never happened was the result of 'several accidents' which contributed to 'the several successes' of a small disparate clique. But not even the leaders of this group 'who have been the grand instruments towards this change' had the 'industry and foresight' to contrive the rebellion.[2] Nor, indeed, did they want it. Pym, Hampden, Holles, St John and Essex were represented as essentially moderate men, who were driven to desperate ends by radicals, not because of the revolutionary situation in the country, but because of moral failure on both sides. Ultimately Clarendon's great rebellion was caused by the failings of all responsible sections of the community to perform their trust: King Charles 'whose kingly virtues had some mixture and allay that hindered them from shining in full lustre'; the king's principal counsellors, especially Henrietta Maria, the great lords and the judges, who at many critical stages up to the dismantling of the king's government in the early months of the Long Parliament had given such bad advice, and who, at the time of the attempted arrest of the five members, were not only working against the king's best interests, but also failing to consult his supporters in the Commons; members of parliament who 'by their supine laziness, negligence and absence' had allowed 'a handful of

men much inferior in the beginning, in number and interest
. . . to give laws to the major part'; and finally, by implication,
at least, the 'supine sottishness of the people' who allowed
themselves to be traduced.[3] Clarendon makes it clear that at
almost any stage of the crisis, good counsel (especially, one
feels, had it been given by himself) could have averted war, but
as this was lacking the country drifted into civil conflict.
Clarendon believed, therefore, that the English constitution
was intrinsically sound. It had simply been unhinged by
'perverse actions of folly and madness, making the weak to
contribute to the designs of the wicked, and suffering even
those, by degrees, out of the conscience of their guilt, to grow
more wicked than they intended to be'. But the wounds
inflicted by such perversions could, after a suitable period of
bloodletting, 'by God's mercy . . . be again bound up'.[4]

Harrington, by contrast, was far from thinking that at the
time of the Civil War the English constitution was basically
sound. Indeed, he believed that the rot had set in as early as
the reign of Henry VII (fictionalised as 'Panurgus') who by
initiating the statutes which deprived the nobility of their
military tenants and their right to recruit retainers 'first began
to open those sluices that have since overwhelmed not
the king only but the throne'. For Harrington argued that
the 'yeomanry or middle people' were beneficiaries of the
weakening in military status of the aristocracy and that the
crown was the loser. The yeomanry, freed from their military
dependence on the great lords and also aided materially by the
statute of alienations and the so-called 'new invention of
entails', gained in military strength and wealth; the crown,
faced by a *domos* of independent freeholders, no longer
depended on the strength of 'the few' and had no certain
means of power. From now onwards, Harrington suggests,
decline was inevitable. Coraunus (Henry VIII) further upset
'the balance of the commonwealth' by the dissolution of the
monasteries, bringing 'with the declining estate of the nobility
so vast a prey unto the industry of the people'. 'The wise
council of Queen Parthenia' (Elizabeth I) was too shrewd not to
appreciate the strength of the 'popular party', but the consequence of 'the perpetual love tricks that passed between her
and her people into a kind of romance' was that the nobility

became 'wholly neglected'. Thereafter, the last king of *Oceana* discovered that when there was an 'irreparable breach' – for which, Harrington hinted, the clergy were largely responsible – between ruler and ruled, as there was no longer an effective nobility, subjects could be controlled only through the use of force. The result of this conflict was a foregone conclusion: the king could not succeed by arms, which by 1642 had long been under his subjects' direction.[5]

Such an argument could hardly have been further from Clarendon's reasoning: where Clarendon stressed essentially short-term reasons for civil war, Harrington emphasised that the constitution had been undermined by the early Tudors; where Clarendon argued that the war could have been averted almost until the outbreak of hostilities, Harrington suggested that *at some point* conflict was inevitable; where Clarendon observed that strife stemmed from 'many concurrent causes', Harrington's explanation was essentially mono-causal; where Clarendon used a detailed political chronology to emphasise moral failings at all levels, Harrington concentrated on a broad social and economic argument, devised to fit his theory of republican government.

Notwithstanding these differences the *History of the Rebellion* and the *Commonwealth of Oceana* have this in common: both works are of fundamental importance in the evolution of the historiography of the English Civil War. Given this they may be taken to represent two distinct types of interpretation: the one that sees civil war arising out of personal failure; and the other that views the Civil War as essentially a product of social change. The historians who tend to favour the former explanation may be further subdivided into Whig historians who regarded the Stuarts as attempting innovations within the framework of English government and the sceptical Whigs, like Hume, who did not consider that there was an ancient constitution to subvert and who viewed the early Stuarts in a more favourable light.

## II

In an age when every writer was expected, in Gibbon's words, 'to hang out a badge of party', Hume's *History of Great Britain*, first published in 1754, stands out as a work apart. As a philosopher, Hume claimed to be above party, and considered that his displeasing 'the zealots of both parties' was a sign of his genuine impartiality. Indeed, as Duncan Forbes has shown,[6] Hume's work contained a fine blend of Whig and Tory elements. In his defence of traditional liberties Hume was decidedly Whiggish, but he believed that contemporary Whig historians had misinterpreted the seventeenth century, 'forgetting that a regard for liberty, though a laudable passion, ought commonly to be subordinate to a reverence for established government'. Justice, not liberty, was the object for which government was established and this was obtained by the crown's firm guidance of the national will.

Charles I, therefore, may have in some respects violated public liberty – although ultimately it was the religious puritans who made civil war inevitable – but he could not justly be accused of having destroyed a fixed constitution, since the constitution was not absolute and might have developed in unpredictable ways. Thus Hume's *History* is detached; it lacks pride in English institutions; and it is essentially non-progressive – to Hume there was nothing inevitable about the progress of civilisation or the successful establishment of political liberty.

For well over half a century Hume's *History* remained the most influential work on seventeenth-century England. Indeed, for successive Whig historians such as Charles James Fox, George Brodie and Henry Hallam, Hume was a 'felt presence'[7] and an obvious subject for attack. Despite their broadsides, Hume's *History* survived in popular esteem at least until the mid-nineteenth century and the publication of the great masterpiece of Whig historiography, Macaulay's *History of England* (1848–61). Macaulay deliberately set out to demolish Hume's reputation and condescendingly described him as 'an accomplished advocate' whose work was nothing more than a 'vast mass of sophistry'.[8] Although, as Professor Burrow has pointed out,[9] Macaulay was in some respects distinctly Humean, he offered a view that fundamentally undermined Hume's dispassionate, cosmopolitan approach to English history. According to Macaulay the English constitution was in a state of continuing development. English liberties had originated in the thirteenth century when England had become a nation, but the old constitution could not be preserved unaltered and by the seventeenth century there was need for redefinition. By then the crucial question was 'not whether our policy should undergo a change but what the nature of the change should be'. As for Harrington and Hume, the medieval constitutional equilibrium had been tilted by a shift in the military balance between crown and subject. But for Macaulay the key was the rise of professional standing armies rather than the decline of feudalism. The likelihood was that by the early seventeenth century the English king would, as on the continent, have gained an independent military force that would have turned him into an absolute monarch, unless 'placed under restraints to which no Plantagenet or Tudor had ever been subject'. It was this threat which had justified the actions of the Long Parliament and ultimately led to civil war. Given Charles I's 'faithlessness' 'contempt of the law' and 'habitual perfidy', and the lack of a reversionary interest around which opposition forces might have rallied, no other course could have been followed.[10]

The academic standing of Macaulay's *History*, however, did not long survive the publication of the final volume, which appeared (in 1861) at a time when the nature of English historical scholarship was undergoing a profound change. The German historian, Leopold von Ranke, was perhaps the most important continental influence on this development. His *History of England* was written in the 1860s at the height of his powers, and may be regarded as the culmination of a life spent writing the histories of and tracing the diplomatic links between the states of Europe. As a consequence of this, his English *History* bristles with continental comparisons and insights, and this is perhaps its greatest strength. But more important, as far as English historiography is concerned, is the manner of its composition. Not only was it written dispassionately but it was also based on an extensive use of English and European primary source material, appropriately referenced and partly laid out in extensive critical appendices.[11] Two further influences on the development of the English historiography were, first, the creation of distinct schools of history at the universities of Cambridge and Oxford – where William Stubbs in his inaugural lecture as regius professor characterised his predecessors as 'men to whom the study of history ... is in ... [no] way indebted';[12] and second, the increasing accessibility of primary source material: the new Public Record Office was opened in 1862 and the Historical Manuscripts Commission was founded in 1869.

The swing in fashion away from literary and towards 'scientific' history may be traced by comparing the different receptions given to S. R. Gardiner's *History of England from the Accession of James I* at each stage of its publication. In 1863, after the first two volumes had appeared, the *Athenaeum* reviewer could condemn Gardiner for belonging to 'the dry old school of historical writing, in which facts stood for ideas and dates for pictures'. 'We do not every day meet an author with whom we could so easily agree,' he continued 'if, in reading him, we could only keep awake.' Six years later the next two volumes were no more cordially received, but in 1875, after the appearance of two further instalments, even the *Athenaeum* found Gardiner's treatment 'dignified and impartial'.[13] Thereafter, Gardiner's success was assured and praise grew with the appearance of every volume. On the other hand, by 1882, Macaulay's *History* was criticised as being 'unhistorical'.[14]

Gardiner did indeed bring new dimensions to the writing of history: his historical methodology differed markedly from previous seventeenth-century English historians. Gardiner claimed that he was concerned to do justice to both Whig and Tory viewpoints, or at least not to misinterpret them, by avoiding 'the constant avowed or unavowed comparison' of past with present. Professor Seeley, who in 1873 instituted the Historical Tripos at Cambridge, and von Ranke were singled out as his mentors in this respect. Their approach to historical research was directly contrasted with that of Macaulay and another contemporary Whig historian, John Forster, whose attitude to the development of the past was condemned as being 'altogether destructive of real historical knowledge'.[15] As a consequence of these beliefs and in a conscious attempt to avoid bias, Gardiner adopted a strictly chronological approach in order to try to establish, by the testing of all the available evidence, the true course of events. He reacted strongly against Macaulay's use of hindsight and deliberately put out of his mind his knowledge of succeeding events, thereby attempting 'to put himself in the position, without the partisanship, of a contemporary and to watch events as they unfolded under his gaze'.[16] Any deep analysis of causation was eschewed and comment was kept to a minimum. The results of Gardiner's methodology, however, were hardly scientific, despite his plea for 'the scientific study of history as a whole'.[17] Given the way he worked – writing quickly, sending off a few pages of manuscript at a time to the printers, rarely revising and bringing out his eighteen volumes over a period of nearly forty years – inconsistencies were inevitable. Objectivity, too, proved an impossible goal: Gardiner could escape neither the pulls of Whig historiography nor his own Liberal Nonconformist background. His sober tone and the wealth of detail he provided could not hide his lack of sympathy for the crown. Yet although it is easy both to cavil at some of his interpretations and to question his random use of concepts such as 'the nation' or 'the religious opposition', his *History of England* remains one of the masterpieces of Victorian scholarship. What is more, despite the fact that many of our present domestic sources, particularly parliamentary diaries, were unknown to Gardiner, on English issues his narrative – especially of the pre-civil-war years – has not been superseded. And on foreign questions he remains unchallenged – no historian of early seventeenth-century England has yet emulated his mastery of diplomatic sources. That he is still held in esteem by today's historians, of whatever tradition, is a mark of his great achievement.[18]

In the early twentieth century those historians who have attempted political explanations of the causes of the English Civil War – C. H. Firth, Godfrey Davies and G. M. Trevelyan were, perhaps, the most influential – in essence followed existing interpretations. Sir Charles Firth, an amanuensis and friend of Gardiner in his latter years, who in *The Last Years of the Protectorate* (1909) continued Gardiner's narrative down to 1658, largely agreed with the concept of a Puritan Revolution. Firth's student and collaborator, Godfrey Davies, on the other hand, was more sceptical. In the introduction to

*The Early Stuarts* (1937) Davies argued that the 'great rebellion' was a better label than the 'puritan revolution' and that 'the struggle, though at no time a class war, was to a large extent a revolution of the middle classes against personal government'. Nevertheless, like previous historians, Davies accepted the Whig progressive view that the change from personal rule to parliamentary government was 'preordained'. Trevelyan, in *England Under the Stuarts* (1904) – in some ways, especially in its breadth of vision, a finer book than the Davies volume – was less sure. Some transformation in the balance of the constitution, he argued, was probable in 1603, 'but whether in such a land liberty had still a chance of survival or whether the universal tide of monarchy in Europe would not after all prove irresistible even in England' very much depended on 'the hazard of events and . . . the prejudice and passion of men'. It was only with the meeting of the Long Parliament that 'the time had come when British freedom might be secured', but even then it was 'by no means the inevitable outcome'. Despite Trevelyan's hesitancy over the likelihood of the parliamentary constitutional victory, the reader is left in no doubt as to where the author's sympathies lay. As befitted the great-nephew of Macaulay, Trevelyan portrayed Pym and company as the patriots, 'enamoured of liberty, or of religion, or of loyalty each for her own sake, not as the handmaid of class greed'. 'This', Trevelyan continued, 'was the secret of the moral splendour of our great rebellion and our civil war.'[19] More than half a century later Trevelyan continued to adhere to the fundamentals of this interpretation, as he made clear in his introduction to the later revised edition of *England Under the Stuarts*.

But in the period intervening between Trevelyan's first and last prefaces to the book, many historians had moved away from political interpretations towards social and economic explanations of the Civil War.

## III

It was not that previous historians had neglected social history. One of Hume's fundamental themes was that the Commons owed its influence to the growth of commerce; Macaulay at the beginning of the *History of England* states his intention 'to relate the history of the people as well as the history of the government'; and two chapters of *England Under the Stuarts* are devoted to 'the general conditions of English life'. But of the historians so far mentioned, only Harrington regarded the outbreak of war as resulting *primarily* from social and economic tensions. And it was Harrington who was the starting point for the first twentieth-century economic theory of the causes of the civil war: the rise of the gentry.

It would be fair to postulate that Harrington and R. H. Tawney were both equally responsible for the gentry controversy. Tawney himself had rejected a purely political approach to history at an early stage of his academic career. He felt it did not explain the questions that he thought were worth asking – most famously answered in *Religion and the Rise of Capitalism* (1926) – about the development of society, and in particular the relationship between economic and political power. But it was not until his celebrated British Academy lecture of 1941 that he turned towards an economic explanation of the causes of the English Civil War. It was in this lecture that he placed Harrington in the forefront of what was to become one of the most keenly contested historical arguments of the post-war period. Tawney saw in Harrington a kindred spirit who not only believed that politics could only be properly understood with the aid of history, but who also adopted a determinist approach towards the English Civil War. He argued that Harrington's theory, whilst being simplistic, was, in so far as it explained 'the transference of political power in changes in the distribution of real property', the key to an understanding of the upheavals of the period. It is not my purpose here to discuss the details of the academic gladiatorial combat that took place over the next twenty years, as to whether the aristocracy declined and the gentry rose in fortune in the century before the Civil War.[20] Now that the storm has subsided, however, it is possible to place the debate in some sort of historiographical context. What is clear is that none of the leading participants succeeded in explaining the Civil War in economic terms. H. R. Trevor-Roper in his famous riposte took Tawney to task for leaving the great rebellion unexplained and divorcing social from political history.[21] But although he and some of the other leading gladiators, like Lawrence Stone, tried to use the findings from their investigations of aristocratic and gentry fortunes to explain the outbreak of war, none did so successfully. As in many academic debates assertions ran ahead of hard evidence. The results of the debate, however, were not entirely negative. As we shall see, Trevor-Roper's insistence on the importance of both court and country element in the crisis was a conceptual advance on which other historians were to build; and, more importantly, the very limitations of evidence cited by the leading participants in the 'storm over the gentry' were a stimulus for further research on the period.[22]

For a later generation of seventeenth-century historians, led by Christopher Hill, as for the Whigs and R. H. Tawney, history was not to be studied for its own sake but for the light it shed on present problems. Like Tawney, Hill, who started his career in the 1930s, soon became dissatisfied with the standard Victorian authorities and tried to replace them with a full-blown Marxist interpretation of the civil-war period. Hill's *The English Revolution*, published in 1940, was clearly a tract for the times, written in the shadow of fascism with the avowed intention of determining the significance of the English Revolution for his generation. Previous Whig and Tory interpretations were dismissed as 'one-sided' and instead the Civil War was presented as a class war and the English Revolution as a revolution by the bourgeoisie, a necessary stage in the overthrow of the feudal state and the free development of capitalism. Hill's later writings – especially those written in the aftermath of the Hungarian rising of 1956 – have been much less openly propagandist, but the Marxist interpretation of the civil-war period has not been abandoned. Hill's splendid text book, *The Century of Revolution* (1961), for example, is based on Marxist assumptions, and in an article written as late as the mid-1970s, he has argued that the English Revolution, *in its outcome*, was a bourgeois revolution in the Marxist sense. Even though it was brought about neither by the wishes of the bourgeoisie nor by the leaders of the Long Parliament, he emphasised that it was 'the ultimate consequence of stresses and strains produced by the rise of the capitalist mode of production'.[23]

It is indicative that in the above article Christopher Hill acknowledged his debt to two other Marxist historians, Eric Hobsbawm and Edward Thompson, rather than to one of his many students of seventeenth-century history. For, unlike Namier, Hill has not founded a historical school, and with the exception of Brian Manning[24] few scholars have followed Hill along the Marxist path. For historians brought up in post-war Britain it has been the growth of opportunity afforded by the opening up of new archives and new universities, rather than dogma, that has dictated the direction of early seventeenth-century research. This is shown by the plethora of scholars who are and have been engaged in county and regional studies, the stimulus for which was afforded in part by the gentry controversy, in part by the opening of new county record offices and private archives since 1945, and in part by the PhD hurdle.

Local historians had been drawn towards the seventeenth century long before 1945. Almost before the Civil War had ended a multitude of tracts and local histories appeared about the most dramatic events of the conflict, and the great county histories of the eighteenth century produced a mass of local information on the period. But it was not until the reign of Victoria, when a wide variety of local texts on the seventeenth century were made available, that there was a serious re-examination of the local history of the Civil War.[25] Few Victorian county studies are worthy of note but at the turn of the century Firth's Ford Lectures on the English soldier during the civil wars – later published as *Cromwell's Army* – influenced the writing of a number of scholarly county civil-war studies. Writing in the early 1930s, in the preface to *Cornwall in the Great Civil War and Interregnum*, Mary Coate, who acknowledged her debt to Firth, observed that the Civil War and Interregnum could 'only be fully understood through regional surveys of the country' and listed eight other such studies as having already appeared. The earliest of these works, such as Ernest Broxap's *The Great Civil War in Lancashire* (Manchester, 1910), are essentially narrative political and military studies; the best of them – Coate's *Cornwall* and A.C. Wood's *Nottinghamshire in the Civil War* (Oxford, 1937) – are analytical and also have a social dimension. These two studies in particular rise well above antiquarianism, but, whilst endeavouring 'to keep the parish pump linked up to the mainstream',[26] they do not seek to challenge or modify the interpretations of Gardiner and Firth. In recent years, however, local studies have done more than simply illustrate the accepted national picture.

In the case of local studies of gentry families the findings of a number of scholars have cast doubt on the general conclusions advanced either by Tawney or any of his adversaries. One historian has suggested that for his region 'the perdurable gentry' would be an appropriate description. In East Anglia, as also apparently in South Wales, the gentry 'endured' rather than 'prospered' or perished – continuity rather than change is the keynote in these regions. Other scholars have concluded that the fortunes of landowning families depended more on individual character than on any other factor – an observation which upsets any general theory of the rise and decline of sections of the gentry class as a whole.[27] Those historians examining county society and government on a wider plane have been no more content to accept the *status quo*. Indeed, the studies of Alan Everitt and his followers have revolutionised our understanding of the nature of seventeenth-century society. In *Suffolk and the Great Rebellion, The Community of Kent and the Great Rebellion* and a number of seminal articles,[28] Everitt rejected the traditional emphasis on central institutions and stressed the need to investigate the local world of the county community, which he saw as 'a self-conscious and coherent society with a distinct life of its own', developing at a different pace and in different ways from the economy of the country at large. 'In many respects', he wrote elsewhere, 'the England of 1640 resembled a union of partially independent county-states or communities.' The consequences of this for the traditional interpretation of seventeenth-century politics were immense. For whereas Gardiner and all the local studies that followed in his wake had assumed that 'the nation' was fully conscious of the actions of their national leader, Everitt and his school suggested that the political horizons of the gentry were limited by the boundaries of their own shire or their 'country'. According to Everitt, tensions in seventeenth-century society arose not because of the king's wilful disregard of the political feelings of the nation, which in Everitt's eyes did not exist, but because of 'the unresolved tension between the provincial's loyalty to his local world and his loyalty to the state'. Everitt's conceptualisation has not been without its critics but many young scholars owe him a considerable intellectual debt and partly as a result of his influence a new breed of local study, urban as well as rural, has been spawned.[29] This has, in turn, occasioned a reinterpretation of parliamentary politics.[30]

## IV

It is more difficult to summarise the present state of play in early seventeenth-century studies than it has been at any other time this century. This is not simply because of the post-war boom in books on the period, which one historian has recently characterised as being the academic equivalent to the Ruhr basin,[31] but mainly because there is no agreed stand-point from which to view England before the Civil War. Past 'progressive' interpretations, whether Whig or Marxist, have long since ceased to be wholly acceptable to many professional historians but no-one has come up with a satisfactory alternative. Oliver Cromwell's famous confession – 'I can tell you, sir, what I would not have but I cannot what I would' – may be considered an apt comment on the state of confusion in which historians of these decades find themselves,[32] were it not for the fact that many scholars cannot even agree on the extent to which they disapprove of the Whig interpretation, quite apart from what constitutes a revisionist[33] or how far revisionism should go.

Two attempts to construct alternative interpretations have met with hostile receptions. In *The Court and the Country: The Beginning of the English Revolution* (1969), Perez Zagorin built on a concept first used by Trevor-Roper in the gentry controversy, and in an essay on the 'general crisis' of the seventeenth century, he saw the Civil War in terms of a 'fundamental cleavage' within the governing elite between 'the crown and its adherents on the one side, and its opponents on the other', or, to use the labels that he identified were then in contemporary use, the court and the country. He thereby rejected the Marxist theory of class war but his teleological investigation of 'the organisation, tactics, principles and ideas of the movement of opposition to the Stuart regime ... from the formation of the country opposition in the 1620s to the emergence of the parliamentarian party in 1641–2' begged too many questions and directly underpinned the Whig account.[34]

Three years later Lawrence Stone published a much more far-reaching interpretation. He had been a scarred campaigner in the gentry debate and in his massive book on the aristocracy, published in 1965, he had argued that the 'socio-political breakdown of 1640–2' was in part made possible by the prior decline in the power and authority of the peerage.[35] By the time *The Causes of the English Revolution, 1529–1642*, had appeared in 1972, the reasons for the breakdown, according to Stone, had multiplied. All previous interpretations, he noted, from Clarendon's 'Great Rebellion', through Macaulay and the Whigs' and Gardiner's Puritan revolution, to the Marxists' bourgeois revolution and Trevor-Roper's 'revolution of despair', had 'a grain of truth', but each displayed only 'one face of a many-sided whole'. The truth, as Stone saw it, was much more complex, and this 'necessitated the construction of multiple helix chains of causation' which stretched far back into the reaches of the early Tudor period. This involved not only an examination of the long-term factors, the Tudor 'preconditions' for Revolution, but also an analysis of the 'precipitants', short-term errors of policy which made some modifications of the polity 'very probable', and the 'triggers' that caused the government to collapse and the country to drift towards civil war. The resultant hypothesis was that the Revolution was the consequence of a cumulative 'multiple dysfunction' in English society, government, religion, culture and, ultimately, politics. Thus, although in various passages Stone stressed that the outbreak of civil war was not inevitable – in his introduction, indeed, he notes that as an observer of the student upheavals of 1968 and 1970 he became conscious how those in authority might determine whether a

revolutionary mood would lead to 'physical violence' or
'peaceful accommodation' – the logical outcome of his neat
package of preconditions and precipitants was that opposition
to the crown grew in a linear progression from the Tudor
period onwards. Despite the apparent sophistication of Stone's
approach – the book contains a sociological chapter on theories
of revolution – in his analysis, as G. R. Elton pointed out, there
was nothing that would have surprised Gardiner or Pollard. 'It
is only by directing all developments towards the distant end of
1640', Elton continued, 'that the debates and dissatisfactions
which are the experience of any live society assume the guise of
necessary causes.'[36]

Over the course of the past twenty years, Professor Elton has
been instrumental in directing our attention away from 'a high
road to civil war'.[37] In his extended review of Zagorin's book,
for example, he raised important questions about the conflict.
Were the court and country labels really helpful in explaining
the political divisions of the period? Did many people want civil
war even as late as 1642? Was civil war, in any case, really so
out of the ordinary in the England of 1642? Perhaps con-
ceptually the most important articles were the three pieces
Elton published in the mid-1970s in the *Transactions of the
Royal Historical Society*, entitled 'Tudor Government: The
Points of Contact', in which he suggested that Tudor stability
depended on the sharing of power and that at all levels
mechanisms existed, particularly parliament and the court, 'to
give reality to the principle of participation'. If the Tudor
Parliaments were an instrument for stability rather than
opposition, and if the Tudor Court, rather than parliament,
was the centre of political conflict, the implications for the
early Stuart period were profound. Elton's conceptual block-
busters, together with the investigations of other scholars who
normally work in earlier periods, like J. S. Roskell and G. L.
Harriss – two medievalists who have made occasional forays
into the parliamentary history of the seventeenth century[38] –
prompted a direct challenge to the progressive interpretations
of the past. This was aided by the findings of historians of early
modern Europe, particularly J. H. Elliott and H. G. Koenigsberger,[39] who have examined the fortunes of continental
estates. Two themes, in particular, have proved influential in

the subsequent work of revision: first, that the problems between monarchs and European estates, especially after the outbreak of the Thirty Years War, can at least partly be attributed to the soaring demands for money to which the estates were subjected; and second, that the reasons for the survival and extinction of seventeenth-century European parliaments were less to do with rational developments, like institutional and procedural advances, than with unpredictable forces, such as the relationship between different parts of multiple kingdoms and external invasion.

It is ironic that Conrad Russell, an historian with the most impeccable Whig pedigree, should lead this revisionist challenge and paradoxical that a consciousness of this pedigree has assisted him in the process of revision.[40] Over the past few years his work has placed early Stuart parliaments in a much wider context than hitherto. His research has shown that a proper study of seventeenth-century parliaments cannot be made without consideration of the various pressures – particularly those produced by the strains of war – that acted on the members of those assemblies. Through his vision we see parliaments from the perspective of both government and local constituents. Russell's books and articles, together with the independent analysis of Kevin Sharpe and others,[41] have vigorously questioned the Whig orthodoxy. It is difficult to summarise their collective view: the revisionists should not be seen as 'a school' and the extent of agreement between them – particularly, perhaps, over the extent and influence of aristocratic patronage – should not be overemphasised. Yet it is fair to suggest that their researches have all questioned the power of parliament, the extent to which there was a permanent opposition in the Commons and whether the raising of major issues was not more influenced by court intrigues, local pressures and war than matters of principle or grand constitutional design. As a consequence, although they do not deny that the Apology, Bate's Case, the impeachments of the 1620s and the Petition of Right were important events, they reject the views of those who see them as great civil-war milestones, and suggest instead that the civil war was essentially 'an accidental war'.[42]

This reinterpretation has been so influential that one scholar has recently commented that 'examination scripts on both sides of the Atlantic show that his [Russell's] views are fast becoming the new orthodoxy'.[43] Whig interpretations are so deeply embedded in the historical consciousness of us all, however, that it is not surprising to find that the first sustained sweep of the seamless web of early Stuart history since Hume should have met with some resistance. Professors Hexter, Hirst and Rabb, among others, have clung to the essentials of the traditional interpretation.[44] Again, there is no complete agreement between the neo-Whigs: Hexter and Rabb, for instance, argue that there is a need to go back at least to 1604 'to find a coherent context for the succession of angry confrontations that took place in James's and Charles's reigns', whereas Hirst seems to suggest that the 1620s was the break point in the relationship between crown and parliament. Nonetheless, they would all stress the importance of continuity in explaining the Civil War. Moreover, they all emphasise the central position of parliament in the constitution and all insist that the tensions within that institution arose primarily from debates over issues of principle. Whilst they acknowledge a debt of gratitude to the revisionists for returning politics to the centre of the civil-war stage and for refining the traditional *simpliste* notions of the old Whig historians, they are not prepared to go along with Kevin Sharpe's view that we should be returning 'to the drawing board' rather than 'repairing the old canvas'.[45] It is again ironic that despite the vast mass of literature that has been written on this subject in recent years, despite our methodological advance in the use of other disciplines, such as economics, sociology and even psychology, to help interpret the past, and despite an increased sophistication in our use of conceptualisation and nomenclature, we are now little nearer agreement than were Clarendon and Tom May as to the causes of the Civil War.

It is too early to judge whether a consensus will emerge. First, agreement still needs to be reached about what we need to find causes for: a civil war or an English Revolution. Was the English Civil War an integral part of the English Revolution? Or was it merely a rebellion by the political elite to force Charles I's hand but not to overthrow him? *Pace* Harrington, did war cause 'the dissolution of this government' rather than being itself caused by 'the dissolution'? Second, more work needs to be done, particularly on the 1630s – the testing ground of non-parliamentary government – and the Long Parliament, 1640–2. As Conrad Russell observed ten years ago, before we attempt any analysis of why the Civil War broke out, we need to know how it broke out.[46] Historians have now had the 'foolhardiness' to try to update Gardiner but that work is still in progress. Third, a franker exchange is needed between the revisionists and the neo-Whigs. While the controversy has generally been conducted in a gentlemanly manner, it does, in part, resemble the storm over the gentry. Some of the neo-Whigs need to adopt a less acerbic tone – Professor Hexter's use of argument *ad extremas* resembles the rhetoric of his 'patriots' in the early seventeenth-century Commons but does little to advance his cause – and to avoid obvious misinterpretation. On the other hand, the revisionists should be careful of overassertion, and are obliged eventually to suggest an alternative to the Whig edifice that they have helped to undermine.[47] Otherwise, as Professor Elton long ago observed,[48] we shall be in danger of concluding that the Civil War cannot be explained: and that is the road to antiquarianism, not history.

Even if the revisionists emerge victorious, their alternative explanation of the causes of the Civil War will not for ever remain the standard orthodoxy. For what emerges above all from this survey is that there is no such thing as absolute historical truth and, correspondingly, that there is no authoritative, received version of events in history. As Burckhardt observed, history 'is on every occasion what one age finds worthy of note in another'. Each generation needs to reinterpret the past in the light of the present. Moreover, because we are all conditioned by the age in which we live, bias in history is inevitable. The three-century debate on the causes of the English Civil War shows that historians – even those like Clarendon and S. R. Gardiner who have a claim to be called 'great' – are, and always have been, as John Rushworth admitted in the 1650s, 'crook-sided, warped and bowed to the right or to the left',[49] to a greater or lesser degree.

# 2. The Jacobean Religious Settlement: The Hampton Court Conference

## PATRICK COLLINSON

### I

THE death of Queen Elizabeth was an event which her subjects had feared for so long that when at last it happened and left the world to all appearances unchanged they were taken by surprise. The aged Archbishop of Canterbury, John Whitgift, 'trooped up to the cross in Cheapside' to hear James I proclaimed and observed to his relief that it was business as usual in the City: 'not one shop window shut up for fear of any disturbance'.[1] As the new era began, so it continued, with little of the expected sense of dislocation. Looking back from the other end of the seventeenth century, one writer referred to 'the long reign of Queen *Elizabeth* and King *James*' as if it made a single epoch.[2]

In the affairs of the English Church, continuity was equally the order of the day. 'The Phoenix of her ashes reigns over us' was the comment of one rising churchman on the new Supreme Governor.[3] There was no mass eviction of ecclesiastical personnel such as had marked the beginning of the last two reigns, no royal visitation to interrupt the normal routine of ecclesiastical administration and signal the arbitrary imposition of some new religious policy. Archbishop Whitgift, who under Elizabeth 'did all in all for the managing of clergy-affairs',[4] continued to do so; and when, within a year, he died, control of the Church passed to Richard Bancroft, an efficient disciplinarian after his own heart, whose career he had

27

advanced. Bancroft began by drawing up a comprehensive statement of the laws of the English Church, the Constitutions and Canons of 1604 which were to remain in force for three centuries and more. But this was not so much a New Deal as a codification of existing laws and procedures, symbolising not the end of the Tudor Church but its perpetuation.

Nevertheless, as the new king himself was to observe at the Hampton Court Conference, there was a sense in which every new reign necessarily involved steps to 'establish' the Church, 'both for doctrine and policy'.[5] Admittedly James went on to confess his reluctance to tamper with things which were 'well settled already'. But Elizabeth's refusal to contemplate any change whatsoever, expressed in her motto *Semper Eadem*, was acknowledged to have been a personal eccentricity. Moreover, her successor had grown up in a foreign church with an entirely different constitution, which conformed more closely than the Church of England to what Calvinists liked to call 'the best reformed churches' overseas; and as a theologian, and no mean one at that, James was a professing Calvinist himself. To say, as one observer did, that the English bishops as they prepared to welcome their new master feared 'the ruin of their estate',[6] was to exaggerate, but they cannot have felt entirely easy.

Minority interests – catholic, puritan, sectarian – which had been subject to varying degrees of intolerance and repression under the old regime were correspondingly encouraged by the 'Scotch mist' which, according to one religious enthusiast, would soon blind the eyes of the prelates and 'turn into a parching sun'.[7] Even the Family of Love (an obscure and much maligned sect) thought it worthwhile to present the new ruler with an optimistic address.[8]

James was not likely to declare himself a sudden convert to familism. And although as a genuinely tolerant ruler he was inclined to lighten the burden of the Elizabethan penal laws on the English catholics, he was scarcely more likely to convert to Rome. (Once he was securely on his throne, he was reported as saying: 'Na, na, gud faiyth, we's not need the papists noo.'[9]) But the hopes of relatively orthodox protestants were more realistically aroused. Consequently, in considering the prospects for religious change which were available in 1603, we are

concerned chiefly with the aspirations of those 'hotter'
protestants who were generally if rather loosely known as
puritans, and who for decades had agitated for measures to
complete a protestant settlement which in their opinion had
stopped half-way.[10]

Puritanism was not a distinct and coherent philosophy but a
tendency (compare 'Militant Tendency' in the modern Labour
Party) and puritans were not a sect on their own but a presence
within the Church, believing what other protestants believed,
but more intensely. The authority of Scripture was the formal
ground of protestant faith, but in puritan circles the language
and imagery of the Bible actively permeated every aspect of
existence. Protestantism detached itself from catholicism as a
perverted and even antichristian religion. But puritanism
rejected 'popery' more fiercely, denouncing the popish
elements which continued to contaminate the worship and
discipline of the English Church. There were degrees of
puritanism. Extreme puritans rejected the Book of Common
Prayer outright. Moderate puritans merely objected to certain
ceremonies, such as the white linen surplice which the clergy
were required to wear (a popish rag), and the sign of the cross
which they were obliged by law to trace on the infant's
forehead in baptism. Their nonconformity, for which from
time to time they suffered various penalties and privations,
consisted of an obstinate refusal to use these things, or to
endorse them by subscription. Extremists believed that bishops
were necessarily antichristian, and they claimed to have discovered a more scriptural form of church order in the New
Testament and in the presbyterian practice of Geneva and
other 'best reformed churches', some of them no further away
than the foreign 'stranger' churches in London. Moderates
distinguished between bad bishops and good and were content
to work within existing structures. But by definition all
puritans were more or less dissatisfied with things as they were,
with the sins of their neighbours and with their own short-
comings, and most of all they fretted over the wretched condition of the ordinary parish clergy, which they compared
unfavourably with the reformed ideal of a 'godly, learned,
preaching ministry'. There was probably no such creature as a
puritan in the singular. Puritans were always plural, close with

one another but careful to shun what they deplored as the 'company keeping' of others, in taverns and alehouses. In spite of the doubts currently expressed by some historians, Elizabethan puritanism is properly described as a movement, and as a kind of church within the Church.

This movement, so far as it concerned the clergy, was most fully developed in the 1580s, a period of intense anxiety for English protestants. Local conferences were set up with a certain formality and from time to time despatched their delegates to provincial and even national meetings, held in London when parliament was in session. Through skilful orchestration, the public was confronted with the appearance of a ground swell of popular indignation, directed against a hierarchy which by its policy of suspending and depriving nonconformists seemed to have declared war on the preaching ministry. This lent some credibility to the petitions and parliamentary bills in which a small minority of extremists demanded the extinction of bishops and the reconstruction of the Church on presbyterian lines. But in the face of unswerving opposition from Archbishop Whitgift and from the queen herself, this movement proved powerless to attain its objectives by political means. Eventually the campaign was tacitly abandoned, and puritanism was to find a different way forward, working like leaven in the lump to bring about a creeping religious and moral revolution. By the mid-seventeenth century this transformation, with consequences for English culture as profound as any in our history, was far advanced in those districts and sectors of society which proved receptive to the austere spirituality and public morality which flourished on the basis of Calvinist indoctrination.

But in 1603 the puritan conferences were either still in being or could be readily reconstituted, and many veterans of the 1580s remained active and hopeful that in these altered circumstances some at least of their goals were attainable. As James travelled south, he was presented with the so-called Millenary Petition which addressed him as 'our physician to heal these diseases', a tactful reference to one of the king's favourite metaphors. This famous manifesto seems to have carried no names, but it claimed the 'consent' of more than a thousand ministers and others of the king's subjects.[11] A formal, printed reply from the authorities of both universities inspired a secondary wave of petitioning which purported to be the voice of the country, noblemen, gentlemen, ministers and 'the people', 'every sort by themselves'. It was said that 'that only county of Northampton is sufficient to stop the mouths of them that say there are not above some 20 or 23 factious persons that desire reformation of these things'. But from surviving correspondence and 'advices' it appears that some petitions were drafted centrally, by 'the brethren in London', and that signatures were collected by the usual methods of pressure groups, but with some not very plausible attempts to conceal this fact: 'There must be sundry petitions of ministers from sundry parts, but of some few, to avoid the suspicion of conspiracy, which petitions must vary in words. . . .'[12]

From what they knew of James's opinions and intentions, the managers of this campaign were aware of the need to contain their own lunatic fringe. In the preface to the English edition of his book *Basilikon Doron*, published with superb timing within days of the old queen's death, James had commented on the religious quarrels of the time, dismissing certain 'brainsick and heady preachers' but warmly commending 'the learned and grave men of both sides', as if he had an impartial regard for the bishops and the more balanced of their opponents.[13] But although incurable optimists continued for months to circulate rumours to the contrary,[14] anyone with access to the king or knowledge of recent Scottish history must have known that James was unlikely to take sides against the bishops, still less to preside over a presbyterian revolution. For in Scotland the presbyterians were his ideological opponents, not afraid to tell the king to his face that the Church was not his kingdom but Christ's, in which he was a simple member and subject to discipline like any other christian.[15] All this was well enough known for a petitioner to beg the king not to confuse the English puritans with the Scots: 'We are not as they were: we do not as they did'.[16]

The millenary petitioners accordingly spoke 'neither as factious men affecting a popular parity in the Church, nor as schismatics, aiming at the dissolution of the state ecclesiastical'. And they were guarded in their request that ecclesiastical discipline might be administered 'according to

Christ's own institution, or at the least, that enormities may be redressed': which was to draw attention to abuses in the existing system rather than to question the system itself. 'A godly gentleman at Court' told his friends in the country to disclaim any intention 'to take down the framework of bishoprics' and this was underlined in the 'advices' circulated by the London brethren: 'Do not expressly desire the removing of bishops'. Perhaps there was a tussle between presbyterian and moderate elements. The standard form of petition included a patently presbyterian reference to 'the example of other reformed churches which have restored both the doctrine and discipline as it was delivered by our Saviour Christ and his Apostles'. But an accompanying letter gave permission to stop short of this controversial clause. 'Herein we leave every man.'[17]

In the event it scarcely mattered. Within two years it would be plain that James was hardly more responsive to the carefully modulated approach of 'learned and grave men' than to explicit, full-blooded presbyterianism. The Millenary Petition had asked that the sign of the cross in baptism should be 'taken away' and the surplice as an item of clerical attire 'not urged': not a great deal to ask of a foreign, Calvinist prince for whom such things were unfamiliar and exotic. But within a year, James would stoutly defend these very ceremonies, remarking that he had lived among puritans since he was ten years-old but was 'never of them'.[18] So there was to be no 'Jacobean religious settlement' in the sense of the turning of a new page and the phrase is not in use among historians. But if some of the continuities of history can be taken for granted, others call for explanation no less than the more obviously decisive turning points in human affairs. Why was the Jacobean religious settlement little more than an endorsement of the Elizabethan *status quo*?

## II

Part of the answer is hidden in manoeuvres at Court of which there is little reliable record. The bishops were not well known to the king on his arrival. They were not his men but part of the old queen's legacy. But later he would advise his son that they were 'grave and wise men and best companions for princes'.[19] To offset their growing influence, the puritans depended upon a number of pertinacious but socially insignificant agents, together with such patronage as they were able to command. These included a minor Northamptonshire gentleman, Lewis Pickering, whose ability to help followed an opportunistic ride to Edinburgh with news of the queen's death; and Patrick Galloway, a Scottish royal chaplain and client of one of the most influential Scottish lords, the Earl of Mar. When the puritan delegation appeared at Hampton Court, they were described by one observer as 'Galloway and his crew'.[20]

Early in the reign someone (and it was probably Galloway) interested James in a plan to return to parish churches the alienated revenue from tithes which was currently the property of numerous 'impropriators', of which the crown was one of the largest. Impropriation was the greatest single cause of clerical poverty and consequently of a parish ministry which fell short of the rising expectations of an increasingly protestant, and literate, society. The king wrote enthusiastically to the universities, suggesting that they should follow his own example in redeeming the impropriations in their possession to the parishes, in order to provide for 'learned and painful preachers'. But Archbishop Whitgift pointed out that what was proposed would ruin the universities at a stroke and suggested that some more sophisticated means must be found for augmenting the income of the poor clergy. James's diminishing interest in the plan was an index of Galloway's waning influence and of Whitgift's rising ascendancy.[21]

In October the king was presented with alarming evidence of some very unspontaneous petitioning in Sussex, a campaign which had taken his own name in vain and claimed the collusion of 'some that are in especial credit with his Highness'. He responded with a royal proclamation which protested against the 'tumult sedition and violence' implied by recent puritan agitation. Professor Mark Curtis, who argues that at this time the king was not unduly dependent upon the bishops, believes that the proclamation was drafted by Whitgift and Bancroft but subsequently amended by the king himself in order to emphasise his serious interest in the reform of ecclesi-

astical abuses: 'scandals' was the word James chose to use. But
the evidence will not bear this construction. The proclamation
of 24 October, as published, was in every way helpful to the
bishops, ending as it did with a declaration of intent to
preserve the Church 'as we have found it established by the
laws here, reforming only the abuses which we shall apparently
find proved'.[22]

Here, two months before the Hampton Court Conference,
there was small encouragement for any but the most modest
of puritan ambitions. Nevertheless, historians have always
regarded that extraordinary conference as the crux and crisis
of this year of frenetic ecclesiastical activity. Before Hampton
Court many things were possible. In modern political
parlance, the mould had broken. After Hampton Court it
reset, and James told one of his cronies that he 'would be sorry
not to be as constant indeed as she was, who called herself
*Semper Eadem*'.[23]

## III

We have described Hampton Court as 'extraordinary'. As an
informal, *ad hoc* 'conference' without constitutional standing
or agreed modes of procedure, it was extra to any regular
machinery for determining the Church's doctrine, liturgy and
government. Anything decided in this forum would require
confirmation elsewhere, perhaps in Convocation and certainly
by the crown, acting in its legislative capacity, either by Act of
Parliament or under the Great Seal. But Hampton Court was
not without parallel or precedent. Conferences of this kind
were loosely related to academic disputations, and especially to
the formal 'acts' staged in universities on formal occasions, or
for the edification and even the entertainment of distinguished
visitors. In 1600 a young Bohemian nobleman was delighted to
find that 'by great good luck' his arrival in Cambridge
coincided with the annual graduation ceremonies. Where a
modern tourist might be glad to take in a play or a concert,
Baron Waldstein enjoyed witnessing the discomfiture of a
learned doctor of divinity who became 'quite red with mortifi-
cation' when publicly rebuked by the moderator for an

incompetent performance. James I experienced the same sort of pleasure when he told a correspondent that if their own scholars had disputed as feebly as the puritan spokesmen at Hampton Court, the rod would have been applied to 'the poor boys' buttocks'.[24]

But in the crisis of the Reformation, theological disputation could serve a more public and momentous purpose. On the outcome of the disputations held at Leipzig in 1518, or at Westminster Hall in 1559, the religious destiny of whole nations depended. Wherever a choice was posed between two religious paths, debates were staged between the qualified experts of either side, in principle to resolve the problem by rational discussion, but often in practice to advertise and justify a decision already reached at a political level.

The Hampton Court Conference may seem unique in that the presiding moderator was a king, and a king who as an able controversialist in his own right took an active part in discussion. But in 1584 a very similar event occurred in the archbishop's house at Lambeth: a debate between two puritan divines and three bishops, held in the presence of leading magnates, including Lord Burghley and the Earl of Leicester. These 'honourable personages' presided and their approval was the prize contended for. But like James at Hampton Court, they intervened freely in proceedings.[25]

More than twenty years after Hampton Court, a new reign and a new religious settlement were marked by yet another conference, staged on this occasion at York House, the London residence of George Villiers, Duke of Buckingham. The subject for debate, on 11 and 17 February 1626, was theological and concerned the anti-Calvinist doctrine known as Arminianism, represented for the purpose of debate by one of its promoters, Richard Montague, and his writings. In the judgement of the participants the debate could not have been more momentous, concerning as it did the very ground of salvation and the gospel of Christ, which Montague was said by his Calvinist opponents to have perverted. Once again, the moderators were a group of privy councillors, headed by the all-powerful Buckingham who, like Leicester in 1584 and James in 1604, was more of a participant than a spectator. As at Lambeth and Hampton Court, both sides later claimed the victory, a circumstance

likely to arise from the lack of any formal structure to the
debate or any rules. But it soon became clear that at York
House the anti-Calvinists had prevailed in the only quarter that
ultimately counted, the heart and mind of Buckingham's
friend and master, Charles I. Within a few years, control of the
Church passed into the hands of the Arminian faction, headed
by Archbishop Laud. So York House proved the centrepiece of
the Caroline religious settlement as Hampton Court was of the
earlier, Jacobean settlement.[26] These were the English
precedents, parallels and sequences to Hampton Court. There
was also a Scottish background, which no-one knew better than
James himself, who was accustomed to frequent confrontations
with the leaders of the Kirk.

The conference at Hampton Court arose from a long-standing desire of the Elizabethan puritans for an 'indifferent
hearing', only partially satisfied at Lambeth in 1584. One of
Richard Montague's books was called *Apello Caesarem*. If the
puritans had thought of such a clever title they would surely
have used it first. There was talk in the Millenary Petition –
itself an appeal to Caesar – of solving outstanding problems
'by conference among the learned'. Couched in these terms,
the suggestion was calculated to whet the king's appetite for
religious argument. So in spite of the rumoured hostility of the
more conservative bishops, it was reported in the late summer
that the king 'intended a conference'.[27] The date was set for 1
November, but the onset of plague enforced a postponement.
It was on Thursday 12 January that the conference convened,
to begin its work two days later in the Privy Chamber, where
the king conferred with the bishops and five cathedral deans,
in the presence of the Privy Council. On Monday 16 January
came the long-awaited 'indifferent hearing', when four puritan
spokesmen confronted their 'opposites', Bancroft of London
and Thomas Bilson, Bishop of Winchester. The third party to
this crucial debate was the king, an unconventional umpire
who from time to time took hold of both bat and ball and used
them to devastating effect. Finally there was a plenary session
on 18 January, when all parties were informed of the outcome.

The historian of Hampton Court faces formidable difficulties. At first sight, he is not short of evidence. He can
compare four independent accounts of the proceedings,

adding further details from letters written by several observers
and participants, including the king himself. But most of these
sources are episodic and selective. And whereas the most extensive, William Barlow's semi-official *Summe and substance of
the conference*, complained of other versions as 'partial',
'untrue' and 'slanderous', it was itself a skilfully tendentious
piece of propaganda, commissioned by Whitgift, flattering to
the king, supportive of the bishops (whose ranks Barlow was
about to join) and damaging to the credibility of the puritan
delegation. Nevertheless, at 16,000 words it is three times the
length of its nearest rival, usually referred to as the Anonymous
Account, and for all its imperfections is indispensable.[28]

The problems deepen when we look closely into the purpose
of the conference in the perceptions of the participants, and
into their status. For those at either end of the ecclesiastical
spectrum, the conference was a fight to the finish between two
irreconcilable parties. Among the bishops, the committed anti-
puritans tried to win a victory in advance by preventing the
conference from taking place and disrupting it when it was
already under way. Bancroft hoped that this might be done by
reminding the king of an ancient principle that schismatics
ought not to be given a hearing against bishops.

Among puritan militants, the conference was seen as a
decisive contest, to be fought on their side by mandated
representatives or, as Barlow ironically described them, 'agents
for the millenary plaintiffs'. Not a hundred miles from the
Privy Chamber at Hampton Court, 'at the conference but not
in place', there was a gathering of some thirty ministers
representing eleven counties and four towns. This was reminis-
cent of the parliamentary lobbies of the 1580s, with the
delegates mostly survivors of that earlier campaign. They
included Edmund Snape, late of Northampton and now of
Exeter, Josias Nicholls of Kent, who had written a courageous
apologia for the defeated Elizabethan cause, and Arthur
Hildersham, master-mind of the Millenary Petition. The three
London representatives were Thomas Wilcox, who more than
thirty years before had shared with John Field the writing of
that electrifying pamphlet *An admonition to the Parliament*;
and two younger men who had managed the campaign of the
previous summer, Stephen Egerton and Henry Jacobs. The

delegates drew up instructions for their spokesmen at the conference ('ten demands made by thirty reverend divines in the name of themselves and others') which carefully avoided a direct attack on episcopacy. But condemnation of the disputed ceremonies as absolutely unlawful rather than merely indifferent places them some distance to the left of moderate puritanism, as does their request, virtually presbyterian, that 'the minister's right in the exercise of the Church censures and ordination of ministers may be restored'.[29]

This robust statement was not adequately expressed, or represented, by the four spokesmen who appeared for the puritans. These were the 'foreman' Dr John Reynolds, a leading Oxford theologian whom we may call an extreme moderate; a former archdeacon, Thomas Sparke, who had taken part in the Lambeth Conference of 1584; Laurence Chaderton, first master of Emmanuel College, Cambridge, and once, but perhaps no longer, a theoretical presbyterian; and the Suffolk minister John Knewstub, a potent figure inside his own county but obscure and unimpressive outside it. In due course, when more radical spirits conducted their post-mortems, it was said, by Henry Jacobs, that these four were 'not of their choosing, nor nomination, nor of their judgment in the matters now and then in question, but of a clean contrary'.[30]

True, the spokesmen were not in any proper sense delegates. Each of them had received a formal summons from the Privy Council,[31] which was probably acting on nominations made at Court. Thomas Sparke, for example, may have owed his place to a book in which he had defended the king's title to the throne before his accession, allegedly at some cost to himself. Patrick Galloway and his patron the Earl of Mar are very likely to have played a behind-the-scenes role. But according to a dark rumour reported after the conference by Henry Jacobs, the prelates themselves arranged the representation 'underhand'. This may explain the choice of the foreman, Reynolds, who was on good terms with Archbishop Whitgift and as Dean of Lincoln occupied an office which was one of Whitgift's own early preferments. According to Barlow, outside the conference sessions the four spokesmen 'made semblance of joining with the bishops'. In the aftermath, Sparke became an apologist not only for conformity but for episcopacy by divine right. He wrote that he wished that 'the odious name of puritanism' might be buried for ever. A recent historian of religion in Elizabethan Oxford has chosen not to call Reynolds a puritan. Both he and Sparke are better described as moderate men of the centre rather than true partisans.[32]

This was equally the standpoint of some of the bishops and deans who were supposedly in the opposite camp. Bishop Henry Robinson of Carlisle was an old Oxford colleague of Reynolds and probably his closest friend; while Rudd of St David's, Babington of Worcester and Matthew of Durham were all known to be sympathetic to moderate puritanism.[33] The difference between the two sides was further blurred by the presence of individuals whom it is hard to categorise, including the learned theologian Richard Field, who appears on several lists as part of the puritan group but is said to have spoken only once and then 'altogether against them'.[34] Another notable cross-bencher was the dean of the Chapel Royal, James Montagu, who according to his Northamptonshire neighbour Lewis Pickering was the 'watchman of the king's soul' and would later, as Bishop of Winchester, edit James's literary works. As the first master of the new and virtually puritan foundation of Sidney Sussex College and a leading Cambridge Calvinist, he was considered a dangerous man by the more conservative bishops. There was a telling incident in the conference when Montagu whispered in the king's ear and Bancroft called out: 'Speak out Mr Doctor and do not cross us underhand'.[35] Except for the business of the second day, Hampton Court is better described as a kind of round-table conference on a variety of ecclesiastical topics than as a debate between two sides.

## IV

And what of the royal umpire? If the Hampton Court Conference is a series of variations on an enigma, then that enigma is James I. What were his motives in staging the conference? What did he really think of puritanism and of the English bishops? Did he engage seriously with these issues, or did they provide a passing intellectual diversion, something to take the place of hunting in the chilly aftermath of the Christmas holidays? His comment to the Earl of Northampton was: 'We have kept such a revel with the puritans'.[36] Can his religious policy be explained? Can it be defended?

According to the greatest modern historian of seventeenth-century politics, Samuel Rawson Gardiner, the idea of the conference was a good one and offered hope of reuniting the Church of England. But James's flippant and self-gratifying performance threw away this golden opportunity. 'The essential littleness of the man was at once revealed.' But according to the American scholar, Roland Green Usher, James's mistake was not in treating the puritan 'plaintiffs' with contempt but in granting them a hearing. More recently, Mark Curtis has pointed out that the difference between Gardiner and Usher conceals a shared assumption that the conference was a sterile failure, and this he traces to Barlow's biased and misleading *Summe and substance of the conference*. The alternative 'Anonymous Account' suggests that James was far from deaf to the voice of puritan complaint and made concessions to it, although in the event he failed to ensure that the bishops implemented all the reforms entrusted to them. But Fred Shriver disagrees. Barlow's account is probably accurate. Years of fencing with Scottish presbyterians had left James as relentless and resourceful an opponent of puritanism as Elizabeth ever was. He had spent his early months trying to win over moderate puritan critics by gracious means, which was political common sense. But at the end of the day what a Scot later called 'that unkoth motto' 'No bishop, no king' was the cornerstone of his ecclesiastical thinking.[37]

The difficulty of correctly interpreting the confused and biased accounts of a sometimes disorderly debate can be dramatised if we focus on a particular episode, as it happens the most famous moment in the entire proceedings. This came towards the end of the second day, when Dr Reynolds presented the case for the 'plaintiffs'. Reynolds had begun the day by explaining that the matters 'disliked or questioned' would be presented under four heads: purity of doctrine, reform of the ministry, reform of church government and Prayer Book matters. As can so easily happen in meetings, the first item on the Agenda, doctrine, occupied a disproportionate amount of time, although this may have been justified for Reynolds by his sense of priority as an academic theologian. If Reynolds had been invited to devise a new religious settlement he would have begun, and perhaps ended, by rewriting the Church's confession of faith, the Thirty Nine Articles. From the point of view of a high Calvinist, the doctrine of grace and salvation expressed by the Articles was in need of clarification and reinforcement, to meet the serious challenge recently mounted by theological revisionists in both universities. This could be done most conveniently by adding a more recent statement, the so-called Lambeth Articles, composed by Archbishop Whitgift, himself no enemy of scholastic Calvinism, in an attempt to make theological peace in Cambridge.[38] Reynolds continued, complaining that other Articles were less than candid in their treatment of baptism and confirmation; that there ought to be a new and standardised Catechism; and a new and improved translation of the Bible was needed. Although this last proposal was the source of the only tangible achievement of Hampton Court, the Authorised Version of 1611, it was at this point, while particularising the faults of existing translations, that Reynolds tried the king's patience by descending into trivia.

It was already afternoon when the foreman, having spent a much shorter time on contentious Prayer Book matters, finally reached the third of his four categories of complaint which, in spite of its major importance, had been left until last: 'That the church government might be sincerely ministered, according to God's word'. Decoded, these disarming words could mean the end of bishops and their replacement by church discipline on the Genevan model. But the Dean of Lincoln intended no such thing: only a modification of existing institutions. Excommunication, the soul of a rigorous pastoral discipline and its ultimate sanction, was in current practice a penalty routinely employed by lay officials as the principal means of enforcing the authority of the ecclesiastical courts against recalcitrant offenders, and as such it was debased. Reynolds proposed that these censures should recover their authentic character as solemn, spiritual sentences to be pronounced by the bishop in person. But the bishop was not to act arbitrarily.

Reynolds went on to sketch a model of what, later in the century, would be known as limited or 'reduced' episcopacy. As the prime unit of discipline there should be regular meetings of the clergy on a local basis, much like those which had sustained the preaching activity known as 'prophesying' before the queen had put a stop to it in the days of Archbishop Grindal. Matters which could not be settled by the ministers at this level would be referred to the archdeacon, and from him to the episcopal synod, where they would be resolved by the bishop, sitting 'with his presbytery', that is, with representatives of the clergy. The underlying motive was to mitigate 'lordly prelacy' and to restore a human, pastoral face to the impersonal and legalistic system of ecclesiastical justice inherited from the pre-Reformation Church. Ideas of this kind continued to attract attention far into the seventeenth century, either on their own merits or as a compromise between the rigidities of the episcopal and presbyterian principles. But as mere paper projects, they were to remain one of the might-have-beens of English church history.

According to Barlow, the king had made similar proposals for the reform of excommunication in his conference with the bishops and deans on the first day. So now he interrupted Reynolds to assure him that this matter was already in hand. But when Reynolds went on to use the word 'presbytery', James launched into a tirade which contained the most memorable of his utterances at Hampton Court. A presbytery agreed as well with monarchy as God and the Devil. 'No bishop, no king.' In Barlow's account, this outburst concluded with words which he made the climax and pivot of his narrative and which, if publicly uttered, must have annihilated the puritan delegation: 'If this be all, quoth he, that they have to say, I shall make them conform themselves, or I will harry them out of this land, or else do worse'.

Was the outburst involuntary, or controlled and tactical? And did Barlow exaggerate its dramatic effect? He suggests that James mistook the drift of Reynolds's remarks, 'thinking that they aimed at a Scottish presbytery'. In Scotland, a presbytery was a local court constituted of ministers and lay ruling elders, the very essence of presbyterianism and the body which English presbyterians called a *classis* or conference. And yet in context Reynolds's proposals bore some resemblance to the working compromise between the rule of presbyteries and of bishops which was a matter of experiment in Scotland and with which James, of all people, should have been perfectly familiar. But perhaps the king was not so much confused as exhausted, and Reynolds guilty of a tactless error in timing. For Barlow suggests that it was after the king had proposed an adjournment 'because it was late' that he launched into this new and important subject; and that the day's business ended abruptly with James's tart response.

But the Anonymous Account would have us believe that far from speaking out of turn, Reynolds was *required* by the king to proceed to this final topic of ecclesiastical discipline. And if this observer agrees that Reynolds met with a withering stream of abuse for his pains, he suggests that James soon cooled down and that it was after his tirade, not before, that he expressed some interest in a modification of ecclesiastical discipline on some such lines as Reynolds had proposed. Discussion of other matters followed and the day ended, not with the denunciation reported by Barlow (which was perhaps an aside rather than a public rebuke) but with an eirenical statement in which James suggested that he might 'yield' to better arguments than those so far presented and appealed for unity against the common Romish adversary. According to yet another report, he then 'favourably dismissed' the puritans for that occasion.[39]

The celebrated outburst may have occurred as a spontaneous reaction to the dreaded word 'presbytery', but it is more likely that James, who was not a stupid man, deliberately grasped the opportunity which Reynolds unwittingly offered him. This was more than a tactical opportunity to throw the puritan spokesman off balance. It was a chance, hitherto lacking in the conference, to assert the high claims of monarchy. James was an educated man with an interest in various topics, among them witchcraft, catholicism and tobacco, or, as on this occasion, the state of the Church. But first and foremost he was a king (and had been since the age of one!) who while writing and discoursing on these subjects was also promoting his kingship. As Stuart Clark has shown, his approach to every question was typical of the mentality of his age in its tendency to argue from opposites and antitheses.

Thus, since the Devil was opposite to God, to know God it was helpful to come to terms with the Devil, and 'by the falsehood of the one to consider the truth of the other'.[40] In much the same way 'presbytery', precisely because it was so averse to monarchy, was a mode of discussing its opposite. Thus whether or not the hapless Reynolds really 'aimed at a Scottish presbytery', it was necessary for the exaltation of monarchy to pretend that he did. He had appealed to the king against the bishops and in so doing had acknowledged the royal supremacy. But James suggested that like John Knox he and his kind would make use of the supremacy for just as long as it suited their purpose and no longer. 'But if once you were out and they in place' (he said to the bishops) 'I know what would become of my supremacy. No bishop, no king, as before I said.'

## V

At this moment, late in the afternoon of 16 January 1604, a well-informed fly on the wall would have concluded that the puritans had lost their duel with the bishops, game, set and match. Dr Reynolds had put forward a scheme of reform which incorporated several of the king's own ideas (although he may not have appreciated this), only to be humiliated and accused of ideological hypocrisy. And the fly on the wall would have been at least half right. The puritans were in what is nowadays called a 'Catch 22 situation'. To have demanded a full-scale presbyterian revolution would have resembled the charge of the Light Brigade: magnificent, but not war, still less diplomacy. Yet when they moderated their demands to an acceptable level they were treated with amused contempt; or so the Barlow account would have us believe. With the benefit of hindsight it appears that in the event the puritan campaign of 1603–4 may have achieved the worst of all possible outcomes. The king was impressed by the puritans as agitators and conspirators (as S. R. Gardiner suggested, this was evidence in itself of 'a presbyterian temper'[41]) but not with the gravity of their demands. The more moderate, even trivial, their case, the less excuse for disturbing the peace and unity of the Church.

In the aftermath of Hampton Court, the bishops, headed by the new primate, Richard Bancroft, set out to induce obedience by imposing on the clergy the new book of Canons, which included a requirement to subscribe to articles which positively endorsed all those features of the *status quo* to which the puritans had for so long objected. Many refused and an unprecedented number were turned out of their livings or excluded from their pulpits: perhaps as many as a hundred and certainly a much higher number than the total of those deprived under Archbishop Whitgift's subscription campaign of 1584.[42] But for every nonconformist who remained defiant, many more made their peace with the authorities. This was a painful crossroads, where one path led into the wilderness of separatism and another into conformity. It was not the end of puritanism, but it proved to be the end of the puritan movement in the form of a concerted effort mounted from within the Church to alter the fundamental terms of the Elizabethan settlement by political means.

This was Bancroft's handiwork. But Bancroft was the king's choice as primate and he met with no discouragement from that quarter. Indeed, John Chamberlain reported that only the king was 'constant to have all come to conformity', and a recent historian agrees that at times even the archbishop was left 'trailing in his wake'.[43] When the leading gentlemen of Northamptonshire petitioned him on behalf of their deprived and suspended ministers (and the petitioners included the kindred of Dean Montagu, the 'watchman of his soul') the king overreacted, almost as if Northamptonshire had gone into rebellion. It was at about this time that he told Robert Cecil: 'I have daily more and more cause to hate and abhor all that sect, enemies to all kings, and to me, only because I am a king'. Nonconformity was tantamount to *lèse majesté*, and intolerable.[44]

But our fly on the wall, if attentive throughout the Hampton Court Conference, would not have mistaken the king's distaste for puritanism for a total lack of interest in correcting ecclesiastical abuses. James seems to have intended the conference to perform not one but two almost separate functions. The business of the second day was to hear what the puritans had to say, perhaps with the prime purpose of reminding them of their obedience. But on the first day, with no puritan 'plaintiffs' present, the king put to the bishops and deans doubts and anxieties about Anglican doctrine and practice which may have been partly prompted by puritan propaganda but which are just as likely to have arisen from his own reflections. On the third day, he discussed various proposed reforms with the responsible parties to whom they were entrusted before admitting the puritan spokesmen to hear his answers to their complaints. Is it too paradoxical to suggest that he might have taken a more extensive and sustained interest in such matters if the puritans had not robbed him of the initiative?

The views which James expressed, sifted from his racy and sometimes even scatological vein of discourse, were well-informed as to the issues and consistent with the opinion which he never tired of repeating: that the English Church was a basically sound body which after forty-four years in its present condition was naturally in need of some medical attention. On the doctrine of grace, he was an expert critic, well able to detect the pitfalls into which both extreme Calvinists and their enemies were liable to descend, but more of a Calvinist than otherwise. Unlike the more conservative bishops, and very unlike Queen Elizabeth, his Calvinism led him to believe that the ministry of the Church ought, as a matter of course, to be a learned preaching ministry. So on the final day of the conference he committed to the bishops as a weighty matter the provision of sufficient resources to provide for 'the planting of a learned and painful minister in every parish'. On a point of fascinating detail, at least for James, he was surprised to find that the Book of Common Prayer allowed midwives to christen infants, implying a superstitious regard for baptism. This was one of the very few things altered in the Jacobean recension of the Prayer Book. But on the other hand he rejected on reasonable grounds the puritan arguments against the surplice and the sign of the cross. If these survived in the liturgy it was not because of the king's indifference.

There was never much chance that the Hampton Court Conference would make the Prayer Book, or the Church, safe for delicate puritan consciences. Some of Reynolds's proposals for the modification of episcopal government were reflected in the king's list of 'things as shall be reformed', which included a surprisingly radical ruling that 'the jurisdiction of the bishops shall be somewhat limited': specifically by associating 'some grave ministers' in the processes of 'ordination, suspension, degradation etc'.[45] These reforms were not totally neglected but in the Canons of 1604 their effect was minimised. Canon 35, relating to ordination, merely required the bishop to use the assistance of his cathedral chapter or failing them of three other 'sufficient preachers' of his diocese in the laying on of hands. And Canon 122 insisted that sentences against clergy should be pronounced by the bishop in person, assisted by his chapter or 'two other at the least grave ministers and preachers'.[46]

As a round-table conference, concerned with what James himself had called ecclesiastical 'scandals'[47] and which we may describe with more tact as the unfinished business of the English Reformation, the conference was almost equally abortive. There were two damaging legacies of the old Church, both untouched by earlier religious settlements: the artificial poverty of thousands of parochial livings, where the tithes had been siphoned off into alien hands, first the monasteries and other religious corporations and now the lay persons to whom this property had been conveyed at the time of the Dissolution; and the degradation of ecclesiastical discipline inherent in the administrative use of excommunication as the ordinary penalty for contempt of court. So long as there was no action on these fronts, the Church of England was neither feeding its sheep, nor shepherding them responsibly. (As the Scot Robert Baillie later remarked, 'episcopal courts were never fitted for the reclaiming of minds'.[48])

At Hampton Court, the proposal to rehabilitate excommunication by finding a more acceptable substitute for its current use was 'very easily yielded unto of all sides' as a reform which was long overdue and the king endorsed it. Yet James's first parliament lacked the legislative will to proceed and the problem was shelved for solution until the nineteenth century, by which time it had ceased to matter.[49] The augmentation of clerical stipends was equally uncontroversial and proved to be equally unattainable. As James had discovered already, it was one thing to establish the cause of the disease, in a word impropriation, but quite another to prescribe a cure.[50]

Superficially the king can be blamed for failing in the aftermath of Hampton Court to lead a determined onslaught on these Augean stables. And indeed James I was no Hercules. But for an adequate explanation of why it was that the Church of England remained in these respects more in principle than reality a reformed Church it would be necessary to look beyond the indolence of a monarch who preferred hunting to administration. We should need to investigate the legal and institutional rigidities of early seventeenth-century society and to come to terms with a mentality which ascribed to parliament and the law a defensive rather than a socially creative role, especially where private property was concerned. And with the best will in the world impropriations presented great difficulties to any would-be reformer of the system. They were a form of property vested with perfect legality in the hands of the class which composed the legislature, and which used it, for example, to provide for younger sons or to create a dowry or jointure for a daughter. Outright expropriation was unthinkable, and devices to compensate the parishes out of the proceeds of impropriations were legally unenforceable. The long-term consequence was that the Church faced the multiple challenges of its future starved of resources at the level of the local community and incapable of flexible responses to the changing needs of society.

## VI

At this point the reader may wish to ask what an essay on the Hampton Court Conference is doing in a book with the title *Before the English Civil War*. It is a good question. In the past, as we have seen, before the days of what has come to be called 'revisionism', it was possible by taking up a position in 1604 to enjoy an almost uninterrupted view of the outbreak a full generation later of what used to be called 'the Puritan Revolution'. Puritanism had been unnaturally suppressed, the abuses which had nourished it were unreformed, and eventually with a certain inevitability it would burst its bonds with a new and terrible energy. It was with an eye to this future that Gardiner took James I so severely to task for the cheap victory won at Hampton Court by his facile tongue. 'James went his way, thinking little of what he had done.'[51] But that prospect is, or ought to be, obscured by the intervening history of the Jacobean Church, a subject which historians have strangely neglected.[52] The story told in this essay is true, or as nearly true as conflicts of evidence and the limited skill of the author have allowed. Yet it provides an almost misleading introduction to the ecclesiastical history of the next twenty years. Contrary to all the indications of Hampton Court and its sequel, this was so far from assuming the shape of a relentless struggle between puritans and Anglicans that any attempt to write it in these terms would be a dismal failure.

At Hampton Court, James laid the ghost of Scottish presbyterianism. (And in Scotland it was no insubstantial wraith but remained a body of formidable opposition to his regality.) But we may well ask what his longstanding duel with presbyterianism on the Scottish model had to do with English conditions. A minority of conservative bishops, Bancroft mainly, had won and proceeded to consolidate a revengeful victory against an old opponent: militant and political puritanism. But that and the subscription struggle which ensued, for all the agitated paperwork which it has left behind, belonged more to the Elizabethan past than to the Jacobean future. Few bishops saw the Church as Bancroft saw it, as a battlefield. Most would probably have agreed with Bishop Rudd of St David's that they and the puritans were united in 'substance of religion'.[53] Many of the bishops whom James was to appoint or promote, perhaps a majority of those who displayed any kind of merit or distinction, shared with puritans a common regard for the Calvinism which was still the dominant religious tendency.[54] They included Bancroft's successor as Archbishop of Canterbury, George Abbot, and his fellow metropolitan, Tobie Matthew of York. As Calvinists, these Jacobean prelates believed in the preaching ministry, promoted it, defended it and sometimes took an energetic part in it themselves: notably Matthew who is known to have preached over two thousand sermons in the course of forty years of high ecclesiastical office, and who in his eighties was credited with preaching more sermons in one year than all the popes in history.[55] Such bishops shared the passionate concern of Jacobean puritans for the reformation of manners and most of them were convinced Sabbatarians. One bishop, Lewis Bayly, wrote the most popular religious book of the age, *The practice of piety*, which in the first half of the seventeenth century seems to have held the position occupied in other epochs by Thomas à Kempis or Bunyan.

This rising tide of consensual, evangelical Calvinism all but submerged the old differences between conformity and non-conformity. These controversies were not dead. In 1618 Bishop Thomas Morton of Chester (and later of Lichfield and Durham), one of the most admired of Jacobean prelates, published many hundreds of pages in defence of the three disputed ceremonies of the surplice, the cross in baptism and kneeling at the Communion.[56] But now such things assumed minor importance in the perceived priorities of the religious public. Besides, in many churches they continued to be observed in the breach. Meanwhile, in spite of the absence of any general, legislative attack on the deficiencies of parochial finance, the Jacobean age witnessed a striking improvement in the academic qualifications and general competence of the clergy. Whereas in many parts of Elizabethan England graduates had been very thin on the ground, by the time of James's death there were very few entrants to the profession who lacked any kind of university experience.[57] Although this is a perspective which most historians would find it hard to share, contemporaries believed that they were living in their Church's golden age when, as a late seventeenth-century writer put it, 'the Clergy of the *Reformed Church of England* grew the most learned of the world'.[58]

If it had not been for the destructive controversies and conflicts which were to follow, in the tragic reign of Charles I, the verdict of history might have been that this upward climb to a plateau of modest respectability and even, here and there, some excellence, was what constituted the true Jacobean settlement of religion, rather than anything discussed at Hampton Court. Or we might regard it as the coming to a certain maturity of the Church of the Elizabethan Settlement. It would be absurd to absolve James of all blame for the calamities which followed, after his time. But at least he cannot be charged with the greatest calamity of all and the cause of much else that was disastrous, the advancement of Archbishop William Laud. When Buckingham recommended Laud for his first episcopal promotion, James made a characteristically shrewd comment: 'Take him to you. But on my soul you will repent it'.[59]

# 3. The Personal Rule of Charles I

## KEVIN SHARPE

THE period of government without parliaments from 1629 to
1640, variously described as the 'eleven years tyranny' and 'The
Personal Rule of Charles I', has been little studied (at least as
far as the central government is concerned) since Gardiner
completed his commanding narrative nearly a century ago.[1]
Yet the 1630s is not only a decade of unusual fascination,
worthy of investigation in itself. Because we may learn from
those years so much about King Charles, so much about the
nature and problems of early Stuart government, a study of the
Personal Rule is also essential for an understanding of the
crises which led to civil war. To some, perhaps, the place of
that decade in the story of civil war is clear: the period of
government without parliament intensified the conflicts
between crown and subjects which had been set in motion since
the succession of James I; accelerated, that is, the fateful
journey towards civil war past many a milestone of divisive
controversy. As Professor Rabb has recently put it, 'the
attempt to do without parliament in the 1630s was in the long
run untenable ... Resistance to Charles's policy was
inevitable'.[2]

But was it? To those on the road during the 1630s the
journey seemed far from a headlong rush towards conflict.
Even looking backward from a knowledge of later events,
Edward Hyde, no uncritical flatterer of Charles I, recalled, as
we have seen, the Personal Rule as a decade of calm and
felicity.[3] His analysis prompts a number of questions. How,
after two decades of alleged constitutional conflict between
king and Commons, was Charles able to rule without con-
sulting his subjects in parliament? How, if parliament was

central to the government of England, was it possible (and even easier) to continue the business of government without it? Why did the gentry families represented in parliament, indeed in many cases former MPs themselves, assist with the collection of levies and the enforcement of policies which made rule without parliament possible? Unlike the kings of France, Charles I had no standing army and no agents of the central authority in the localities: his government rested upon co-operation. Why and how far was that co-operation secured after 1629?

In order to begin to answer these questions, we must investigate the circumstances in which the decision to govern for a time without parliaments was made. We must attempt to understand the aims and ideals of the king and his counsellors for the government of Church and state. We must see how those aims and ideals became policies and how, through the organs of central and local government – the Privy Council, the courts, the lieutenants, the bishops, the sheriffs, the justices and the constables – policies were translated into actions. We must pay no less close attention to the responses and to the nature of the responses, within Whitehall and in the counties and dioceses, to those policies and to the methods by which they were executed. Finally we must attempt to suggest why and when the co-operation upon which personal government depended began to break down and why the Personal Rule collapsed. These are questions which can only be touched upon here, but they are questions which need to be asked and more thoroughly investigated.

## II

Why then did Charles I in 1629 dispense with parliament for a decade? Hitherto his short reign had exhibited no hostility to those assemblies. Before he became king, Charles had been, as Rudyerd described him, a prince bred in parliaments.[4] During the first four years of his reign parliaments were summoned more frequently than at any time during the previous seventy years. And, at least in the declaration of war against Spain, royal policy had been framed in accordance with the wishes of the Commons. Indeed it was these very factors – the experience

of parliaments and the heeding of their counsel – which, in the
end, persuaded the king to dispense with them. Looked at
from Charles's point of view parliament had proved reluctant
to finance a war which it had advocated. The failures, defeats
and abortive campaigns of the 1620s, humiliating to a ruler as
obsessed with honour and shame as was Charles, were the
direct consequences of inadequate supply. Months after those
failures, in April 1629, the Council discussed questions arising
from the king having been engaged, at the entreaty of parliament, in three wars for which it had voted insufficient revenue.
These were understandable questions. Acceptance of parliamentary advice and expectation of parliamentary supply went
hand in hand.[5] Secondly, the House of Commons had
instituted judicial proceedings against the Duke of Buckingham, who was not only a favourite fully in the king's
confidence, but the architect of the foreign policy advocated
by parliament and, at least in Charles's estimation, the general
best qualified to conduct the war.[6] It is hardly surprising if
Charles expected that in time of war domestic quarrels,
especially those stemming (as he believed them to be) from
jealous pique and personal interest, should be subordinated to
unity in the face of the enemy. Then when after three years of
warfare, MPs assembled in 1628, they came to parliament not
to offer their support, but to present as grievances the very
measures – forced loans, billeting, martial law – which their
own counsel, their failure to supply, indeed the very facts of
war had necessitated. Few today question the emergency
powers assumed by government in the name of common safety
at a time of crisis. Few in 1628 questioned the need for some
emergency power or doubted that it rested in the king's prerogative. But those who came to Westminster in 1628 did
argue that the modes and the men through which those
necessary powers had been exercised had led to an abuse of
their purpose, to a breach of the rights and privileges guaranteed
by law. With those engaged in trying to fight a war, these
distinctions carried little conviction. To tie the government in
wartime to the normal processes of law was to end its capacity
to fight. Or as Sir James Bagg expressed the point to Buckingham, 'Magna Charta...is now made a chain to bind the king
from doing anything'.[7] The king's decision to dispense with

parliament originated from the failure to fight the war and from a feeling that the deliberations of the Commons bedevilled any action. It was a vision shared by many at court and not a few throughout the country. Within the House of Commons, Sir Thomas Wentworth experienced the same sense of frustration with parliament's fondness for debate, not action. Members of parliament he regarded as 'a generation of men more apt to begin business than obstinately to pursue and perfect them; and the part they delight most in is to discourse rather than suffer'.[8]

If the renewed attack on the duke, during the last weeks of parliament, presaged ill, the close of the session at least brought five subsidies. Charles had promised to resummon the House and evidently embarked upon preparations to ensure the success of the second session. In July Buckingham surrendered some of his offices and was reconciled to some of his enemies. Clarendon suggests that he also considered a complete change of policy; a suggestion confirmed by Dorchester's belief that the duke had found 'his own judgement to have been misled'. Though preparations for the relief of La Rochelle continued during the summer of 1628, there was much noise of 'trading for a peace'.[9] Whatever Buckingham's intentions, they were cut short by Felton's dagger on 23 August. Buckingham's death was one of those incidents that changed the flow of traffic. For all his loyalty to the man and his memory, Charles now came into his own as master of affairs. More importantly, many estranged and alienated from the court returned to positions of favour and influence. And with the removal of the minister named as the cause of all grievances, there was good expectation of a harmonious session of parliament. Sir Francis Nethersole expressed that optimism bluntly only a day after the duke's assassination: 'The stone of offence being now removed by the hand of God, it is to be hoped that the king and people will come to a perfect unity'.[10]

Not all thought the problem so simple. There was disagreement at court about whether to recall parliament, some maintaining that the duke's death would give members of the Commons an opportunity 'to make appear their formal distempers were rather personal than real', others suggesting a period of respite and reform, before a second session in the spring. By the end of September it was decided to resummon parliament in January. Dorchester thought it the wisest course, 'for the *aegritudo* in men's minds requires time to take it away and the medicine of a constant and settled government . . .'.[11]

Metaphors of illness and cures pervade the language of 1628 and 1629.[12] The diseases discovered had not only affected relations between king and parliament. The war years had revealed symptoms of more fundamental disabilities and sores which, to the king and Council at least, threatened to infect the whole body politic: the weakness of the militia, divisions within the church, the pursuit of private interests before the public good, the decline of respect for authority, even a rejection of the wholesome purgatives which might have cleansed and restored the commonweal. It was a sense of impending fatality, of a terminal cancer of disorder threatening the collapse of all authority which governed the behaviour of king and Council during the winter of 1628.[13] That same sense, those same fears were articulated in the language of necessity, that is the needs of the state. But if the word 'state' is used more frequently in the letters and reports of this period,[14] it should not be understood in its modern sense, as an abstract authority detached from society, but as a description of the commonweal, that is of the common good. At the end of Hilary term 1628, Charles urged the judges leaving on circuit to see above all 'that every man in his quality and calling should have care of the common good, the rather because not every particular man, but the whole commonwealth is interested in it'.[15] The strains and stresses of war had not only brought about the crisis of parliaments; the safety and survival of the commonweal had been called into question.

King and Council embarked, as we shall see, upon a course of treatment: reform and retrenchment at court, the end of the sale of honours, reinvigoration of conciliar and local government. But for all the difficulties and frustrations of recent experience, Charles had by no means given up with parliaments. Rather the feverish activity of the autumn and winter of 1628 was an expression of the realisation, eloquently expressed by the Secretary of State, that 'it imports more than anything else that the next meeting should be without the late disorders'.[16] It is important to grasp that having commenced a programme of reform, Charles I met his last parliament for a decade in a mood of not unmerited optimism.

That optimism, as we know, was misplaced. The session of 1629 proved contentious, abortive, unproductive and chaotic. The Commons refused to pass an act legitimising the collection of tunnage and poundage, remained querulous about the religious issue, despite the king's declaration, and departed from Westminster after an unruly and disordered scene followed the order for their adjournment. The ill humours of the state had not been purged. Charles resolved not to call another parliament for a time, until, as his proclamation declared, his people might see his good intentions more clearly. The *aegritudo* referred to by Dorchester required longer and more radical treatment. There was business, not debate, to be conducted. As Attorney General Heath told Carlisle in reporting the dissolution: 'Now is the time to put brave and noble resolutions into action'.[17]

There can be little doubt that thereafter, whatever road the course of politics took, the king was his own master. Though foreign ambassadors, familiar with a Richelieu or an Olivares, tried to predict the rise of another favourite, none emerged to assume Buckingham's former place of influence and power. The arrangements which had followed Buckingham's death settled as an established pattern: 'The King holds in his hands the total directory leaving the executury part to every man within the compass of his charge'.[18] Even the queen, to whom Charles became a devoted husband and with whom he secluded himself whenever possible, was allowed almost no part in public affairs and showed no desire to exercise influence.[19] The state papers and registers of the Privy Council certainly reveal breadth of counsel and full consultation within the Council and the committees of the Council. But they indicate too that the decisions made, the aims and priorities pursued were often those of Charles himself.[20]

### III

What were those aims and priorities? What were the ideals and purposes, for ideals and purposes there were, which underlay the directives and proclamations issued and published by king and Council during the decade of Personal Rule? It is not always possible to detect from the official language of public documents the minds most at work in their formulation. Those which were of the king's own devising, and those which, formed by the genius of another, bore only his stamp cannot always be differentiated. But the language of the king's own letters and speeches, the articulation of ideals in the culture of the court, the alterations made by his hand to official papers, the comparison of documents passing through the Signet Office with the business reported in the Council register enable us to form a fairly clear picture of what mattered most to Charles.[21] Central to all his directives was an obsessive concern with order – in matters both large and small. Always an aspect of his personality, it was a characteristic developed by experience: by the profound impression made on the prince by the decorous gravity of Spain; by (in contrast) the dislocation and chaos of the wars; perhaps by the social unrest which bad harvests and unemployment threatened.[22]

It was an obsession most visible in the Royal Court and Household. In the Memoirs of her husband, Lucy Hutchinson recalled vividly the change of style from King James to King Charles: 'The face of the Court was much changed in the king, for King Charles was temperate, chaste and serious, so that the fools and bawds, mimics and catamites of the former Court grew out of fashion'.[23] It was a change of style which is more clearly detectable after 1628. In March 1629, for example, Charles announced his resumption of the ancient forms at Court. With the ordinances of Henry VIII as his model, he ordered greater care concerning the distinctions and degrees of rooms and persons; he issued directives governing the behaviour of attendants when the court went abroad. In January 1631 royal instructions of greater detail delineated by rank those with rights of access respectively to the Privy, Presence and Bed Chambers; they commanded due distance to be kept when the king and queen were in public. Charles literally withdrew himself from the easy familiarity which had characterised the reign of James and from which, perhaps, court favourites had sprung. The style of Charles's court reflected the image of the king: formal and reserved.[24] But it was not only in the sphere of morality and manners that the concern·for order was revealed. Charles instigated a pro- gramme of reform and retrenchment at Court, a programme which, if never very successful, at least curtailed the curve of rising extravagances. During the 1630s, the Court and House- hold were, as Professor Aylmer concluded, relatively par- simonious. The reforming Jupiter who in *Coelum Britannicum* renounces the sins of extravagance and licence was not purely a character of the dramatic imagination inhabiting only the idealised world of the masque.[25] As always with Charles I, the image and the reality informed each other.

The concern with order was not confined to the Court. Indeed it is important to understand that for Charles I the Court was not to be, as some historians have maintained, a retreat from the world of reality, but rather a model for the reformed government of Church and state. Fear of the collapse of all authority and the dislocation of society directed the king's attention to the reordering of society and government. Where there were no laws, the Council was to act to tackle problems, where statutes had already prescribed measures, the Council was to ensure that they were enforced.[26] The Book of Orders, perhaps the best known statement of Caroline social policy, was undoubtedly a response to the immediate circumstances of hardship and the threat of riot which they imposed. But, as has recently been emphasised, it is remarkable too as an innovative attempt to deal not only with the immediate problem and consequences but also with the symptoms of dearth and poverty. The Book of Orders looked to longer-term solutions and their enforcement. In informing his brother of the new orders in November 1630, the Earl of Manchester described that wider purpose clearly: 'It is time for Councillors to care [for] those things that concern government in these loose and dear times, lest mischief follow of it. The diligence of some justices and the good fruit of their pains show that there want no laws to reform all things, but good executioners of laws. Notice must be taken of such as use diligent and they known that are negligent to which end we are in purpose to have a commission'.[27] Manchester went on to explain that the commission would oversee relief·for the poor, the putting of youths to apprenticeship, the regulation of alehouses and the suppression of rogues and vagabonds. The Book of Orders, in other words, was the start of a programme for the reformation of society and the reinvigoration of local government.

That programme, because it depended upon men of substance and ability, brought an end to the sale of honours. Profligate grants of office and title had been a feature of Buckingham's supremacy no less under Charles than under James. Soon after the duke's death, however, Charles resolved to grant no more. When a widow petitioned for the nomination of a baronetcy promised her by Buckingham, 'the king told her he would not grant any more of that kind'.[28] Action was taken to rectify the consequences of undiscriminating patronage. In June 1629 Charles ordered that no peers with Irish or Scottish titles should be of the commission of the peace, unless they also held estates in England. Sir Edward Moundeford reported the new policy: 'There is a general reformation in hand for court and county . . . offices shall be given by desert. Sheriff-wicks shall be given as rewards of honour to the best-deserving of the counties'. The 1630s saw a return to the careful maintenance of aristocratic privilege.[29] It was one characteristic of the old society of degree and deference for which Charles increasingly yearned.

The king attached great importance to the role of the nobility and gentry in the governance of the localities. Proclamations ordering gentry dwelling in London to return to their country seats, published since the late years of Elizabeth's reign, were reissued in stronger language and enforced with great vigilance. The prosecution of town dwellers in Star Chamber was not just a fiscal device to bring money into the Exchequer. Charles was 'very jealous in the prosecution of his proclamation against town dwellers' and endeavoured, by ordering a detailed census of inhabitants, to ensure that it was enforced.[30] The re-establishment of authority in the localities, in the hands of the most important local families, was a central beam of his social reconstruction.

That reconstruction incorporated action to suppress taverns and tobacco, to end depopulation and dearth, to foster fishing and the drainage of the fens.[31] How far the king's intentions went may, perhaps, best be seen in London, 'our royal chamber and the principal state of our residence'. As London embodied the ills of the age so it was, when reformed, to be the proof of the cure. The treatment ranged from the work of the commission for buildings to the regulation of hackney coaches, even to schemes for the levelling and draining of streets, and the improvement of London Bridge.[32] All were part of Charles's design to reduce the sprawling anarchy of the metropolis to order, calm and decency.

It is in the context of these concerns, of this looking back to an (idealised) society of harmony and deference that we should understand Charles's religious policy. If order was Charles I's private religion, then it behoved all the more that the religion of the realm be ordered. Gardiner, in a perceptive phrase, captured the central tenet of royal policy: 'the incongruity of dirt and disorder with sacred things'.[33]

It is not usual to refer to the religious reforms and enactments of the 1630s as the policy of Charles I. The name of Archbishop Laud stamped itself on the religious history of that decade at the time and has borne his imprint ever since. And yet it was the king's policy. It is important to recall that Laud did not become Archbishop of Canterbury until August 1633 and that, until then, such influence as he exercised beyond his see of London, formidable though that was, he owed entirely to royal favour and support. In 1633 Laud was elevated to oversee a programme with which he was known to be in sympathy, but which the king (albeit with his advice) had already devised. In 1626 and again in 1628 it was Charles who had attempted, over-optimistically and unsuccessfully, to stifle the growth of controversy by a declaration prefatory to the new edition of the Thirty Nine Articles, a declaration which forbade 'unnecessary disputations' and ordered that 'all further curious search be laid aside'. In December 1629 the king issued instructions to the bishops, enjoining their residence, diligent performance of their duties and careful maintenance of their sees. Afternoon sermons were replaced by catechising and lecturers were ordered to read divine service (in full vestments) before delivering their sermon.[34] Even after his elevation to Canterbury, the tone of Laud's letters suggests that it was the king who led and the archbishop who followed. The decision in the St Gregory's case, for example, was the king's, not Laud's: Laud specifically explained to John Williams that it was

Charles and not he who disapproved of communion in the body of the church, not the chancel.[35] Throughout the 1630s royal letters reflect the king's personal concern with the Church, with the proper maintenance of the clergy and episcopacy, and with due observance of the forms of worship established by the Book of Common Prayer.[36] Charles determined to end theological controversy, to reform and to reestablish respect for the hierarchy of the Church and to order its service with a view to uniting the realm in a liturgy common to every parish. It was an ideal close to that of Elizabeth in 1559. It was now an ideal which embraced not only England, but all three kingdoms, and even the plantations. Supervision of ministers going to the colonies, instructions to the Lord Deputy of Ireland, and most of all royal policy towards the Scots all bear witness to 'that good conformity and unity in the church which his Majesty is careful and desirous to establish throughout his dominions'.[37]

It had been necessary to reform the Court because it was the temple of God's lieutenant on earth. It was essential to order the Church because it was the palace of an invisible king. An ordered Church was also the foundation of the perfect commonweal which was the king's grand design. When he decided to govern without parliaments, Charles I did not resign himself to a hand-to-mouth struggle for mere survival; he embarked upon an ambitious renovation of the fabric of Church and state.

## IV

Policies and ideals without the instruments of their enactment belong to the world of utopia, not to that of affairs. Some indeed have argued that during the 1630s Charles was but a dreamer, concocting fantasies of a monarchical Elysium, ignorant of the obstacle to its realisation and unconcerned with the measures by which ideal is translated into practice. Nothing could be further from the truth. No decade of seventeenth-century history was more concerned with (to borrow a phrase from the 1650s with which the 30s have much in common) the instruments of government.

In the first place, the Personal Rule saw the reinvigoration of the Privy Council. During the years of Buckingham's hegemony, the Council was eclipsed by private counsel, compromised by division and weakened by the exclusions of magnates powerful in their localities. During the war years and especially after 1628, the Council was formed into an efficient advisory body and an effective organ of government. Former enemies of Buckingham returned to the Council board.[38] The Lords President of the Marches and the North, and the Secretaries for Ireland and Scotland were added, presumably to facilitate communications with the outlying provinces and kingdoms. In the absence of a favourite, king and Council resumed their partnership for the government of the realm. The Council met regularly, usually twice weekly. The king himself was more frequently in attendance, especially after 1635 with the death of Weston and, more significantly, the launching of the ship-money fleet.[39] If the formal registers of the Council (like the formal journals of the Commons) provide the best evidence of the bulk and range of business, it is the notes of a secretary to the Council such as George Weckherlin which offer a valuable glimpse inside the Council chamber.[40] They suggest full debate, vocal differences, extensive research and renewed discussion prior to action. They indicate an ordered and efficient institution.

Pressure of business necessitated procedural developments. Committees of the Council, formerly *ad hoc* conventions, became standing bodies with regular times of meeting and their own clerical bureaucracy. The Irish committee, for example, met every Wednesday morning, and the committee for war (significantly in session until 1634) on Thursday afternoons. Committees generated subcommittees, such as that for St Paul's cathedral, a subdivision of the committee for charitable uses.[41] Royal requests for regular surveys, censuses and reports vastly increased the paperwork coming to the Council and, by consequence, improved its own record-keeping. Council orders of April 1632 required that the title of each subject discussed be entered in the margin of the appropriate page and indexed at the end of the book. In October of the next year, the clerk began to compile an abstract of unfinished business of the month, so that matters left incomplete would not lapse but would instead be given priority. Precedents were drawn up to facilitate the resolution of problems by references to past practice.[42] When we read through the Council register, when we peruse the clerks' notes or the memoranda left by Windebanke and others, we cannot but be struck by the efficiency of the Council — by the sophistication of the procedure, by the diligence and continuity of its personnel. The 1630s might well be known for the winning of the initiative by the English Privy Council.

The Council was but the first link in the chain which connected the motor of central policy with the wheel of local action. There were no permanent agents of the central government to enact its will in the localities. And Charles I showed no desire, even had it been possible, to change the traditional structure. But he did attempt to revitalise the existing machinery and especially to improve the means by which the orders of the Council were communicated to the counties. In the absence of a parliament, that seminar of the English localities, it was all the more important to secure the other 'points of contact' between Council and county.[43]

Perhaps the most useful were the justices of assize making their twice-yearly circuit. At the end of Hilary term 1628 the Lord Keeper addressed them before they went, ordering them in the king's name to 'certify his Majesty of the state of the several places of the kingdom and how they found the counties governed and that they should cherish such as they found diligent and careful in the execution of justice and certify the names of such as they found negligent and careless'. The Book of Orders of January 1631 further extended and formalised the role of the justices as roving reporters and superintendents of royal policy. In the summer of the same year Charles exhorted them especially to oversee the execution of his orders and to ensure that the gentry maintained their seats in the country. In 1635, the justices went out to explain and to justify the second writ of ship money. Not without cause were they described by the Lord Keeper as 'visitors of the kingdom'.[44]

But that of course was *exactly* what they were: occasional visitors to counties and provinces of which they otherwise had little knowledge. As such they were of limited value both as agents in and as reporters from the localities. There were

potentially more effective instruments. In May 1629, one
Lionel Sharpe, lamenting the parliament's misunderstanding
of the king's good intentions, advised Secretary Dorchester,
that 'to make the king known, there are no fitter instruments
than the lord lieutenants and the bishops. They might make
known the excellent mind and nature of the king to his
people'.[45] It may be that king and Council endorsed this
analysis. During the 1630s the number of lords lieutenant was
increased so that almost every county had its own lieutenant
and most more than one. Sons of magnates were joined in the
commission with their fathers, perhaps in order to familiarise
them with their charge and to establish a degree of continuity
in office. Those not required at court on the king's business
were ordered to reside in their lieutenancies and to oversee
personally the organisation of the militia and the mustering of
troops.[46] Similarly, the bishops were placed on the commission
of the peace and permitted to leave their seats only by licence
from the king. They could, if they were as diligent as Bishop
Wren, be an invaluable source of information and a reliable
agent of royal policy.[47]

   And yet for all this the English counties were not governed
from the centre. At the vital end of the chain of command
were the unpaid local officers — the gentry deputy lieutenants
and justices of the peace, the parish constables and church-
wardens from the lower social orders. In so far as he derived his
authority from letters patent under the Great Seal, was responsible for his behaviour to the Council and was reluctant to lose
the prestige attaching to the position, the justice of the peace
was the king's man in the county. But in so far as he there held
his estates, there enjoyed the society of friends and neighbours,
there felt responsibility for his tenants and inferiors, there
himself paid the rates which he helped to levy, the justice was
the pinnacle and embodiment of local society — bound by
interest and expectation to protect its customs and represent its
needs. The absence of parliament, and the Book of Orders
itself underlined the duality of the position. Local government
depended upon local knowledge. This remained essentially the
monopoly of local men. The lords lieutenant who diligently
attended the Council, or wantonly sported in the West End,
knew all too little of the counties in their charge. Devoid of any

other agents, the Council was forced to rely upon the pro-
pertied gentry who resided on their estates. The compositions
for knighthood demonstrated that dependence. At first the
Privy Councillors compounded with offenders. But, after a
poor start, the commission was extended into the localities and
leading gentry were appointed because they alone would know
who, possessed of £40 of annual rent, should have come
forward:

> We are well assured that by your industries and knowledge
> of the persons of men and their estates you may . . . better
> the same in many things, for whereas our commissioners . . .
> were led for the most part by subsidy rolls . . . they might
> easily mistake the true values of men which you by your
> better knowledge of them may be more truly informed of.[48]

With or without parliaments, the government of early Stuart
England rested upon co-operation and consent.

## V

To what extent then was co-operation secured? Did the
members of parliament who returned to their localities in 1629
seek to obstruct the government by Council? Were the aims
and ideals of Charles I anathema to the gentry rulers of the
counties? Were the problems encountered by king and Council
manufactured by constitutional conflict or inherent in the
structure of the English polity?

Such questions are hard to answer qualitatively. Silence, or
even letters of support from the localities, could conceal
diligent activity, grudging compliance, at times even outright
resistance. The certificates performed according to the
requirements of the Book of Orders ranged from the brief 'all
well' to the multipage report.[49] And whilst we should not
equate detail of information with extent of activity, we may
still deduce something from it. As Rowland St John advised
Edward Montagu: 'It is observed to be a rule of discreet policy
in general businesses to make a general answer, lest by
descending too far into particulars something should be

fastened upon which may produce an unexpected prejudice'.[50] Vagueness, in other words, could cloak a multitude of sins. It is impossible to calculate how many avoided composition for knighthood by a false return of their income, but the excuses certainly arouse suspicion.[51] On the other hand, few doubted the need for measures to deal with grain shortage and unemployment. Few questioned the legality of knighthood fines. For all the evasions, the Book of Orders was successful and the compositions for knighthood brought £173,537 into the Exchequer.[52] If there was opposition, it did not in the end prevent payment. Beyond that all we can say is that the curve of response ranged from grudging to enthusiastic.

At two points it is possible to be more specific: the quest for an 'exact militia', and the levy of ship money. In so far as the one required soldiers and the other money the response to each can be measured. The effort to increase the numbers, sharpen the skill and modernise the equipment of the local militia was beleaguered by a multitude of problems. After 1604 and the repeal of 4 and 5 Philip and Mary caps 2 and 3, the authority of lieutenancy lost its foundation on statute and rested entirely on the prerogative — exposed to challenge from those with more enthusiasm for legal niceties than for military exercise. In February 1632, one Walters, an attorney, refused to contribute to the musters in Northamptonshire and stood 'upon the letter of the law'.[53] But there were more serious difficulties even at the centre. In the first place the lords lieutenant who first received instructions were often the very members of the Council which had issued them. Absent from their commissions and preoccupied with other business they were content to pass the burden of supervision to the deputies who 'best understand the state of the county and men's abilities therein'.[54] But no less than the justices, among whose number they ranked, the deputy lieutenants were first and foremost local men. With an authority that some questioned and with little support from absentee superiors, they were obliged to muster the reluctant pikemen and corsleteers (many perhaps their own tenants) and, in the case of the horse, the gentry of the county, their social equals and fellow justices. It is hardly surprising that it was always the number of horse which was most deficient.[55] The difficulties which faced the deputies were exacerbated by memory of the war years during which they had assisted with the loan, imposed martial law and billeted unruly troops on unwilling households, often without funds to reimburse them. That memory, as it fuelled their unpopularity, so it sapped their authority. The repeated injunctions of king and Council suggest that orders were not obeyed. In 1638 Charles admitted that former directories were 'not finding effects answerable to our expectations'.[56] The perfect militia proved an unrealisable goal.

But was the programme an unrelieved failure? The answer to that must be no. The very complaints about musters during the 1630s, and about deputy lieutenants in 1640, suggest that some effort was made locally.[57] And study of the extensive militia records among the papers of Sir Thomas Jervoise, a deputy lieutenant of Hampshire, indicates clearly that for all it fell short of the ideal, the militia of that county saw some improvement. Jervoise and his fellow deputies were diligent in their attention to business. Even where there was less enthusiasm for service, the Council was not completely helpless. Sir John Holland, deputy lieutenant for Norfolk, felt acutely the need for action after signs of Council disapproval: 'The Council's letters requiring diligence and expedition, the tax of our late remissness from our lords lieutenants are all spurs to quicken us in this service... The lords, I believe, will listen after our diligence and there will be them at leisure to give intelligence'.[58] The county militia never rose to the standards for which Wentworth would have laboured. Foot-dragging was common and hard to prevent. But if the achievement fell short of the expectation, the horse and foot of the county militia were driven to greater activity, more frequent exercise, perhaps greater expenditure on arms than had been, or was considered desirable.[59]

The great success story, however, was ship money. Ship money was a rate, not a tax, collected at first from the maritime counties, but after 1635 from the whole country. It owed its origins to royal diplomacy, and especially the king's negotiations with Spain.[60] It was never a source of ordinary revenue and was received not into the Exchequer, but into the Treasury of the Navy. It is important to bear in mind that ship money was not, and was never demanded (whatever was intended), as a regular or permanent levy. Each writ was a *separate* request for aid in time of national emergency; the preface to each writ explained and justified the need to equip a fleet for the year. It may be that the early responses of the country reflected a genuine recognition (after the debacle of 1628) of the need for a strong navy in a war-torn Europe.[61] It is significant certainly that when the writ was extended from the maritime counties to the country at large, the point at which the legality might have been questioned, only 2½ per cent of the sum requested failed to come in, and the amount raised, £194,864, was never exceeded. The success story continued as we shall see, and it was not until 1639 and 1640 that the collection of ship money collapsed.[62] So much for the figures. What may we learn from the success and final failure of ship money about Charles I's government, and reactions to his government, during the years of Personal Rule?

The first response to the writ was bewilderment in the localities: doubts about *how* to proceed to rate the maritime towns and individual inhabitants. The first writ of 1634 left the assessment of the corporate towns to the mayors and civic authorities meeting together. This immediately posed problems, as the mayor of Dover explained to the Earl of Suffolk, Lord Warden of the Cinque Ports: 'Such is the distance of these towns and cities ... that [we] are at an exigent, and know not where to begin or what to do'.[63] The Council learned by the experience. When the writ was extended the next year, they suggested the amount to be paid by the corporate towns within the counties. Beyond those suggestions, the assessment was to be made by the sheriff, who was exhorted to have 'more than ordinary care and regard' in the apportionment 'to prevent complaints of inequality in the assessment whereby we were much troubled the last year'. In general he was advised to rate according to the houses and lands within the county, or to follow the other public payments 'most equal and agreeable' to the inhabitants.[64] But if this were an attempt to resolve all the earlier problems, it failed. Rating disputes remained the biggest headache.[65] Complaints about unequal assessment and favouritism came to both the sheriff and the Council. Often they contradicted each other. On the one hand the Council had ordered the sheriff to rate according to property; on the other it enjoined that poor cottagers should be spared and those of no estate but considerable personal wealth be assessed in their stead. Amid these conflicting dictates there was room for much confusion, protest and mis-understanding. The most diligent sheriffs perhaps met with the greatest difficulties. Sir George Sandys, sheriff of Kent for part of 1636 and 1637, was well respected in his county for his efforts to give all complaints a hearing and to settle all disputes fairly. Not surprisingly, as a result, 'there was in some places not less than six if not seven warrants or orders from him and his undersheriff in one and the same matter, each contradict-ing the other'.[66] At times the Council created the problem. Continuing to act as the final and impartial arbiter of disputes, it overruled and contradicted the assessment made by a sheriff according to its own directions.[67] Ship money exemplifies the problems of early modern government: problems of interest, division and localism, most of all the problem of dependence — the dependence of the Council upon the sheriff, of the sheriff on the constable, ultimately the dependence of all upon the preparedness of those assessed to pay.

And yet because ship money was collected, because the pro-portion returned of the sum expected was far higher than subsidies, better than any contemporary levy and certainly more impressive than modern taxation it must also be regarded as evidence of what could be done when the Council and local officers devoted themselves to the task. By making the sheriff solely responsible for payment, the Council ensured a devoted servant of central policy in the county. Because his own interest was at stake, the sheriff laboured to overcome the difficulties and to raise the whole sum. Why then did ship money collapse?

Here we should return to an earlier point: ship money was not a regular tax, but a levy for a specific purpose. The Council itself seemed to act upon that assumption. The writ of 1638 demanded less than a third of the sum previously required, presumably because the Scots War focused attention upon a different emergency, one which would require troops rather than ships. The return, as we have seen, was low and the next year, when the Council (unwisely) raised the sum to earlier heights, the response was poorer. For ship money was

now demanded along with other more pressing, more costly
and certainly more disruptive requests for men to join the army
at York and money to equip and transport them.[68] Sheriffs
preoccupied with raising troops could not devote their
undivided attention to the collection of ship money. In some
counties they even acquiesced, under the pressure of time and
circumstance, in using the money they had garnered to speed
the troops North. The most diligent collectors met with
resistance, especially from the lower orders, those most
affected by the demands of the war. And when they lost the co-
operation of the parish constables, when they could no longer
distrain goods, nor sell confiscated property, the sheriffs were
powerless.[69] When the sheriff could do nothing, the
exhortations and threats of the Council lost their force. The
collapse of ship money in 1639 takes us back to the problems of
the later 1620s: problems that arose when England was called
upon to fight a war. It points too to the weakness of the Council
when there was too much business to supervise, too little co-
operation in the counties. The success and the failure of ship
money reflect the strengths and weaknesses of early modern
government.

In discussing ship money we have confined ourselves to the
practical problems of government. We have said nothing of the
constitutional grounds.[70] Complaints were confined to rating
1637, there is little to say. Before Hampden there are almost no
recorded instances of objection to the levy on legal or
constitutional grounds.[70] Complaints were confined to rating
disputes; protests were limited to unfair assessments. Some
have argued that these complaints cannot be distinguished
from more principled objections. Rating disputes, they argue,
were the respectable veils which covered more principled
objections. Those principles plaintiffs not unnaturally silenced
when appealing to the Council for more practical measures,
such as redress of unfair assessments.[71] Such arguments must
be taken seriously. When we reflect that Tintinhull hundred,
Somerset, the home of that irrepressible parliamentarian, Sir
Robert Phelips, produced more rating disputes than any other
hundred in the kingdom, we are bound to suspect some
opposition from principle.[72] Certainly we should not lightly
assume constitutional acquiescence from silence. For at least

one adviser sympathetic to ship money considered that 'in every place there are some malevolent spirits that labour to poison and censure the most honourable actions, blasting this for an imposition, an innovation against the liberty of the subject'. . . [73] But yet the absence of vocal protest remains remarkable. Sheriffs who might have drawn some advantage, certainly some sympathy from the Council, from attributing delays to nice constitutional scruples seldom refer to objections of principle. More often administrative difficulties are set in contrast to a general willingness to pay – a willingness which is more convincing when endorsed by the sheriff and translated into action and money. In Gloucester in November 1634, for example, though feeling was strong that the city was overrated, 'the chief inhabitants encouraged the payment rather than the service should be retarded'. [74] Purses were more in evidence than principles. Doubtless there was in letters to the Council an element of loyal rhetoric which at times concealed resentment and antagonism; doubtless ship money was paid, like any tax, with resignation rather than with enthusiasm. But before 1637 there is little *evidence* at least that its legality was widely questioned, and some suggestion that it was becoming more accepted.

It was John Hampden who raised the issue of principle and so took ship money to the law. [75] Hampden's case, the arguments of counsel, the eventual decision for the crown by the narrowest majority are well known. The news spread widely at the time. [76] During the year of decision, many delayed payment in anticipation of the judgement, perhaps in hope that the king might abandon the levy. But whatever his place in the portrait gallery of martyrs for English constitutionalism, Hampden should not loom too large on the canvas of Personal Rule. As the Earl of Leicester was informed by his secretary, ship money was in debate, 'but in the interim the money is in collecting'. The case may also have caused as much concern to the country as to the crown. Clarendon suggests that before Hampden's case many were pleased to pay a levy which they were not bound to. And even before the final judgement, one newswriter was 'of opinion it had been better for the people that this question had never been put to dispute, for if the judgement be on the king's side, . . . then it will be as a

perpetual case and law and may for ever be continued'.[77] He
may have been right. As we shall see, in the year of Hampden's
case more than 90 per cent was collected. If the trial delayed
payments and raised the question of legality, the final decision,
unwelcome though it was, may have resolved more legal doubts
than it aroused.

## VI

And so we come to the fundamental question. Did the Bishops'
War accelerate the journey along the high road to civil war, or
force a detour into a conflict which had never been in sight?
Could Charles have succeeded, could the Personal Rule have
continued without the rebellion of the northern kingdom?

The question itself is inappropriate, for it assumes that
Charles had decided permanently to govern without parliament. This was not the case. The declaration of 1629, that the
king would call another parliament, 'when our people shall see
more clearly into our interests and actions' should, I think, be
taken literally. Wentworth seems so to have understood it. In
1635, triumphant after the success of parliament in Ireland, he
reflected upon the situation at home:

> Happy it were if we might live to see the like in England;
> everything in his season; but in some cases it is necessary
> there be a time to forget, as in others to learn, and howbeit
> the peccant.... Humour be not yet wholly purged forth,
> yet do I conceive it in the way, and that once rightly
> corrected and prepared, we may hope for a parliament of a
> sound constitution indeed ...[78]

If Wentworth saw a high road stretching before him, its
destination was a world of harmony in which king and
parliament would work together. But what of others?

After the unruly scene of 1629, the early 1630s were marked
by calm and quiet, at Court and throughout the country.
Clarendon recalled that 'there quickly followed so excellent a
composure throughout the whole kingdom that the like peace
and plenty and universal tranquillity for ten years was never

enjoyed by any nation'.[79] Peace brought the expansion of trade
and the benefits of neutrality in a Europe at war. The
merchants soon abandoned their protest about customs duties.
Some MPs imprisoned in 1629 made their apologies and were
pardoned. Sir John Eliot himself faded from the public eye. His
death in the Tower in 1632 attracted little attention: 'Sir John
Eliot is dead in the Tower who is no otherwise considerable
here but among the dead.'[80] The events of 1629 had caused
concern to MPs themselves and to the many who heard news of
them in the country. In 1630 there may well have been support
for government initiatives like the Book of Orders which
tackled pressing problems neglected by legislation. When
Charles I went on progress to Scotland in 1633, he was
evidently a monarch popular with his people. The king, it was
reported, 'enjoyed the love and dutiful demonstrations of his
subjects in every place'; he received 'the acclamations of his
people everywhere and their expressions of joy and
contentment'.[81]

The calm and peace continued. The ordinary budget was
better balanced. Ship money was generally paid despite the
difficulties. Undoubtedly there were tensions and grievances:
Charles's religious policy, framed to unite the realm in a common liturgy, divided the Church and alienated some of the
gentry. But those tensions and grievances neither stymied
government nor threatened revolt. Most, Clarendon tells us,
thought that 'imperium et libertas were as well reconciled as
possible'.[82] In the many volumes of correspondence, public and
private, we find few demands for a parliament. Nor should
that surprise us. James I had called no parliament from 1614 to
1621. After 1624 war necessitated frequent sessions; with the
peace those circumstances changed. In 1629 parliament was
still an event; it was not an institution.[83]

On the eve of Hampden's case, in October 1637, John
Burghe penned his weekly despatch to Viscount Scudamore,
then ambassador in Paris. The political climate, as he
described it, was far from threatening:

  All things are at this instant here in that calmness that there
  is very little matter of novelty to write, for there appears no
  change or alteration either in court or affairs, for all business

goes undisturbedly on in the strong current of the present time to which all men for the most part submit, and that effects this quietness. And although payments here are great (considering the people have not heretofore been accustomed unto them) yet they only privately breathe out a little discontented humour and lay down their purses, for I think that great tax of the ship money is so well digested (the honour of the business sinking now into apprehension and amongst most winning an affection to it) I suppose will become perpetual; for indeed if men would consider the great levies of monies in foreign parts for the service of the state, these impositions would appear but little burdens, but time can season and form minds to comply with public necessities.[84]

Time indeed might well have done. But even without the Scots would Charles have had that time? For all his vision down the long road to parliamentary government, Gardiner remained unsure: 'How long this state of things would have endured if no impulse had come from without it is impossible to say'.[85] There were undoubtedly difficulties and problems which *might* in the long run have made personal government unsustainable. The co-operation of those who bore the massive burdens of collecting knighthood fines or ship money could not for certain be secured indefinitely. Yet the diligence exhibited by many, even in 1639 and 1640, must not be underestimated. The relative youth of the royalists in 1642 suggests, perhaps, a maturing generation supportive of the king's personal rule. To contemplate what might have happened had the Scots not risen is no idle parlour game; it is an exercise of the historical imagination, central to an understanding of the past.

In the end we come back to the Bishops' Wars. At first the troubles in Scotland presaged no major crisis. In January 1638, Sir John Finet, Master of Ceremonies, devoted more correspondence to his problems of seating ambassadors at the masque than to the news of events in the North. Only by April did he begin to fear that the Scots question would not be settled 'without mischief'.[86] It is important to reflect that when he resolved to enforce obedience by arms Charles was evidently optimistic — not only of victory, but of the willingness of the

localities to co-operate with the levy of men and money. If this
was misplaced optimism, it was at least shared by others and
not without sense. For all his opposition to English involvement
in Europe, Wentworth supported the decision to fight the
Scots. In November 1639, Colonel Gage could not perceive
'why it should not be feasible to raise and maintain a good
army at the charge of the shires of England, as it hath been to
compass the contribution of the ship money. I am confident
that if in the country there were fit ministers and willing to
second such a design, it would be effected with a great
facility'.[86] Even that condition did not seem beyond hope of
fulfilment. The Scots were old enemies and ballads sung in
1639 gave voice to English jingoism. Sheriffs and deputy
lieutenants worked loyally to conduct the troops to York. But
the war proved unpopular and changed the whole course of
affairs. Why?

War revived the problems and grievances of 1628. The
demand for coat and conduct money raised legal, administrative and fiscal problems. In many counties the cost of
equipping soldiers equalled (and at times surpassed) that of
ship money which was still demanded. The levy of troops from
the trained bands gave rise to fears of invasion in a realm
schooled by ship-money writs to anticipate imminent danger.
Hampshire, remote from Scotland, offered excuses instead of
men, on the grounds that the coast was vulnerable. The loss of
young adult males caused more than emotional disturbance to
many a village or hundred. Parts of Cornwall protested that
the removal of men led to a labour shortage which resulted in
the flooding of the tin mines. Grievances were expressed most
vocally by the lower orders, those most affected in any age by
the demands and miseries of war. The most diligent sheriffs,
deputies and justices faced recalcitrance and riot. The Council
could offer little help. Central policy now threatened local
order. It was impossible to preserve them both. The issues at
stake were not constitutional. 'What had changed between
1634 and 1639 was not the gentry's opinion of Charles's
constitutional arguments, but the breakdown of peace, quiet
and order in the local communities.'[88] In 1640, the gentry no
less than the king met resistance from below.

The decision to summon parliament, for all that it defused

the electric atmosphere, exacerbated some of the problems. Even in 1640 ship money was paid well in Hampshire until the issue of writs for elections to parliament. Few thereafter would pay a levy which might be questioned or when subsidies would certainly be granted. Similarly the deputy lieutenants of Devonshire, mindful of 1628, feared being criticised in parliament.[89] With the war and the summoning of parliament all was again in flux. Personal Rule was at an end.

War undoubtedly provided the opportunity for the expression of discontents. But more significantly, because on a wider plain, it created problems and grievances not in evidence before. At court, the decision to fight the Scots meant the end of domestic reform, a crash from financial stability to indebtedness and the distraction of the Council from the business of normal government.[90] In the counties, that decision, like the wars of the 1620s, strained the fabric of local government and threatened the peace of local society. The problems which faced Charles I from 1638 to 1640, problems similar to those which faced the kings of France and Spain, caused no less difficulty to the republican regimes of the 1650s. They were problems rooted less in the constitution than in the structure of English government. Charles was too conservative ever to seek to change that structure. It was his achievement to have governed so ambitiously and so successfully within it. If local intransigence and a stand on local customs are milestones on a high road of English history, it is a road which leads past civil war, indeed beyond the Restoration. It is a road which leads not to the triumph of parliament, but to the erosion of provincialism: a road which ends with the railways?

## Acknowledgements

I am grateful to the Duke of Buccleuch KT for permission to see the Montagu MSS cited in note 39 and to Lord Downshire for permission to see the Trumbull MSS cited in note 40.

# 4. Spain or the Netherlands? The Dilemmas of Early Stuart Foreign Policy

## SIMON ADAMS

That your Majesty will be pleased to enter into a more strict alliance with the States of the United Provinces and other neighbouring princes and states of the Protestant Religion, for the defence and maintenance thereof against all designs and attempts of the Pope and his adherents to subvert and suppress it.

The Nineteen Propositions, 1 June 1642. Proposition 17

## I

THE foreign policy of James I and Charles I was shaped by two fundamental tensions which, although they were experienced by all the leading European states of the early seventeenth century, took on a particular significance in the context of English politics. (The union of the crowns creates a problem of nomenclature, but since the English political debate forms the central subject of this essay, 'England' and 'English' will generally be used throughout.) The first of the two – the fiscal tension between crown and subject – was the product of a major structural problem: that of conducting efficient military operations in the light of the contemporary inflation of military costs. The second tension was an ideological one: the impact of the religious division in Europe created by the Reformation. By the end of the sixteenth century a popular consensus had been created in English politics that English foreign policy should be conducted to a greater or lesser degree in defence of the protestant cause on the continent. The Thirty Years War appeared to imperil the future of that cause – although it neither involved the British Isles directly, apart from the brief Franco-Spanish invasion threat in 1626–7, nor endangered any immediate economic interest. For James I and Charles I, however, the central issue of the war was the defence of the Stuart dynastic interest in the hereditary lands of the Elector Palatine Frederick V. A major debate ensued over the nature of English foreign policy and the means by which it should be pursued and by 1640 the conduct of foreign relations had become one of the many issues that divided the English political nation.

## II

The structural difficulties of the Stuart monarchy have been the subject of much recent scholarly attention. In his major study of the parliaments of the 1620s, Conrad Russell has argued that 'it was this burden of war ... that brought relations between central and local government, and hence between king and parliament, to the point of collapse. The crisis of 1626–8, like the crisis of 1640, was the result of England's administrative inability to fight a war'.[1] However, the nature of these structural difficulties depended on the type of war to be fought and the means to be employed. The inflation of military costs was a result not only of the general increase in the size of armies following changes of weaponry and tactics during the sixteenth century but also of the King of Spain's possession of vast resources of colonial wealth.[2] The wealth from the Indies enabled him to engage in warfare on a scale which, as the Privy Council in 1602, parliamentarians in 1621 and 1624 (see below), the Dutch, Frederick V and Cardinal Richelieu all recognised, would quickly exhaust his enemies.[3] They in turn were forced to look to the economic bases of their military machines and seek either to expand their powers of taxation, create their own colonial or mercantile empires, or contest his control over the Indies.

The English monarchy possessed few intrinsic fiscal assets.

The windfall expropriation of monastic and chantry lands had enabled Henry VIII and Edward VI to fight a war on a massive, if ultimately disastrous, scale between 1542 and 1550. The Earls of Leicester and Essex in the reign of Elizabeth, the Duke of Buckingham in 1624 and the Earl of Bedford in 1640 were all associated with schemes for the expropriation of episcopal and dean and chapter lands; but further change in the constitution of the Church did not receive royal approval.[4] The sources of ordinary revenue were inadequate to support large-scale military operations. The crown lands were diminishing in value, while customs receipts were too vulnerable to the vagaries of trade and the hazards of war to be relied upon. The increased importance of customs receipts for the revenue of the crown encouraged neutrality, as both Charles I in April 1636 and the Count-Duke of Olivares in January 1637 observed.[5] Major military operations were, therefore, dependent on either of the two sources of extraordinary revenue (parliamentary subsidy or various forms of prerogative taxation), the advancing of mercantile enterprise, or a mercantile/colonial war.

The need to reach agreement with members of parliament – and in consequence to permit discussion of policy – made reliance on parliamentary subsidy for military finance an unattractive prospect. There was, however, no consensus of constitutional opinion opposing parliamentary involvement in affairs of state. Queen Elizabeth had attempted to avoid discussion of foreign policy but her counsellors expected and encouraged her to seek parliamentary support for the intervention in the Netherlands in 1585–6 and an open debate on intervention was held in the second session of the Parliament of 1586–7.[6] Jacobean policy and practice were ambiguous. In June 1607, during the course of the still mysterious affair of the petition of the merchants trading with Spain, the Earls of Salisbury and Northampton delivered a formal lecture to a joint committee of Lords and Commons on the inability of the Commons to discuss major affairs of state.[7] Yet three years later, in June 1610, Salisbury reversed his position and attempted to persuade the Commons to grant a subsidy for the support of James's military intervention in the Cleves-Jülich crisis (see below) by appealing to them as

men of extraordinary quality ... we deal not with you
economically, we talk not of corn or grain, but as with
statesmen and wish you to bend your cogitations to view how
foreign states stand and how their affairs have relation to the
state of this kingdom.[8]

During the first session of the Parliament of 1621, Sir George
Calvert, the Secretary of State, opposed a motion in the
Commons to consult with the Lords on policy on the grounds
that 'it is a strange thing for a king to consult with his subjects
what war he mean to undertake. This were means for all his
enemies to know what he intends to do'. The second session,
however, was initiated on 21 November by an address to a joint
committee of Lords and Commons by three Privy Councillors –
Lord Digby, Lord Cranfield and the Lord Keeper – on the
current state of policy. During the subsequent debate on the
Petition and Remonstrance of 1 December, the Commons took
the position that they had thereby been specifically invited to
discuss foreign affairs, although James replied that an
invitation to discuss the Palatinate did not include policy as a
whole and specifically not the marriage of Prince Charles.[9]

The inconsistencies and shifts of position suggest that
opposition to parliamentary discussion of foreign policy was
not so much strictly constitutional as political and was
motivated by the fear of being forced into a disliked foreign
policy by popular pressure. In this respect the apparent
toleration of parliamentary debate of foreign affairs between
1624 and 1628 was more apparent than real. It did not represent a constitutional concession and, moreover, Buckingham
never intended to subordinate his foreign policy to
parliamentary desires in the first place. His refusal to take
them into account in the conduct of his policy underlay many
of the disputes of 1625–8.

In the absence of financial support from parliament, the
crown could turn to various prerogative fiscal measures, as
James began to do on a large scale after his rejection of the
Great Contract in 1610. But as a form of military financing these
measures – as the benevolences of 1620 and 1622 showed –
were unreliable. Not only were the returns limited, but the
collection met with constitutional resistance from men who in

fact accepted the aims of the king's foreign policy, as was the case with Viscount Saye and Sele in 1622.[10] Following the outbreak of war in 1625 and the dissolutions of the Parliaments of 1625 and 1626, the emergency powers of the prerogative were employed to justify a number of devices: the forced loan of 1626, the use of martial law to discipline unpaid soldiers and sailors, and the proposed ship-money levy and excise of 1628. Once again these produced more resistance than they were worth, as did the later ship-money levies and the methods used to raise troops for the Bishops' War. In this respect it was not so much the power of the crown to fight a war that collapsed in 1640, but the power to do so under the prerogative.

The weakness of relying on domestic taxation to finance major military operations had been recognised in the reign of Elizabeth and during the course of the war with Spain the strategy of subsidising land operations by a naval war against the Spanish Indies and by the interception of the Silver Fleet had been devised.[11] It was for such a campaign, combined with a land attack on the Spanish Netherlands – and not a simple open season for privateers – that parliamentarians like Sir Dudley Digges and John Pym in November 1621 or Sir John Eliot in March 1624 called, when they advocated a 'war by diversion'.[12] While Elizabethan practice had not lived up to expectations – nor did the attempts of Buckingham to revive the strategy in 1625 and 1626 – the concern with economic and diversionary warfare was shared by Richelieu, Gustavus Adolphus and most of the other participants in the Thirty Years War. During the 1620s the Dutch stood on the defensive on land while conducting an offensive at sea – a strategy which obtained its greatest success when Piet Hein captured the Silver Fleet in September 1628. In retaliation, Olivares sought to attack the basis of Dutch commercial strength in the North Sea and the Baltic through the creation of the *Almirantazgo del Norte* (Admiralty of the North) in Flanders in 1624.[13]

Only in the brief period 1625–30 did a state of war exist with Spain. During the years of peace, when penetration of the Spanish Indies did not receive official sanction, attempts to expand the colonial and commercial strength of the kingdom created friction with the Dutch. Disputes over trade had become increasingly more significant during the last decade of

Elizabeth's reign: after 1609 the whale and herring fisheries, the cloth export trade and the East Indies provided further sources of tension. By the 1630s the appeal to force was becoming increasingly more attractive. One motive for the creation of the ship-money fleet was the desire to bridle the 'growing greatness of the States, by whose insolencies he [Charles] is every day much awakened'. In 1636 the fleet's control of the Narrow Seas was seen as a means of augmenting the king's revenue through the enforcement of the licensing of the Dutch herring fishery.[14]

The growing tension with the Dutch directly affected naval and military policy, for the substantial naval and military establishments that James had inherited in 1603 were very much products of the Anglo-Dutch alliance against Spain. The navy required heavy capital expenditure, as the increased functional specialisation of shipping of all types caused the size and cost of such major warships as the *Prince Royal* of 1610 or the *Sovereign of the Seas* of 1637 to inflate dramatically. The attack on Cadiz in 1625 showed that converted merchant ships were no longer adequate alternatives to purpose-built warships. James, however, placed a lower priority on naval preparedness than on political accommodation and the Earl of Nottingham's maladministration of the Admiralty was tolerated until 1618. Buckingham's attempts at reform were hindered as much by the absence of a clear role for the navy as by shortage of funds.[15] The Stuart concentration on a continental war left the navy, after the failure at Cadiz, with little to do except convoy amphibious expeditions or chase Dunkirk privateers, which the slow speed of the larger English warships made a generally fruitless task. Plans for more ambitious maritime enterprises – the cruise against the Barbary pirates in concert with Spain in 1620 and the campaigns against the West Indies in 1624 or against Dunkirk in 1625 in alliance with the Dutch – never got very far. The rebuilding of the fleet in the 1630s was primarily intended to further Charles I's rapprochement with Spain. In the First Maritime Treaty, of 27 July 1634, under the pretext of clearing pirates from the Channel, Charles offered to provide sufficient warships to keep open Spanish communications with Flanders if Philip IV would subsidise the cost.[16] The unwillingness of the

Spaniards to pay for the fleet unless it was to be used directly against the Dutch left Charles with an expensive navy – to be maintained by the ship-money levies – with little to do except to make demonstrations of strength by its annual cruises in the Channel.

James I had kept a significant proportion of Elizabeth's military forces in being after the treaty of 1604 through the expedient of transferring the troops in the Netherlands to the service of the States-General while still retaining their allegiance. In 1616 the garrisons of the former cautionary towns were similarly transferred. By 1621 there were four English and two Scots regiments in the States service – some 13,000 men, a third of the Dutch standing army. As a reciprocal gesture James allowed Spain to recruit among British catholics to keep up the regiments originally raised by English catholic émigrés in the reign of Elizabeth. Although this permission was temporarily withdrawn after the Gunpowder Plot, during the 1620s and 1630s there were on average 4000 British troops in the army of Flanders.[17] The troops in the States service provided the basis for a British regular army in the event of a war with Spain; and the Parliament of 1624 allocated funds from the subsidy to reinforce the existing British brigade with four new regiments in English pay. But the general trend of Stuart foreign policy inhibited the effective employment of these troops, although Buckingham obtained the use of 2000 for the Cadiz expedition in 1625 and one regiment was sent to Denmark in November 1626.[18] Buckingam turned instead to the hasty levying of men from the county militias, the poorhouses and the gaols to supply the Count of Mansfeld in 1624 and the expeditions to Cadiz in 1625 and to La Rochelle in 1627 – a practice Charles also followed in the levying of the Duke of Hamilton's expedition in 1631 and for the armies employed against the Covenanters in 1639 and 1640.[19] Sir Horace Vere's Palatine regiment of 1620–2, on the other hand, provides evidence that not all Stuart military expeditions were necessarily disasters – but Vere and most of his officers were seconded from the Dutch service and the regiment was equipped and supplied by the States.[20] The foreign employment of the trained English troops had the further significant effect of leaving the crown without forces to quell domestic opposition. In 1626 proposals to recall some of the Dutch regiments to enforce the loan were rejected on the grounds that their reliability in such circumstances could not be guaranteed. Charles's request for 6000 men from the army of Flanders in February 1639 for use against the Scots would only be granted by Olivares in exchange for the use of the English fleet.[21]

## III

The structural difficulties of the Stuart monarchy cannot, therefore, be fully explained without taking the ideological implications of the redirection of policy from a Dutch to a Spanish alliance into account. The Anglo-Dutch alliance was based on a shared response to two major questions about the contemporary religious confrontation: whether the course of events pointed to a struggle for religion in which the only stable alliances would be confessional ones, and whether such a struggle was part of the divine plan (and therefore inevitable) or a major catastrophe. The events of the latter half of the sixteenth century had led many both in Britain and in the protestant communities on the continent to believe in the existence of a papal-led catholic league for the extermination of heresy, which could only be countered by a protestant alliance. The events of the years 1609–11 – the creation of the Catholic League in the Empire in 1609, the assassination of Henry IV in July 1610 and the marriage alliance between France and Spain in 1611 – appeared to suggest that this league was being revived. In April 1612 Sir Ralph Winwood, the English ambassador in the Netherlands, and Maurice of Nassau agreed on the necessity of forming a protestant counter-alliance against 'the general league complotted for the subversion of religion'.[22] The Bohemian revolution of 1618 was seen in turn as a divinely-inspired opportunity both to break up the catholic league and then to bring about the fall of the papal antichrist. Sir Henry Wotton reflected in October 1618 that

the actions in Bohemia give us leave to be wanton, about which, although *modus non placet*, I mean the throwing of councillors out of windows and other circumstances of popular sollevation, yet considering upon what just causes and what pernicious discoveries it began, I am sorry the remedies were so violent that were so just.[23]

Sir Edward Herbert, the future Lord Herbert of Cherbury, then ambassador in Paris, strongly supported the acceptance of the Bohemian crown by the Elector Palatine in September 1619.

God forbid he should refuse it, being the apparent way His providence hath opened to the ruin of the Papacy. I hope, therefore, his majesty will assist in this great work.[24]

The Archbishop of Canterbury, George Abbot, echoed Herbert's views.[25] For these men, and those who thought like them, the Thirty Years War was above all else a struggle for religion in which the Anglo-Dutch alliance should be expanded into a general protestant alliance to support Frederick both in the Palatinate and in Bohemia. As the Earl of Pembroke commented in December 1624, it did not matter if the war 'be styled rather a particular war for the kingdom of Bohemia, than a war for religion ... I know in the consequence they cannot be severed'.[26]

Neither James I nor Charles I shared this view of the state of Europe. James remained consistently loyal to predestinarian Calvinism but he regarded a confessional war as a disaster to be avoided at all costs. His involvement in the resolution of protestant doctrinal disputes was more inspired by his wider, if fitful, interest in a general ecumenical settlement of the confessional confrontation than by any desire to create a protestant political front.[27] During his dispute with the Papacy over the oath of allegiance in 1606–9 he had identified the Pope as antichrist; but when asked by the Venetian ambassador Foscarini in May 1612 whether he believed a catholic league was in existence, he considered it to be a worrying possibility rather than a fact. Two months later he was reported as taking 'an apprehension out of the concurrence of many particulars that there is some great work in hand amongst the catholics'.[28] His scepticism about the league was, however, revived when the Queen-Regent of France agreed to join him in mediating the second Cleves-Jülich crisis in 1614, and later when Philip III agreed to accept his mediation of the Bohemian crisis in 1618. His position as mediator, acceptable to both sides, was the key to his response to the Thirty Years War.[29] Equally important was his dislike of the revolutionary implications of Calvinism, which not only coloured his attitude towards the Dutch republic but also underlay his refusal both to support Frederick V's acceptance of the Bohemian crown and to provide military assistance to the Huguenots – as in the case of the revolt of the Duke of Soubise in January 1625 – unless the edict of Nantes was abrogated. His only commitment to Frederick – the protection of his hereditary rights in the Palatinate – was inspired by dynastic loyalty and he intended to honour it by diplomacy rather than by war.

James's views on the confessional struggle and the subversive aspects of Calvinist politics were little different from those Elizabeth had held but his dynastic interests and his attitude towards Spain and France marked a distinct break with the past. A central feature of his foreign policy was his intention of marrying his sons to either Habsburg or Bourbon princesses. Elizabethan policy had been based on a deep suspicion of both France and Spain, but James's policy was marked by a growing respect for Spanish *gravitas*, already present in the 1590s, and a growing contempt for French unreliability. In April 1617 Buckingham reported that 'his majesty said that he perceived the Monsieurs continued their accustomed fiddling and giddy fashion'; in October James told the Count of Gondomar that he intended to conduct his foreign policy as a 'friend and brother' to Philip III.[30] Buckingham drew the comparison again during the voyage to Spain when he commented that he was dealing with men who 'carried their business wisely, honestly and constantly, and not like inconstant false Monsieurs', while James during one of the disputes over the marriage treaty with France in March 1625 taunted him about 'your royal frank Monsieurs'.[31]

The Spanish marriage alliance became the focus for the new foreign policy. A royal marriage had first been suggested by Queen Anne during the negotiation of the treaty of London; but for a long period neither James nor Philip III were prepared to make the necessary religious compromises.[32]

Philip, however, was worried that James would take up the leadership of a protestant coalition – such a coalition remained the great fear of Spanish ministers throughout the early stages of the Thirty Years War – and the Anglo-Palatine marriage alliance and the treaty with the Evangelical Union in 1612 added substance to his fears.

In 1613 Don Diego Sarmiento de Acuña (Count of Gondomar after April 1617) was dispatched to London to woo James away from the Dutch-Palatine connection. Gondomar was never confident that James would sacrifice the protestant cause – although he believed that Charles might be converted – but considered that if concessions were made in the marriage terms, the Anglo-Dutch alliance might be disrupted.[33] His great ambition was to convert the Anglo-Dutch to an Anglo-Spanish alliance (with or without the marriage treaty) and he carefully exploited James's increasing hostility towards the Dutch. The initiation of serious, if informal, discussions of the marriage treaty in 1616–17 was accompanied by proposals for the transfer of the Merchant Adventurers staple from Middleburgh to Antwerp and for an Anglo-Spanish naval expedition against the Barbary pirates. Gondomar's relative optimism about the possibilities of the alliance was not, however, shared by the Spanish council and the slow progress of the negotiations caused them to be overtaken by the Bohemian crisis, to the settlement of which the marriage alliance became closely linked. For James the marriage treaty and Spanish acceptance of his mediation of the crisis became symbols of their good faith and the basis for a general settlement of the German war.[34]

Charles I was equally, if not more, fascinated by the Habsburg alliance. His support for a war against Spain during the middle 1620s was largely an emotional reaction to the humiliation he considered he had suffered in Madrid in 1623. His basic attitude towards the French was pungently expressed during the course of the revision of the initial terms of the French marriage treaty in a letter to Henry Rich, Viscount Kensington (the future Earl of Holland) of 13 August 1624.

The Monsieurs have played you so scurvy a trick, that if it

were not for the respect I have for the person of Madame, I would not care a fart for their friendship. I mistrust them wholly; and if they insist upon these new grounds, let them go hang themselves.[35]

The marriage to Henrietta Maria did little to change his mind and his policy during the 1630s was largely based on his respect for Spanish honour. In 1635 he was reported to have commented 'the Spaniards are my friends on whom I can rely. All the rest is deception and villainy'.[36] Even after the great Habsburg rebuff of 1636, which drove Privy Councillors who had previously supported the alliance to propose a war with Spain, Charles remained loyal. Only after the Spanish collapse in 1640 and in the face of his own domestic difficulties did he turn elsewhere.

Charles also shared his father's desire to obtain the restoration of the Palatine through a general settlement of the German war that would be accepted by the Habsburgs, rather than by means of an anti-Habsburg military alliance. A most significant change of policy, which can be attributed to his Arminian sympathies, was the repudiation of a commitment to the protestant world. The protestant interest he considered a political force no different from any other and not the cause of true religion. Charles was also prepared, though discreetly at first, to enter into good relations with the Papacy, on the grounds that 'as the Pope is a temporal prince, we shall not be unwilling to join with him, as we do with other Catholic Roman Princes, in anything that may conduce to the peace of Christendom and of the Church'.[37]

## IV

The emergence of the new Stuart foreign policy produced a type of political factionalism unknown in the reign of Elizabeth. The frequently bitter disputes over foreign policy in the Elizabethan Privy Council remained (after 1570 at least) debates over means rather than ends; but Stuart political factions took on an ideological cast and struggles between court factions and the foreign policy debate became closely interlinked. The succession to Salisbury's offices in 1612–14 was disputed by two factions with conflicting approaches to foreign policy; in 1624–5 Buckingham purged the majority of James I's hispanophile councillors.[38] Following the duke's assassination in 1628, the structure of the Privy Council was carefully scrutinised and it was observed by Benjamin Valentine that 'the Spaniards' faction grows strong'.[99]

The hispanophile faction tended to rally about the king himself, but their opponents lacked a leader imposing enough to create a total polarisation. With the brief exception of Prince Henry between 1610–12, there was no cadet member of the royal family to act as spokesman for the protestant interest. Elizabeth, Queen of Bohemia, occupied an important symbolic position but her sex, physical absence and financial dependence on her father and brother inhibited her freedom of mano-euvre.[40] Her potential political influence was reflected in James's refusal to allow her to reside in England in 1621, and for a brief period during the voyage to Spain in 1623 her court at the Hague took on the appearance of an opposition in exile; but from 1624 onwards Buckingham and Charles were careful to keep her pacified. Moreover, the birth of Prince Charles in May 1630 decisively weakened the position of Elizabeth and her children as a reversionary interest. Both the queen consorts, Anne of Denmark and Henrietta Maria, could exert considerable influence when interested; but both were catholics and Anne of Denmark was strongly pro-Spanish.[41] Henrietta Maria possessed a pro-French following, the core of which was provided by the men involved in the making of the marriage treaty of 1625: Henry Rich, Viscount Kensington and Earl of Holland, James Hay, Earl of Carlisle, and Henry Jermyn. During the 1630s she became the figurehead of a loose anti-Spanish coalition, but her involvement in Marie de Medici's intrigues against Richelieu prevented her from acting as an agent of French foreign policy and her high-flying monarchial views made an alliance with an essentially parliamentarian interest impossible in the long term.[42]

In the absence of leadership from the royal family, the spokesmen for a protestant foreign policy were found initially among the descendants of Leicester's and Essex's followings: in particular, the 3rd Earls of Essex, Southampton and Pembroke and the 4th Earl of Bedford. Essex possessed the popular

appeal of his father's name, his own religious leanings and his
military service to the Palatines and the Dutch, combined with
a personal hostility to the Court following the divorce scandal
of 1613. In the summer of 1640, Sir Francis Windebank, the
Secretary of State, advised Charles to win Essex's support for
the Scottish campaign, for 'he is a popular man and it will give
extraordinary satisfaction to all sorts of people to see him in
employment again'.[43] During the first twenty years of the
century, however, the leader of the surviving Essex faction had
been Southampton, who was the moving figure behind the
short-lived Essex revival in the faction struggles of 1612–13. In
1620 James refused to allow Southampton to recruit an army
for Frederick and in 1621 was very suspicious of his Palatine
contacts, although in 1624 he gave him the colonelcy of one of
the new regiments raised for the Dutch.[44] On the other hand,
Southampton's dependence on royal pensions limited his
freedom of manoeuvre and his ambiguous religious views
inhibited his leadership of a party with a puritan cast.
Pembroke occupied the position of greatest influence but this
in turn depended on his willingness to co-operate with James
and Charles. In December 1617 Archbishop Abbot warned
that Pembroke 'looketh only to his own ends and whatsoever
leagues, promises and confederations are made within one
hour they come to nothing'. The backing of the impeachment
of Buckingham in 1626 was as far as he would go in open
opposition.[45] Abbot himself was outspoken in support of the
protestant cause but after his accidental slaying of a
gamekeeper in 1621 became, as a Huguenot envoy reported in
1625, 'tellement timide qu'il n'osoit depuis faire valoir
l'authorité et le pouvoir que sa dignité lui donne'.[46] After
Pembroke's death in April 1630 the protestant cause lacked a
spokesman among the senior councillors. Bedford emerged at
the end of the decade as the leader of the aristocratic
opposition. His proposals for the revival of a strong parliamentary and protestant monarchy – the programme of Dr John
Morrill's 'official country party' – were intended to provide the
crown with the means to resume the leadership of the protestant cause.[47]

The ambiguities surrounding the politics of the greater
aristocratic figures can be found equally strongly among the

lesser peers – the Sidneys, Earls of Leicester, Robert Rich, Earl of Warwick, or Philip Herbert, Earl of Pembroke and Montgomery for example.[48] From the weakness of aristocratic leadership two consequences followed. The first was the opportunity for the Duke of Buckingham to assume the role of protestant statesman, as John Preston, the puritan divine, encouraged him to do in 1624–5.[49] The second was the difficulty encountered by the House of Commons in the debates over foreign policy in the 1620s. The Commons were responsive to a call to support an active protestant foreign policy but in the absence of clear leadership from the crown or from the Lords they were left unsure and hesitant.

## V

If the roots of the debate over foreign policy can be traced almost to the accession of James, the issues were not fully clarified until the 1620s and 1630s. Five phases of Stuart foreign policy can be distinguished: the foreign policy of Robert Cecil, Earl of Salisbury from 1603 to 1609, the great debate over policy between 1609 and 1616, the hispanophile policy of James I from 1616 until his death in March 1625, the Grand Alliance of the Duke of Buckingham between 1625 and 1628, and the return by Charles I to an hispanophile policy between 1628 and 1640. The termination of the Elizabethan war with Spain has usually been attributed to the intervention of James himself but, in fact, the outlines of the Treaty of London of August 1604 were laid down by Cecil at least a year before the accession. In a Privy Council meeting of 24 May 1602 it was generally agreed that both the naval war with Spain and the war in the Netherlands had reached a stalemate. It was also appreciated that the United Provinces could now maintain their independence but, on the other hand, the expense of the Irish rebellion 'was not to be endured'. Cecil proposed that once the Irish rebellion was ended and the Stuart succession secured – both of which occurred almost simultaneously in March 1603 – peace with Spain could safely be entertained.[50] The Treaty of London did not resolve the question of trade with the Indies, nor did it prevent continued

English aid to the United Provinces.[51] For Salisbury, the treaty did not create an Anglo-Spanish alliance so much as an opportunity to return to a mediating position between France and Spain such as his father Lord Burghley had desired. Salisbury's hostility to and suspicion of both France and Spain were no secret, but he was also sceptical about a purely confessional policy.[52] Proposals that James should take up the leadership of a protestant alliance – first made by a Palatine embassy in 1603 – were politely declined and the international Calvinist scheme to proselytise in Venice during the Venetian conflict with the Papacy in 1606–9 (in which James was very interested) Salisbury opposed as a French ploy to embroil England with Spain.[53]

Salisbury's policy depended, however, on the continuation of the Netherlands war. The signing of the Truce of Antwerp in March 1609 and the widespread, if erroneous, belief that the conclusion of the war would free Spain to pursue designs elsewhere brought its future into question. The direction of the new policy was determined by the death of Duke John William of Cleves-Jülich on 15 March 1609 and the dispute over the succession to his duchies. Although James's intention was to seek to mediate the dispute, the outbreak of hostilities between the protestant claimants and the emperor in the summer of 1609 and the decision of Henry IV and the States-General to intervene in force during the winter of 1609–10 persuaded him to join the anti-Habsburg coalition. The Cleves-Jülich intervention revived the Palatine appeal to James to become the head of the newly-formed Evangelical Union and this was now coupled with proposals for the marriage of Princess Elizabeth to the future Frederick V. These offers were at first resisted: but the consequences of the assassination of Henry IV in July 1610 further increased the pressure on James to create a confessional alliance. Although James and Salisbury remained sceptical about French participation in a revived general catholic league in 1611–12, they became sufficiently worried to accede to the Palatine proposals. The marriage between Elizabeth and Frederick was agreed upon in the spring of 1611, in the spring of 1612 a treaty of alliance was signed with the Evangelical Union, and James encouraged the United Provinces to do likewise. Although James did not accept the full Palatine offer of formal presidency of the Union, his active participation in a protestant alliance combined with his intervention in the Dutch religious disputes and his public commitment to the maintenance of the Edict of Nantes in the summer of 1612 suggested that he was now following a confessional foreign policy.[54] His real concern – to resolve disputes by mediation – was revealed, however, in his response to the second Cleves-Jülich crisis of 1614, following Spanish military intervention on behalf of one of the claimants, the Duke of Neuburg. French willingness to join with him and Spanish acceptance of his mediation caused him to consider the experiment a success and inspired his optimism over his chances of doing the same in the Bohemian crisis four years later. On the other hand, his failure to obtain Spanish evacuation of the protestant town of Wesel confirmed doubts in both Britain and the United Provinces as to Spanish sincerity and inspired the fear that mediation would result only in the sacrifice of protestant interests.[55]

The death of Salisbury in May 1612 not only put an end to his sceptical influence over foreign policy but also initiated a faction struggle over the succession to his offices between a revived Essex faction led by Southampton, Sir Henry Neville and Sir Ralph Winwood, and the Howards.[56] The general Howard victory strengthened conciliar support for a pro-Spanish policy and a tougher line towards the Dutch. On the other hand, the appointment of Winwood as Secretary of State in March 1614 added a further member to the existing protestant faction. From this point until James's death factional tension over foreign policy in the Council became institutionalised. A divided Council enabled James to play one side off against the other, but it also inhibited the formulation of a clear policy during the years following the Bohemian revolt.[57] While one faction encouraged James to seek mediation through the Spanish alliance, the other encouraged Frederick to expect eventual assistance from England.[58]

Between 1618 and the final collapse of the marriage negotiations in 1623 James sought to obtain a general settlement of the Bohemian Revolution and its consequences within the context of the Habsburg marriage alliance. His policy was upset first by Frederick's acceptance of the Bohemian throne in September 1619 and then by the Spanish invasion of the

Palatinate in August 1620: but the hope remained that if James obtained Frederick's submission to the Emperor Ferdinand II and the surrender of his Bohemian claims, Spain would agree to the restoration of the Palatinate. The Spaniards were not opposed to a settlement, especially one which would enable them to escape from the marriage alliance without alienating James entirely. By the time of his death in March 1621, Philip III appears to have decided that the marriage could not be made without the conversion of Prince Charles and the removal of all penal legislation against catholics. The same position was taken by Olivares in 1622–3, who saw the arrival of Buckingham and Charles in Madrid in March 1623 as an indication that James had agreed to these concessions. Restoration of the Palatinate would pacify James and dissuade him from creating a general protestant alliance on Frederick's behalf – though Olivares appears to have been less worried by this threat than Gondomar.[59] Madrid's willingness to accommodate James on this issue had, however, to be balanced against the desires of the Archduchess Isabella (who wished to retain control of those parts of the Lower Palatinate occupied by Spanish troops in 1620–1), Ferdinand II (who had no intention of permitting the return of Frederick to Heidelberg), and the Duke of Bavaria (who had been promised the Palatine electorate and the Upper Palatinate in return for his assistance to the Imperial cause).[60] In 1622, Madrid attempted to resolve its dilemma by proposing the restoration of Frederick's heir, Frederick Henry, following his conversion, education at the Imperial court and marriage to a Habsburg archduchess.

James did not fully appreciate the Spanish terms for the marriage alliance and the restoration of the Palatinate until the voyage to Madrid in 1623. During 1621 and 1622 he tried, in the interests of a general settlement and the avoidance of a religious war, to prevent the expansion of the German war, though at the price of alienating his erstwhile protestant allies. Frederick's defeat at the battle of the White Mountain in November 1620 and the collapse of his position in Bohemia increased his dependence on English assistance and worked to James's advantage; but it was not in fact until 26 August 1623 that Frederick finally agreed to comply with his mediation. To prevent the war from spreading, James discouraged the intervention of other powers which, for example, Christian IV of Denmark had attempted to organise at the Segeberg Convention in March 1621, and tried to keep the German war separate from the revived Spanish-Dutch war.[61] Yet the military position in the Palatinate had to be stabilised and to do so he was forced to call a parliament in January 1621.[62] The House of Commons was inspired equally by the apocalyptical appeal of the Bohemian adventure, the Spanish invasion of the Palatinate, the termination of the Truce of Antwerp and Louis XIII's campaign against the Huguenots to offer support for the protestant cause in their declaration of 4 June 1621 and the Petition and Remonstrance of 1 December: but at the price of severing the Spanish alliance.[63] James, who was aware that Madrid did not completely favour the transfer of the Palatine electorate to Bavaria, was not prepared to go this far and, rather than terminate the negotiations with Spain, he dissolved the parliament.[64]

The policy of mediation collapsed following the fall of the Lower Palatinate in 1622 and the discovery of the ultimate Spanish terms in 1623. The conversions of Charles and Frederick Henry were not negotiable, while Buckingham and Charles were moved by their experiences in Madrid to seek a war of revenge by means of a grand anti-Habsburg coalition. James, however, was not won over and until his death continued to look for a more satisfactory offer from Spain.[65] Nor did he surrender the direction of policy to Buckingham. Most of the major decisions taken during the twelve months preceding his death – the refusal to declare war against Spain, the refusal to accept any alternative to the Spanish marriage for Charles except a French marriage (which prevented a marriage to a protestant princess), the requirement of a French military alliance before a campaign for the Palatinate was undertaken, the hiring of the Count of Mansfeld, the refusal to allow Mansfeld's troops to be employed in the attempted relief of the siege of Breda in January 1625, and the open offer of naval assistance to Louis XIII in the suppression of Soubise's revolt (which Buckingham clearly wished to make conditional) – reflected the king's desires and requirements. These decisions lay behind many of the major disasters that attended Buckingham's foreign policy and he was to some extent justified in stating, as he did to the Parliament of 1626, that he was only carrying out the policy of the late king.[66]

It was, however, Buckingham who was responsible for the major error – which underlay the eventual failure of his French alliance policy – of accepting in the spring of 1624 the optimistic reports of Kensington that the French were eager to enter both a marriage and a military alliance and discounting the warnings of Herbert, the resident ambassador.[67] This over-optimism – combined with the need to keep James pacified – led Buckingham down the road of increased concessions to France in the marriage treaty in return for hoped-for reciprocal concessions over the military alliance. His failure was to a large degree a personal one, caused by a mixture of over-confidence, inexperience and, later, pique: but it was also a reflection of one of the central dilemmas of this phase of the Thirty Years War. English intervention, and any alliance system treated around it, would of its nature be motivated by the defence of the protestant cause, which, as Richelieu and his colleagues were well aware, could never be openly supported by Louis XIII, no matter how willing he might be to see an anti-Habsburg coalition created.[68] To the same degree that they failed to appreciate English protestant suspicion of France and the French alliance, Buckingham and Charles also failed to appreciate the strength of *dévot* opinion at the French court.

Buckingham compounded the initial miscalculation about the French alliance by creating on the strength of it an elaborate structure of further alliances with the Dutch and Christian IV during 1624 and 1625. The weakness of the edifice was revealed during the winter of 1625–6, when the French refused to attend the convention of the Hague in November, Buckingham himself was refused permission to enter France afterwards, and the French signed a separate peace with Spain at Monzón on 23 February 1626. The collapse of his French policy led Buckingham into a second war of revenge and in 1626–7 he sought to engineer the overthrow of Richelieu by means of a coalition of French dissidents, the Dukes of Lorraine and Savoy, and the Huguenots. The Huguenot rebellion proved to be less easy to incite than he had been led to believe and his failure to open the sea route to La

Rochelle by the capture of the Ile de Rhé in the summer of 1627 sealed its fate.[69]

The disastrous results of his foreign policy lay behind many of Buckingham's difficulties with parliament. In 1624 the House of Commons displayed its willingness to support the protestant cause by providing funds for rearmament and military assistance to the Dutch. This was not the open-ended financial commitment the duke had desired, but he had to accept it in order to avoid a confrontation between parliament and the king. He took the calculated risk of violating the Subsidy Act by providing £62,000 from the subsidy for the raising of Mansfeld's expedition.[70] The near-criminal mismanagement of this expedition, the violation of the Act, and the suspicions engendered by the negotiations with France created an atmosphere in the Parliament of 1625 which made it impossible to obtain funds on terms the king and duke found acceptable. The war Charles and Buckingham had entered into was not that intended by parliament in 1624. In 1626 supply was clearly contingent on the impeachment of the duke. In 1628 parliament again showed itself willing to support a protestant foreign policy and five subsidies were voted. They were intended for the support of the King of Denmark; but were employed instead in an abortive second attempt to relieve La Rochelle.

The assassination of the duke in August 1628 created a brief period of political uncertainty similar to that of 1612–14, but the new course of policy was settled comparatively rapidly. The treaty of Suza in May 1629 terminated Buckingham's private war with Richelieu. It was less clear, initially, whether Charles could be persuaded to continue the war against the Habsburgs in alliance with the Netherlands and Sweden (as Viscount Dorchester, Secretary of State until his death in 1632, advocated), but the dissolution of the Parliament of 1629 showed that the terms under which parliamentary support might be obtained were unsatisfactory.[71] Informal negotiations for a settlement with Spain had been initiated by Rubens in 1627 and a treaty was concluded in Madrid in November 1630. Although the terms amounted to little more than a repetition of the 1604 treaty, the more important aspect of the settlement – which established the framework for Charles's foreign policy during the next decade – was the understanding over the restoration of the Palatinate. Philip IV provided a written assurance that Spain would agree to the restoration of Frederick V as part of a general settlement; Charles saw this as a formal recognition of Frederick's rights, which Philip would honour in return for his good will. Olivares, however, would not jeopardise the interests of either the emperor or the Duke of Bavaria unless he received something more substantial: an active alliance against the Dutch, as was outlined in the so-called Cottington Treaty of 2 January 1631.[72]

The successful intervention of Gustavus Adolphus in 1631–2 threatened to jeopardise the understanding by offering Charles the opportunity of restoring Frederick in alliance with Sweden. Charles resisted considerable domestic pressure to join the Swedes and in 1633, instead of exploiting the Habsburg weakness, offered to provide a fleet to keep open the sea routes to the Spanish Netherlands. Olivares, however, demanded an open war against the Dutch as the price of a Palatine restoration, although he also hoped that by undertaking the convoying of Spanish ships Charles would be forced into war by a naval encounter in the Channel.[73] The course of the war determined the success of the mutual attempts to obtain maximum advantage through minimum concession. The First Maritime Treaty of 27 July 1634 was overtaken by the Habsburg victory at Nordlingen on 27 August 1634, but Charles's negotiating position was restored by the French intervention in the spring of 1635. In 1635–6 he sought to use a revived offer of naval assistance and his rejection of a Franco-Dutch invitation to join an anti-Habsburg alliance as gestures of good will to persuade Philip IV to honour his commitment to a final restoration of the Palatinate. The Earl of Arundel and Lord Aston were sent to Vienna and Madrid to conclude the settlement, but in September 1636 it was discovered that the successful Habsburg invasion of France had raised the price of restoration to the open use of the fleet against the Dutch and the supply of troops to assist the emperor in Germany.[74]

The failure of these embassies produced a major reaction in the Privy Council in favour of joining an anti-Habsburg coalition in the spring of 1637. Once again such a policy was resisted by the king, though it is difficult to say whether he might not have agreed in time to a limited show of force, if the Scottish rebellion had not broken out. The Scottish rebellion, which Charles believed was to some degree instigated by Richelieu and the Dutch, drove him back towards a Spanish alliance, but now as much for the defence of his position as for the return of the Palatinate. 1639–40 saw a final series of negotiations for immediate Spanish financial assistance in return for a commitment to a joint war against the Dutch after the Scottish rebellion was crushed. On this occasion it was the Spanish collapse in 1640 that prevented implementation of the agreement and Charles in turn was forced to capitulate to demands for the recall of parliament in the autumn of 1640.[75]

## VI

The crisis of 1640–2 made public the critique of the Stuart foreign policy. The disasters of Buckingham's policy figured prominently in the Grand Remonstrance and both the Nineteen Propositions and the Propositions of Uxbridge included the creation of an active protestant foreign policy as part of a settlement.[76] Yet the very inclusion of foreign policy as an item in a settlement of the Civil War revealed that a protestant foreign policy was no longer part of a political consensus but the programme of a section of the political nation. The collapse of the consensus over foreign policy was an aspect of the collapse of the consensus over religion created by the challenge of Arminianism to the 'Calvinist heritage'.[77] The hispanophile foreign policy provided justification for the claim that Arminianism was a popish plot. The Stuart foreign policy was not without its logic and represented one solution to the dilemmas posed by the Thirty Years War, but it was a solution that offended many of the most engrained of English political attitudes. James and Charles may have preferred to ally with the leading dynasty of Europe rather than with republicans and Calvinist incendiaries, but too many of their subjects preferred the company of the godly to that of the adherents of antichrist.

# 5. Financial and Administrative Developments

## DAVID THOMAS

### I

In 1611 Sir Julius Caesar noted that King James knew 'that no king's estate can endure whose expenses exceed the quantity of his receipts and that all appetites whose object is pleasure, and all affections whose object is bounty will in all wise and religious princes give place to reason'.[1]

For a wise prince, the kingdom James I inherited in 1603 offered considerable potential. Queen Elizabeth had died owing about £422,000 but of this, £120,000 was owed as a result of forced loans of 1597–9 and nobody expected these to be repaid. James was entitled to collect about £355,000 from the uncollected part of the 1601 grant of subsidies, as well as various sums owed to Elizabeth at home and in the Netherlands.[2] Not only did Elizabeth die more or less solvent, she also left James one valuable asset: for all their considerable talents, neither she nor Burghley had been able to obtain the maximum level of revenue from the crown's basic sources of income. The customs, the largest source of royal income, were by no means exploited to their full potential; the Book of Rates, which laid down the notional value of goods for the purpose of allowing duties to be assessed, had not been revised since 1558 despite forty years of inflation. Moreover, the prospect of peace meant a possibility of more trade and consequently, more customs revenue. At the same time, it would allow the crown to reduce its spending on defence.

The crown lands also had considerable potential as a source of income. Elizabeth had not managed her properties as a

103

source of revenue; she had conducted no surveys for the purpose of good estate management, had failed to increase rents in a period of inflation, had made few changes in the way in which the lands were administered and had not spent money on repairs and maintenance. To some extent, the lands had been used as a source of rewards for peers and courtiers who had been granted favourable leases and had been appointed to minor offices, such as stewardships of manors, which increased both their incomes and their local influence. In the sixteenth century the rent of crown lands had failed to rise as quickly as that on private property: the rent on the Seymour manors, for instance, rose ninefold over the century; that on certain crown manors increased only threefold in the same period.[3]

James had therefore acquired a throne whose income had considerable potential for improvement. If he could have found a way to improve the administration of his customs and his estates, he could have achieved a large increase in his receipts. If he could have restrained his appetite for pleasure and his generosity and if he could have avoided wars, then his receipts might have exceeded his expenses.

## II

Unfortunately, James was unable to restrain his desire to spend money on himself, his followers and his friends. This aspect of his character was described by Salisbury to the 1610 Parliament when he said 'his disposition is so worthy, judgment, wisdom and learning great, as he held the same opinion which other learned authors do that there is no greater slave than money and not worthy to be accompted among wise men, it being good for nothing but for use, let alone it will rust'.[4] In fact, things were made relatively easy for James, since peace meant that spending on military affairs could be reduced. Expenditure on the navy was more than halved between 1602 and 1607; the expenses of the ordnance were reduced by 60 per cent. Moreover, the changed constitutional position following the accession of James meant that it was no longer necessary to garrison Berwick: by 1607 spending on the garrison there had fallen from £17,000 to £5500, and as the soldiers of the garrison gradually died expenditure declined to less than £1000 a year.

Unlike Elizabeth, James had a family, and as he constantly remarked, providing for them was an expensive business. As Prince Henry grew up, the cost of his household increased from £3660 in 1604–5 to £35,765 in 1610–11. The unfortunate proximity of the wedding of Princess Elizabeth to the death of the Prince of Wales put an enormous burden on the crown. In one financial year, James spent £116,000 or nearly a fifth of his total income on the funeral and the marriage.[5]

It is, however, impossible to acquit James of the charge of extravagance. Salisbury admitted that 'the king hath given away very much . . . his three first years were his Christmas'.[6] During the first four years of his reign, he distributed £68,000 in gifts, £30,000 in pensions and £174,000 in debts owed to the crown. By 1610 his annual expenditure on fees and annuities to royal servants and courtiers was £80,000. This was £50,000 a year more than Elizabeth had spent. As well as being generous, James was also very lavish in gratifying his own pleasures. Between his accession and 1612 he satisfied his desire for jewels at a total cost of £185,000. His enthusiasm for hunting involved an increase in the number of keepers of the buckhounds from nine to thirty-eight and a corresponding increase in the bill for their wages. At the same time, the Court was run on a much more lavish scale. The Household, which provided food, ran the stables and entertained foreign ambassadors, cost Elizabeth £64,000 in 1602–3; by 1610–11 expenditure had increased by 33 per cent. Spending on the Chamber, which provided non-food services (musicians, footmen, huntsmen, messengers, players, rat catchers, etc.) increased by 63 per cent between 1601–2 and 1609.[7]

As a result of this extravagance, the crown rapidly got into financial difficulties. Between 1606 and 1610 there was a deficit on ordinary expenditure of £334,000. On the accession of James the debt was £422,000; by 1606 it had reached £816,000. Salisbury was able to reduce this considerably between 1608 and 1610 by the collection of the subsidies granted in 1606, the vigorous pursuit of money owed to Elizabeth and the sale of crown properties. Consequently, crown debt fell to £300,000 in 1610. The financial position, however, was still very difficult; in 1610 there was a deficit on ordinary expenditure of £50,000, while the creation of Henry as Prince of Wales and the grant of various concessions to the Parliament cost James £48,000 a year. By 1613 the debt was again up to £500,000 and by 1618 it was £900,000.[8]

### III

One response made by Jacobean officials to the crown's financial difficulties was to try to exact more money from current sources of revenue. The largest source, and the easiest to tackle, was the customs. A new Book of Rates was introduced which pushed up the notional value of goods used as a basis for calculating duties and, as a result, an extra £6000 a year was received. Farming was introduced; the collection of the major duties being leased to a syndicate who paid a fixed rent. This had a number of advantages: the Great Farm of the major duties was leased for £112,400 a year, £28,600 more than the average customs returns for the last seven years of Elizabeth's reign; and farming provided a predetermined and certain revenue, while the farmers rapidly became a valuable source of loans for the crown.

The most significant move concerning the customs was Salisbury's decision in 1608 to levy impositions. The crown had placed extra duties on various goods without the consent of parliament since 1554, but this had only been done on a small scale. In 1606, in Bate's Case, the Court of Exchequer decided that the king could legally levy imposts on goods imported or exported, and the way was opened to the exploitation of this source of revenue on a large scale. The impositions Salisbury introduced in 1608 were expected to raise £70,000 a year.

As well as tackling the customs, Salisbury set out to improve the yield from the crown lands. This was much more difficult than merely levying impositions. John Osborne offered the opinion that 'your Lordship will not tend altogether to make money upon one great means, but upon many little', and so it proved. It was discovered that the crown's mills cost a great deal to repair and so Salisbury began to sell them. Similarly, the lands acquired from the dissolution of the chantries were in such small parcels that they proved uneconomic to administer and so they were sold off. A programme was started to survey and value all the trees in the crown woods. On the manors, efforts were made to increase the rents paid by copyhold tenants; the customary rents paid by the tenants of Gedney manor in Lincolnshire increased from £29 to £230 a year. Surveys of crown lands were instituted in 1608 and produced some dramatic results. In Yorkshire, for example, rents were increased from £3291 to £11,449 a year. All this involved slow, painstaking work, an effort to reverse forty years of neglect by Elizabeth.[9]

Attempts were also made to improve the income from the Court of Wards. Salisbury's *Instructions* of 1610 marked the beginning of a period in which the court was more carefully administered and its officials took care to ensure that a larger share of the profits of wardship went to the crown. Royal income from the Court of Wards increased by 91 per cent between 1603 and 1613.[10]

Unfortunately, these labours were not enough to satisfy the king's voracious appetite for money. On Salisbury's death in 1612, the crown's debts were £500,000 and the deficit was £160,000. Over the next six years, other sources of revenue were tapped. The cautionary towns were sold to the Dutch for £210,000; a voluntary contribution raised £74,000, while some money was raised from the sale of peerages and baronetages. All this was to no avail; there was still a deficit and the debt was growing larger. Some other approach was needed.

The most obvious alternative course was to attempt to cut spending. This had been tried as early as 1605, when Salisbury persuaded James to promise to implement economies. In 1608 Salisbury again prevailed upon the king to agree to issue the Book of Bounty – a list of what suitors could and could not expect. The intention here was to restrict royal gifts to comparatively minor items of revenue: goods of felons and murderers, minor offices, keeperships of parks, etc.; major items such as lands, customs, impositions and monopolies were not to be alienated. In 1609 the most valuable pieces of crown land were entailed to prevent their being sold or given away. Alas, Salisbury had omitted the phrase 'ready money' from the

Book of Bounty and instead of land, James gave cash: in Michaelmas term 1610 alone, the Exchequer paid out £36,000 in gifts. Sir Julius Caesar in 1610, indeed, had drawn up a list of desirable reductions in expenditure amounting to £64,000 a year, 'which', he added, 'I fear will never be done'.[11]

The most famous attempts at reducing spending were those by Lionel Cranfield, who was associated with reform in the crown's administration between 1617 and 1624. For the final two and a half years of this period, he was Lord Treasurer. Cranfield was a talented administrator with a great capacity for detailed work, who used his talents to improve the efficiency of some government departments. In the Household he carefully examined quantities of food purchased and used, and discovered in 1617 that 132¼ oxen and 1248 sheep had not been accounted for. By concerning himself with such matters, by reducing the number of courses served at meals, by addressing himself to the profitable disposal of cast-off fish, bottles and jugs, Cranfield reduced spending on the Household by 22 per cent between 1616–17 and 1621–2. Similarly, in the case of the Wardrobe, Cranfield used his talents as a merchant to good effect by taking care that payment was always in ready money – previously, the crown had been very slow at paying and consequently its suppliers had charged high prices to compensate themselves for the extended credit they were providing – and insisting that only necessary quantities of materials were purchased. He also reduced the number of personnel, put his own servants into key posts and introduced a new form of accounts.

More significantly, Cranfield tried to reduce James's generosity to his courtiers. In 1619 Salisbury's Book of Bounty was reissued and attempts were made to control the grant of new pensions. This was, potentially, a source of great savings for by 1619 nearly a sixth of the crown's revenue was being spent on pensions. In 1621 Cranfield demanded an immediate stop to the payment of pensions and insisted that all new patents be screened by himself. The following year, James promised that no grants of land, pensions or allowances were to be permitted without the approval of the Lord Treasurer and the Chancellor. Unfortunately, Cranfield's attempts to restrict the king's generosity were undermined by avaricious courtiers and excessive spending on pensions which had increased by 22 per cent between 1621 and 1624.[12]

The classical approach to the crown's financial problems – increasing income and cutting spending – was not therefore successful. Cranfield's last revenue account showed a surplus of £50,000, but this ignored the fact that £128,000 was needed for extraordinary expenditure and £72,000 of future revenue had been anticipated. The true situation was that there was a deficit of £160,000.[13] Any attempt to manage the royal finances by simply increasing sources of revenue and cutting costs was bound to come up against major obstacles.

## IV

The first of these obstacles was the way in which the crown paid its servants. In the 1540s royal officials seem to have been better paid than those in comparable jobs on private estates. Unfortunately, the crown did not increase the fees it paid during the following years despite a high level of inflation. As a result, by the end of the sixteenth century official fees were inadequate. Even Burghley complained that 'my fees of my treasureship do not answer to the charge of my stable – I mean not my *table*'.[14] Even though certain officers received free food, bread, ale, firewood and candles, they could not hope to live on their official fees. Equally importantly, there was no provision for them when they became too old or too sick to work.

Royal officials had to live. One of the ways in which they were able to do so was by exacting fees and gratuities from members of the public. Every time anyone had business to transact with the crown, a fee and possibly a gratuity had to be paid to an officer. The experience of Samuel Doves must have been fairly common: 'On the 2nd of February last past, I had a hearing in the Court of Chancery and for that hearing, there stood one in the crier's place; to whom being demanded, I gave him 8s . . . And two men more which kept the door would have 8s more, which I paid. And when I was without the door, two men stayed me and would have 2s more, which I paid. And when I was going out, one man took me by the cloak and would have 5d, which I paid'.[15] Such infuriating and expensive payments were a sort of indirect tax on those who had dealings with the government. They were, from time to time, criticised in parliament.

Some fortunate officers and courtiers had their incomes subsidised by pensions and annuities from the crown. Sir Robert Aitoun, Principal Secretary and Master of Requests to Henrietta Maria, received an official fee of £100, later increased to £126-13-4d. In addition, he had two annuities totalling £640 and a special payment from the Cofferer of the Household of £200 a year. Similarly, the grooms of the king's Bedchamber had annual pensions of £500 to supplement their fees.[16] Because of the perennial deficit, the king could not afford to reward all his servants with pensions, just as he could not afford to increase their fees. Instead, he chose to reward them with shares in his own sources of income, by delegating to them various royal rights.

The most valuable rewards were the farms of the customs. In the first decade of the seventeenth century, various courtiers were allowed to farm the duties on specific items. They normally assigned their rights to syndicates of merchants. Thus in 1604 Robert Cecil sublet his grant of the farm of duties on silks and satins to a merchant syndicate for a profit of £1333 a year. In 1612 he increased this profit to £7000 a year. Other royal servants profited because they were granted exemption from customs duties. In 1604–5 Philip, Earl of Montgomery, Sir James Hay and the Earl of Argyll were given the right to allow aliens to export cloth and pay duty as if they were natives, while Peter Van Lore was permitted to export cloth free of duty. These grants cost the crown £8602.[17]

Further down the scale, courtiers could be rewarded with the right to buy the wardship of a wealthy minor at a low price. They could then either administer the minor's lands themselves, or sell the wardship at a profit. Other, more junior, crown servants could be granted leases in reversion of crown lands. In theory, a lease in reversion gave the grantee the right to enjoy a piece of property after the existing lease had ended. In practice, it gave him the right to compound with (in effect extort money from) the sitting tenants for the renewal of their leases.

In fact, the number of ways in which royal officers could

supplement their incomes at the expense of the crown is too vast to describe. According to Professor Aylmer, 'the exact arrangements were almost as numerous as the individual cases'.[18] Most of these, however, tended to reduce the income of the crown. Some, as in the case of licences to export, reduced it directly. Others did more subtle damage. The grant of the farm of customs to courtiers, for instance, reduced potential income in that it might have been more profitable for the crown to administer the customs itself and it certainly would have been more profitable for it to deal with the merchant syndicates directly. Some of these supplements to the incomes of royal servants had harmful long-term consequences. After the farm of the customs on silks and satins had been granted to Salisbury for nineteen years in 1610, the crown was not in a position to increase its revenue from this source until Salisbury's lease had expired. In practice, this was obviously recognised to be a mistake and in 1613 the crown bought out the lease for £3000 a year. Similarly, the practice of granting leases in reversion meant that the land would be out of royal hands for a very long time and the crown would not be able to benefit from any increase in property values. In 1587 Elizabeth granted a lease in reversion of certain property in Bermondsey for £68 a year; the lease was to begin in 1615 and last for 21 years. By 1636, when the reversionary lease finally expired, the land was worth £1071 a year.[19]

Closely associated with these difficulties in rewarding royal servants were others caused by the terms on which they were appointed. Unlike those of modern times, seventeenth-century civil servants regarded their offices as private property or 'freeholds'. This attitude arose in part from the method of appointment − posts could be purchased from existing office-holders or from senior royal officials. Once acquired, offices were held by various tenures: for life, during good behaviour or during the king's pleasure. Because it was very difficult to dismiss officials who held their posts for life or during good behaviour, it was also difficult to reduce the number of officers. In a test case in 1627, the judges ruled that the keepership of a royal park terminated when the land was 'dis-parked', even though the keepership had been granted for life. However, the judges also ruled that the ex-keeper must continue to receive his fee of £30 a year. When the customs were farmed at the beginning of the seventeenth century, a large number of posts in the crown's customs service became redundant. Unfortunately, there was no money to compensate these office-holders for the loss of positions they had purchased and so they remained in office – an unnecessary burden on the crown. It was, however, felt to be going a bit too far in 1619 when somebody applied for one of these posts which had fallen vacant.[20]

The crown's relations with its servants provided a real obstacle to making the existing financial system work. It was very hard to reduce the number of royal officials, particularly as the crown could not afford to compensate them for loss of office. Many of them relied on having a share of some source of royal income to supplement their official fees. If the crown wished to increase its own proportion of this income, it could do so only (as in the Court of Wards) by reducing the incomes of its officials. If the crown did this, it would either have to increase their fees, a method which would be self-defeating, or it would have to allow them to extort more from the public and this would be politically damaging. The continuous rise in the levels of pensions and annuities paid by the crown and the opposition in parliament to extortions by royal officials may have resulted partly from the crown's increasing its own income at the expense of its officials.

There were other obstacles to the policy of making the existing system work by cutting expenditure and increasing income. It was possible for Cranfield and others to achieve fairly dramatic reductions in spending, but without either an efficient administration or the wholehearted support of the king and courtiers, these reductions could not be maintained. Under James, the number of official messengers had been reduced from over a hundred to forty; at a saving of £2000 a year. By about 1638 the numbers had gradually crept up again and half the saving had been eroded. Similarly, in 1621, Cranfield suspended the payment of pensions, including the £3000 a year paid to the Earl of Salisbury for the loss of the silk farm. This economy programme did not last long – in 1624, the payment of Salisbury's pension was resumed and he was compensated for the period of suspension.[21]

Corruption was a serious obstacle to the existing system. To a large extent, it was the result of the method of rewarding crown servants. Crown servants had to supplement their incomes from their contacts with the public but the distinction between legitimate fees and corruption was very unclear. Many officials abused their positions by accepting bribes, by favouring others at the expense of the crown or by misusing royal resources. As Secretary of State, Robert Cecil invested in privateering ventures, but had his ships fitted out at royal expense. As Lord Treasurer, Suffolk would not pay for the army in Ireland unless the Vice-Treasurer of Ireland sent him a substantial *douceur*. At the bottom of the scale, it was claimed that tenants of crown manors would 'rather give unto the stewards and bailiffs a great bribe upon their new admission, than they will give his majesty his due and reasonable fine, because the same may not be a precedent to their posterity'. Crown lands were often deliberately undervalued to the benefit of tenants and the loss of the owner. The surveyor of the Duchy of Lancaster measured the common land of Colne manor at 2000 acres when it was really 3000 acres and the tenants paid only one-fifteenth of the real value of the land, which contained much coal and limestone. It would seem that land was frequently undervalued when it was being sold by the crown. According to Sir Robert Johnson 'by the corruption, negligence or skill of this age, there was sold the pig in the panier'.[22]

One way round corruption was 'privatisation'. Various official functions were hived off to contractors: the customs were farmed for an agreed rent; the navy commissioners ran the navy at a fixed cost, while Cranfield ran the Wardrobe on similar terms. Unfortunately, this offered further scope for corruption in fixing prices for the contracts. In 1605 Salisbury was both Secretary of State and spokesman for one of the groups bidding for the farm of the customs. In 1611, when negotiations were taking place for the renewal of the lease, Salisbury borrowed vast sums from the existing syndicate. Cranfield ran the Wardrobe at a fixed price which was less than half the previous cost, but he made nearly twice as much from doing so as his predecessors had done.[23]

## V

Because of the problems of making the financial system work, various people came to hold the view that it should be radically altered. James himself seems to have believed that the realm should maintain the dignity of the crown. He told the 1621 Parliament 'that all people owe a kind of tribute to their king, by way of thankfulness to him for his love to them'.[24] This was little more than wishful thinking.

More positive proposals for change were based on the idea of abandoning some of the most unpopular sources of royal income in return for support from parliament. In 1598 it was rumoured that the Court of Wards was to be abolished and replaced by an annual tax on property which had previously been liable to wardship. In 1604 Sir Robert Wroth, a client of Robert Cecil, raised the question of wardship in parliament and the Commons discussed the idea of substituting an annual composition for wardship and kindred royal rights. These proposals were revived again in 1610 in the Great Contract debates when king and Commons nearly reached agreement on a plan to abolish purveyance and wardship in return for the provision of an annual support for the crown. A similar scheme was also considered in the Parliament of 1621.[25] In 1626 various MPs were involved in proposals to increase the king's permanent revenues. According to Sir Benjamin Rudyerd, the Commons intended 'to make his majesty an orderly, warrantable revenue, proportionable to his ordinary charge'. Amongst the schemes discussed were a bill to settle impositions and increase the revenue from the customs, an act of resumption of crown lands, reform of the administration of recusancy fines and a reduction in pensions. It was also proposed to revive the Great Contract.[26]

Attempts to reform the crown's finances by support from parliament were unsuccessful. To a certain extent, this was because the king was unwilling to pay the price of such support. In 1610 there was much concern that in abolishing the Wards, James was damaging his status. As the Lord Privy Seal observed: 'in granting this he blasteth the flower of his regality'. Julius Caesar also argued cogently that the deal was not sufficiently beneficial to the crown. In 1626 the price of parliamentary support was even higher; it was the punishment of Buckingham.[27] To some extent, such proposals failed because MPs were not sure how to levy an annual support for the crown. Even more importantly, they were not sure whether they could obtain the acquiescence of their constituents for such an undertaking. Largely, however, the crown failed in its dealings with MPs over this issue because of the way it had handled its own finances. Salisbury's use of impositions on a large scale in 1608 certainly harmed negotiations over the Great Contract; while the king's failure to curb his own all too conspicuous expenditure made it difficult for him to ask for parliamentary support. In 1610 Sir Edwin Sandys claimed that the rulers of France and Spain spent less on their courts in a year than James did in a quarter. In 1625, after Cranfield's period of office, Sir Edward Coke thought the king's great necessity for money 'grew by want of providence', while Sir Francis Seymour thought that the necessity 'hath not proceeded from want of great sums of money, if we consider what hath been received by former grants in parliament, by prerogative, benevolences and monopolies; but these great sums have come to particular men's purses'.[28]

Yet, ultimately, a settlement of the king's finances based on the agreement of parliament was essential if the crown was to survive within the existing constitutional framework. This was realised by the leaders of the Long Parliament, who in 1640 prepared a constructive programme to settle the king's finances. This included a revival of the Great Contract, an increase in fines on recusants, settlement of the customs and confiscation of the lands of deans and chapters.[29]

## VI

In the 1620s the crown was faced with a new financial situation: the need to raise money to pay for war. The prospect of war strengthened the crown's ability to obtain money from parliament, as parliament was obliged to provide revenue for the king to meet this need. To an outsider, the potential of parliament as a source of finance for war was quite considerable. As the Venetian ambassador observed in 1635: 'his majesty need never lack money either for war or other extraordinary emergencies, as he possesses his richest treasures in the purses and property of his subjects . . . . . one can very reasonably say that parliaments are the Indies and Peru of England, if their goodwill is only cultivated in a tactful and captivating manner'.[30]

The war Charles and Buckingham wanted involved the use of English troops, mercenaries and allies in continental Europe. This was certain to be very expensive. The Council of War in 1621 believed that it would not be possible to defend the Palatinate for less than a lump sum of £250,000 plus £900,000 a year. In 1624 James said that he could not go to war with less than five subsidies for military expenditure and one subsidy to pay his debts. Such a grant, together with the associated clerical subsidies, was worth about £900,000. The next year, the government found that it would need about £1,000,000 for military operations; this included £360,000 for the King of Denmark and £240,000 for Mansfeld. Such sums were enormous compared with the cost when England was last at war. Elizabeth had conducted a successful foreign policy in the 1580s, including defeating the Spanish Armada, for £164,000 a year. In the 1590s she had spent £272,000 a year. Unlike Charles, she had managed to avoid major continental commitments and had relied mainly on her navy and subsidies to her allies.[31]

MPs seem to have been surprised by the level of the crown's demands for finance for the war. Their ability to respond was constrained by their need to maintain the support of their constituents. This problem was made worse after 1626 when many electors had not only suffered the oppressions of billeting and the forced loan commissioners but also had heard the news of the military disasters. Nevertheless, parliament responded generously according to its own lights; granting two subsidies in 1621, three in 1624, two in 1625 and five, an enormous number, in 1628. This was more than had been granted in the 1590s.

Unfortunately, subsidies were of increasingly less value to the crown. The grant of a subsidy was usually preceded by some royal concession, and this could be expensive. In 1610 parliament granted James one subsidy which provided him with £96,000. In the same year, however, James gave concessions worth £28,000 a year. More importantly, the government lacked the apparatus to ensure that the subsidy was efficiently administered. A subsidy was ostensibly a tax on the annual value of a person's land or the actual value of his goods, but the assessment of such values had long been dishonestly low. Under James and Charles, assessments continued to fall and the number of people assessed for the subsidy declined. The average assessment of seventy leading Sussex families, for example, fell from £61 to £14 between the 1540s and 1620s. Occasionally, the government tried to improve the yield of a subsidy. In 1628 the Council sent to the commissioners for subsidies the subsidy rolls of 1563 for their areas and told them that they were expecting the return from the current subsidy to be as good as the return for the earlier date. It was of no use; each of the 1628 subsidies yielded only £55,000 (equivalent to c. £33,000 at 1560s prices) compared with the £149,000 yielded by the one subsidy of 1563. In the 1590s, the crown received about £93,000 a year from subsidies; in the 1620s it obtained only £82,000, despite inflation and the grant of more subsidies.[32]

In the absence of adequate parliamentary finance, the crown raised the money as best it could. In 1625 and 1626, when parliament had failed to grant sufficient subsidies, money was raised from a forced loan. In 1628, for a few days, the crown came close to levying ship money on all counties. For the rest, the money was raised by the sale or mortage of crown lands. £640,000 was acquired in this way between 1625 and 1635. Over £238,000 was received from the sale of captured enemy prizes. Plate was sold and the crown jewels were pawned. Above all, there was a heavy reliance on credit – by July 1627 the king had anticipated £319,000 or two-thirds of his ordinary income – and consequently debts remained unpaid. By December 1627, for example, Charles had failed to provide his ally Christian of Denmark with £600,000 owing under the treaty of The Hague. As late as 1635, according to the Venetian ambassador, the King of Denmark was still trying to recover a large sum of money from England, and felt that he had been badly treated.[33]

## VII

After the 1629 Parliament and the peace with France and Spain, Charles found himself in a new situation. Freed, for the first time, from the need to finance a war, he faced a financial system which had proved inadequate in the past and was over-burdened with debts contracted in the war. The classical approach to royal finance, cutting expenditure and increasing income, had not worked, while the possibility of seeking parliamentary support was not to be considered. Something new would have to be tried.

Charles's attitude to expenditure was hardly radical. The Venetian ambassador, in 1635, said that, in comparison with his father, Charles was moderate and restrained. He did, however, remark on the cost of the Household 'which abounds with many superfluous things, both in the number of officials and ministers of every rank and condition, and by the assign-ment of the daily food allowance, which is given with great pomp and splendour even to excess'. There were other moments of extravagance as in 1635 when Charles spent £10,900 building a wall round the circuit of an enlarged Richmond Park and in 1639 when he borrowed £8000 at 8 per cent interest to buy a diamond. Above all, Charles 'was the most enthusiastic and discerning patron of the arts to grace the English throne and he assembled a collection of pictures and works of art unique in the history of English taste'.[34]

There were various attempted reforms in the 1630s. Of par-ticular significance was an attempt to reform office-holding in the navy. The Admiralty commissioners forbade the granting of reversions to any posts in the navy or ordnance and laid down that in future the tenure of all such offices was to be during the king's pleasure and not for life. Had this reform been extended to all royal servants, it would have done much to curb the problem of office-holding. Other attempts were made to cut departmental expenditure in the Cranfield manner. Spending was reduced in the Wardrobe and House-hold in 1629–30. Permanent savings were achieved in the Wardrobe but the Household cuts could not be maintained – by 1636–7 spending on the Household was 11 per cent higher than the level achieved under Cranfield, and by 1640–1 it was

25 per cent higher.[35] Spending on the navy and ordnance, however, fell in the years of peace before the ship money fleets of 1635–9. Finally the government reduced its expenditure on Ireland, which had been enormously costly under Elizabeth and in the early years of James (in 1607–9, for instance, O'Dogherty's rebellion cost the English Exchequer £119,000) and increased Irish revenues, so that under Wentworth, Ireland began to contribute small sums to the government in London.

If Charles had wanted to ensure the crown's financial survival, however, he should have taken steps to reform his income at home. During the early 1630s, no moves were made to achieve a radical change in the royal revenue. Instead, obsolete financial rights were revived. In 1630 the crown disinterred its entitlement to fine people who had not been knighted at the coronation. There was no pretence that Charles wished people to become knights. People who were ineligible for knighthood on grounds of income or birth were fined, while two men who answered the summons to be knighted in 1626 were not knighted but were fined. Quite simply, the government was using its feudal rights to levy a once and for all payment in place of a parliamentary grant. Its move was quite successful in that it collected the equivalent of two and a half subsidies. In a similar way, the crown used its right to enforce the laws designed to protect the forests and those who lived in them as a way of exacting fines and compositions from those unfortunate enough to own land in or near royal forests. Figures for income from this source are not precise, but it was probably less than one subsidy. The operations of the commission for depopulation, intended to levy money from those who had allowed fields to go out of cultivation, also seem to have raised less than the equivalent of one subsidy.

Charles's government looked for odd sources of income wherever it could. It prosecuted the City of London for the mishandling of its lands in Ulster and had a large fine awarded by the Star Chamber. It enforced the laws controlling building in London, a valuable source of compositions. It even set up a new corporation to administer the suburbs of London, which would provide an income from fines from people who wished to become freemen. The weakness of these sources of revenue was described by the Venetian ambassador: 'All these may be called false mines for obtaining money, because they are good for once only, and states are not maintained by such devices'.[36]

Charles did take some steps towards securing a substantial, permanent expansion of his revenue. Continued improvements in the administration of the Court of Wards increased the income from that source from between £29,000 and £35,000 in the period 1617–22 to between £66,000 and £83,000 in 1638–41. More importantly, substantial sums were raised from the customs. In 1635 the new impositions of 1608 were increased; an extra duty was imposed on wine in 1638 and in the same year, the farm of the customs was increased. Between 1637 and 1640 crown revenue from customs was £300,000–£400,000 a year. Such increases were as unpopular as the original impositions had been. In 1638 the Venetian ambassador commented on the scarcities caused by the high duties and the outcry the impositions themselves caused.[37]

More radical than increasing traditional sources of income were the various revenues which the crown raised from monopolists. In 1628 the crown had contemplated levying an excise on beer, wine or other commodities. This was implemented in the 1630s by granting patentees the monopoly of producing or selling various goods in return for the payment of a rent to the crown. The most successful of these patents was the soap monopoly. Originally granted as a result of a new process to make soap out of vegetable oil, this monopoly rapidly became a restrictive practice which pushed up the price of soap, but paid the crown up to £30,000 a year. Money was also raised on the growing use of tobacco; in 1633 the crown began to sell licences to retail tobacco. At first these licences were issued by the government itself, but in 1637, Lord George Goring was granted an agency to issue such licences in return for a rent to the crown. These monopolies together with others on salt, coal, starch, playing cards, etc. yielded substantial amounts. They were, from the point of view of the consumer, a bad way of raising taxes, in that the monopolists increased prices far more than was necessary merely to levy the tax. According to W. R. Scott, monopolies produced a revenue of £100,000 for the crown, but at a cost of £750,000 to the consumers in higher prices. Monopolies also disturbed the market: that on salt, for example, led to shortages of salt in fishing towns. They also upset existing suppliers. In 1637, John Revell complained that he had leased a soap house for twenty-one years in 1630, but had been prohibited from using it for making soap because of the monopoly and he was being sued for non-payment of rent.[38]

The other source of revenue used by Charles was ship money. In a sense, ship money was irrelevant to the main financial problems of the crown. It was a tax levied to allow Charles to achieve a dramatic increase in the size of the navy. Almost all the proceeds from ship money went for this purpose and the tax did not reduce the Exchequer's contribution to the cost of running the navy. It was an attempt to tax the counties at a much higher level than that for the subsidies. The assessments for ship money appear to have been equivalent to about four subsidies. The tax was surprisingly successful up to 1638: between 1635 and 1638 the government demanded £673,109; 95 per cent of this was collected. In 1639, the total assessment for ship money (£67,750) was much smaller than in previous years, but a fifth of the money (£13,942) was not collected. In 1640, the collection collapsed.[39] The failure of ship money, like the decline of the subsidy, was due to the lack of effective local administration. While the crown had to rely on the gentry to assess their neighbours for the subsidy, or on poor constables to collect ship money, it could not hope to achieve effective national taxation.

Charles failed to achieve solvency before the Bishops' Wars. Crown income increased from about £550,000 in 1630 to nearly £900,000 in the late 1630s, but it still proved necessary to borrow money from the customs farmers and to anticipate future revenues. In 1637 part of the income from the wine licences had been anticipated up to 1651; in 1639 a total of £328,000 of future receipts had been anticipated. Bills were not being paid: in 1636 and 1637, for instance, some of the tradesmen who had supplied goods for the wedding of Princess Elizabeth in 1613 were still trying to get their account settled. Moreover, the crown was increasingly coming to rely on a small circle of individuals to lend it money. Failure to pay debts on time, disputes with London over Ulster and the Royal Contract estates, and the death or bankruptcy of leading financiers had dramatically reduced the sources from which the crown could borrow money. By the late 1630s Charles was able to borrow only from the customs farmers and various individuals like Sir William Russell, Laud and Strafford, who had a close interest in the survival of his regime.[40] These problems were not good signs for the long-term future of the government, even without the trouble from the Scots.

## VIII

On his accession, James had an opportunity to increase the crown's income and could have lived comfortably had he controlled his spending. He did not do so, and his ministers were forced to exploit traditional sources of revenue to the full. They were successful in doing this, except in the case of subsidies where they had insufficient control over the local assessment. These increases in income, however, were inadequate and although attempts were made to control spending, they were thwarted by lack of royal support, corruption, the problems of office-holding and the way in which crown servants were rewarded.

Because such problems were, or seemed to be, intractable, the obvious solution was to look for new sources of revenue. The period presents curious contrasts between the desperate use of expedients which could only have a short-term application – fines for distraint of knighthood or the sale of titles – and serious attempts to effect long-term improvements in the king's income such as impositions and other increases in customs revenue and the monopolies of the 1630s. Unfortunately, the new long-term sources of revenue in this period were all politically unpopular and damaged relations between king and parliament. The major failure of James and Charles was their inability to obtain a new source of supply acceptable to parliament. This was also a major failure by parliament.

# 6. The Nature of a Parliament in Early Stuart England

CONRAD RUSSELL

## I

'I am forced a little to begin in general of the parliament and to call to your memories (though I know you know it already) what a parliament is.'[1] A historian starting out on an apparently elementary task of this sort must share James I's misgivings, yet the things we know already, like the things we can do in our sleep, are ones on which we sometimes need refreshing. Inhabitants of the modern English-speaking world, to whom parliaments are as familiar as the air they breathe, have grown up with a number of what James Mill would have called 'indissoluble associations' with the word 'parliament'. Some of these associations, when applied to the world before the English Civil War or even before 1689, are necessarily false, yet, because they are among the images that the word 'parliament' creates in our minds before we have even begun to think, they are very hard to discard. In fact, like James I, I want to call in question some of the things I am sure we know already, because a number of the things we 'know' about parliament are not known historically. Unless we can dismiss these associations from our minds, we risk committing the same anachronism as was committed by Sir Edward Coke, examining parliaments in the time of 'Ina, King of the West Saxons'.[2]

Minds trained on the eleven-plus examination in England, or on multiple choice questions in the United States, are conditioned to thinking in terms of opposites. Given a pair of familiar names, they will set them up as a sort of see-saw, and tell a story in which, as one goes up, the other has to go down.

This sort of unconscious model-making profoundly influences our patterns of thought. When we know, as twentieth-century historians cannot help knowing, that king and parliament later fought a civil war against each other, we risk finding them fixed as opposites in our minds as firmly as Liberal and Conservative, or as Stephen and Matilda. In doing this, we miss the main reason why 'this bloody and unnatural war' of 1642 was such a profound shock to those who took part in it. We thus risk endowing the participants with motives they could not have had. It takes an effort to remind ourselves that the king was a member of parliament, and claimed privilege for his servants just like other members.[3] Indeed, on occasion, he exercised his right as a member to sit in the House of Lords. To us, the body which remained at Westminster during the Civil War was a parliament, yet Lord Montagu was perfectly right to insist that it was not: it was the Lords and Commons, whereas a parliament consisted of the king, Lords and Commons. 'My heart, hand and life shall stand for parliaments, but for no ordinance only by Lords and Commons.'[4]

For those in whom the tendency to think in opposites has been reinforced by the influence of Montesquieu (a conspicuous offender in this respect), it is also easy to think of king and Commons as representing two different branches of government called 'executive' and 'legislative'. However, England has never had the separation of powers (and still does not). When a parliament was assembled, nothing more than a quick change of hats by some of the members was needed to produce an executive. The Privy Council on occasion met in the Palace of Westminster, in order to allow themselves to take part in parliamentary debates at the same place. When the Commons, in 1572, wanted to name a committee to consider a bill about receivers of crown lands, they sent it to a committee of six, including the Chancellor of the Exchequer and the Queen's Remembrancer, which was to meet in the Chancellor of the Exchequer's house.[5] Lords' committees might include a quorum, or even a majority, of the Privy Council. Such people could hardly have a constitutional conflict with themselves.

Today, when we are used to a permanent institution called 'parliament', it is easy to forget that there is no such subject as 'parliament in the early seventeenth century': there are irregularly recurring events called Parliaments. This difference of linguistic usage conceals a deep difference between seventeenth- and twentieth-century habits of thought. This is a barrier I have discovered by accident: when I first entitled a book *The Crisis of Parliaments*, I did not realise I was making a point of importance. What has since taught me I had done so is the frequency with which colleagues, otherwise well capable of accurate citation, misquote the title of this and of my subsequent book on *Parliaments and English Politics 1621–1629*, and quote me as writing on a singular *Parliament and English Politics*.[6] A linguistic and conceptual habit which produces such persistent error on so straightforward a fact as the wording of a book title is likely to produce other errors also. This, like the incredulity on the faces of an audience when it is pointed out that there was no parliament in session at any time during 1688, suggests that the impermanence of parliaments during the seventeenth century, though a known fact, requires more absorbing than it has yet received.

In an age when 'parliamentary government' has become both a slogan and a fact, it is easy to suppose that parliaments were in some sense part of the 'government' of seventeenth-century England. Yet the JPs of Herefordshire were right to remind Sir Robert Harley, in April 1642, that 'we send you, not with authorities to govern us or others (for who can give that to another that is not in himself), but with our consent for making or altering laws as to his majesty, the Lords and Commons shall seem good'.[7] Before the works of Henry Parker began to appear, most Englishmen did not identify legislation as a key part of 'government': the word was more likely to apply to executive power in general, or more particularly, to the power of appointment.[8]

## II

It is worth remembering what a parliament was not, for otherwise we may not approach our sources with the humility necessary to learn what it was. In the first place, each parliament was the king's creation. The only way a parliament could be brought into being was by the king's writ, summoning members of both Houses to Westminster (or elsewhere) at forty days' notice. The Lords were summoned individually, and insisted, against Charles I's occasional incredulity, that they received their summonses as of right.[9] The Commons, on the other hand, were chosen by authority derived from the king, but not chosen by him. In enjoying authority which ultimately came from the king, without being appointed by him, they could be compared (as they sometimes were) with members of juries. An assembly not summoned by the king's writ, like those of 1660 and 1689, was scrupulously not described as a 'parliament', but only enjoyed the status of a convention. Being summoned by the king for his purposes, parliaments legally existed only during the king's pleasure: the words 'the king's majesty doth dissolve this parliament' brought them to a legal end upon the instant. Indeed, so firm was the legal principle that a parliament was the king's parliament and called to advise him that, except in 1649, a parliament ceased to exist immediately upon the death of the sovereign who had called it. A new king had to issue new writs to hold a new election for a new parliament.

The point was well put by John Hooker, member for the city of Exeter in 1571:

> the king who is God's anointed being the head and chief of the whole realm and upon whom the government and estates therof do wholly and only depend: hath the power and authority to call and assemble his parliament, and therein to seek and ask the advice, counsel and assistance of his whole realm, and without this authority, no parliament can properly be summoned or assembled. And the king having this authority, ought not to summon his parliament: but for weighty and great causes.[10]

James I was quite right to remind the parliament of 1621 that 'a parliament is composed of a head and body. The head is the monarch and the body the three estates. In monarchies only are parliaments held, which were created by monarchs. A strange folly it is in those that would have parliaments to be popular contrary to their own institution'.[11]

Kings had invented parliaments, and made and unmade

them as they pleased. Any power parliaments might have was
derivative: the king was the source of their existence, and the
root cause of their authority. Their power, when it existed, was
power to persuade the king to do what he would not otherwise
have done. Since it had to be exercised *through* the king, there
was a limit to the extent to which it could be exercised against
him. Though Coke and others occasionally quoted fourteenth-
century statutes saying a king should call a parliament once a
year, in practice he called parliaments when he chose. It is
then essential, to understand both why parliaments were
created and why they continued, to ask what benefit the king
derived from their existence. There was a widespread belief
that good kings did call parliaments, but it would be carrying
*noblesse oblige* too far to suppose they called them simply on
grounds of principle. Kings called parliaments for their own
advantage or not at all.

The principle that all parliamentary authority was
derivative was, though, a principle for settled times. In
unsettled times, when there was doubt who the king should be,
or who his successor should be, when he was ill, absent or
insane, had suffered catastrophic military defeat, was
approaching bankruptcy, or had otherwise lost the authority
necessary to govern, things could be very different. In such
times, responsibility for clearing up the mess devolved, *de facto*
if not *de jure*, on influential members of the political
community. A parliament was an excellent device for sharing
the responsibility as widely as possible among them. Periods of
exceptional parliamentary influence of this sort had recurred
cyclically since Simon de Montfort's days, but they were always
temporary: the object of the exercise was not to set up
parliamentary government, but to repair the monarchy on a
more stable basis.

Why did the king call parliaments? In a sense, the reasons
for calling parliaments are as manifold as the individual
parliaments themselves, yet all of them are something to do
with consent. It had been established in Edward I's reign that
members elected to the Commons were deemed, because they
represented their communities, to have *plena potestas*: what
they decided was binding on those they represented.[12] On some
occasions, members tried to refer back to their constituencies

for instructions, but they had no need to do so: whatever they decided was binding on their constituents. The advantages of this fact to the king were potentially immense. If a parliament voted a tax, no one could say 'I never agreed to this': every potential protester was legally bound by the act of his representative. If a law was made about some potentially explosive matter such as the succession or a religious settlement, it could be a great advantage to the crown to argue that this law was binding on everyone because it was the act of the whole realm. This was particularly important to the crown because the men who would have to enforce a law, or collect a tax, were often not merely bound, but personally parties to the decision, because they had been in parliament when it was taken. When a subsidy was to be collected, commissioners were named under the Great Seal (not by the Parliament), and the leading figures among them were normally those who had voted the tax. Their proceedings in the counties were normally begun by a speech from a member of parliament among them, and in defending the grant of subsidy, the member would be justifying his own act.[13] When laws were passed, most members, when they went home, became part of the executive responsible for enforcing the laws they had made. Lord Keeper Nicholas Bacon used to tell members that making laws without executing them was like buying a new set of garden tools, and then never using them. In 1604, James I, in exhorting members to execute the laws they had made, held forth on the divine right of JPs.[14] In both spheres, the requirement of general consent had become established largely because it was to the crown's advantage that it should be so. The king did not create a separation of powers: he put his power in a wider context. It could still be said in the seventeenth century, as Fleta said in the thirteenth, that 'the king has his court in his council in his parliaments'.[15]

More generally, a parliament might be asked about any other business on which the crown thought its interests would be served by a search for general consent. In the words of the writ of summons, they were called 'ad tractandum et consentiendum pro quibusdam arduis et urgentibus negotiis statum et defensionem regni et ecclesiae Anglicanae tangentibus': to treat and consent about difficult and urgent business concerning the state and defence of the kingdom and the Church of England.[16] The wording specifically authorised debate about both religion and foreign policy. It was a convention that a parliament should always be called at the beginning of a war. This was, in large measure, because a war always created a need for an extraordinary grant of taxation. It was also frequently the crown's reasoning that the grant (and any necessary succeeding grants) was more likely to be forthcoming if a parliament had already been a party to a decision to go to war. From 1323 to 1639, I am aware of only one significant war started without the meeting of a parliament, and that, in the first year of Henry IV, was because the king had promised not to ask for a subsidy for one year.[17] Moreover, the assembly of a parliament provided a golden opportunity to offer a propaganda justification of a war to most of those who would be responsible for the administrative effort involved in prosecuting it.

The assembly of a parliament was also an extension of the obligation on the sovereign to take counsel. Few things, if anything, were more central in mediaeval political thought than the belief that a good ruler took counsel from a wide variety of sources. A bad ruler, like Rehoboam, would take counsel from an inner ring of flatterers, who would tell him what he wanted to hear. A good ruler would take counsel from a wide circle of experienced people, who would tell him what he needed to know. There was no better way of ensuring that counsel did not come from a closed circle than to take the counsel of the whole realm. In asking for counsel, whether in the Privy Council or in parliament, the sovereign necessarily authorised a degree of freedom of speech: the good counsellor, like Escalus in *Measure for Measure* or Kent in *Lear*, could be recognised by his willingness to give unwelcome advice which was nevertheless for his ruler's good. This was the basis of the parliamentary practice of free speech, which seems to have long ante-dated a formal privilege of free speech.[18]

In the tradition of counsel, there was always a potential ambiguity. Queen Elizabeth, for example, conceded that all the members were counsellors even if only during the parliament, yet she and James I believed that counsel was to be given when the ruler asked for it, and only on subjects on which the ruler asked for it.[19] It was a view which had always tended to commend itself to rulers. Yet the tradition of faithful counsel could include the obligation to give counsel even if the time or subject, as well as the substance, were unwelcome to rulers. Kings, being wilful, needed to be recalled to their own best interests as often as possible.

Parliaments, as far back as the reign of Henry III, had always tried to persuade kings to do things they did not like. There was nothing in the least new about them sometimes opposing the king's will: that is what a faithful counsellor was for. What did have a profound effect on the way parliamentary business was conducted was the fact that the ultimate object of every political manoeuvre had to be to persuade the king to change his mind. Seventeenth-century parliaments could not simply overrule a reluctant monarch by the deploying of a bare parliamentary majority. They had to bring him, by whatever inducements, to adopt different counsels. By the very nature of the political methods open to them, parliaments were not a rival power centre: they were one more among the manifold pressures the king reacted to when choosing his course of action. As the Earl of Bedford put it in 1640: 'in a parliament speakers make the premises but the aye or no makes the conclusion, so parliaments make premises or major or minor but it kings [sic] that makes the conclusion by granting or dissolving'. Bedford appreciated that however strong his parliamentary base might be, in the end, only the king's fiat could crown his strategy with success. His epitaph, reputed to have been chosen by himself, claimed that he had been 'trusted by King Charles in his most secret counsels'. The Army Plot, taking place at about the time when this was probably composed, showed that Bedford had been guilty of foolish optimism, but at least he understood the nature of the system within which he had to work.[20]

In return for doing the king's business, members of both Houses were allowed an opportunity to do their own business. Any member of either House could propose a bill, and almost no issue was too small to be made a matter of parliamentary legislation. There is no better way to convey the flavour of business involved in bills than to list the bills considered in one day. On 26 May 1604, the Commons considered a bill for relief

of those suffering from the plague,* a bill for deceitful making
of cloth, a bill to prohibit heirs from benefiting from reversal
of attainders if they did not take the oath of supremacy, a bill
for an exchange of lands between Trinity College Cambridge
and Sir Thomas Monson, to confirm letters patent to the Earl
of Nottingham,* to confirm the Queen's jointure,* for the sale
of the lands of Sir Thomas Rowse,* a bill 'against conjuration,
witchcraft and dealing with evil and wicked spirits',* for
allowing Sir Thomas Throckmorton to sell lands,* for preser-
vation of pheasants,* and the expiring laws continuance
bill.*[21] Nothing short of an actual list can convey the miscellaneous quality of business transacted by bill. Some of these
bills would be of general concern, and some, including a high
proportion of the economic bills, would originate from special
interest groups. Many others, such as the bills to break entails
to allow people to sell land, would be of desperate concern to a
few individuals, but of no great concern to the parliament as a
whole.

Beyond the formal business, a parliament also provided, in
Professor Elton's phrase, a 'point of contact'.[22] Many gentlemen who spent their lives carrying out the king's commands
valued the chance to see in real life the man whose image they
were used to seeing on the coinage and the Great Seal. In
return, kings expected to use their parliaments to discover any
particular issue which was causing concern to their subjects.
The Parliament of 1621, in persuading the king that he had
been granting patents to the point at which they became a
grievance, was doing just the sort of thing parliaments were
for. On some issues, the assembly of representatives from all
parts of the realm could allow members to discover that what
they had taken for a series of particular grievances were in fact
parts of one general grievance, calling for a general remedy by
legislation.[23]

The function of a parliament as a 'point of contact' did not
apply only to contact between members and the king. Bishop
Parkhurst of Norwich did not always look forward to
parliaments, yet when he tried to look on the bright side of a
tiresome upheaval, the chance to see his old friend Bishop
Berkeley of Bath and Wells came second only to the chance to
try to pass an Act to deal with his defaulting receiver.[24] For

many people, a parliament was an ideal chance to renew contact with friends or relations who happened to live in other counties. It was also an ideal chance to compare notes with people from other counties, and to acquire a greater sense of England as a whole. As one Elizabethan MP put it:

> We who have never seen Berwick or St. Michael's Mount can but blindly guess at them, albeit we look on the maps that come from thence, or letters of instruction sent from thence: some one whom observation, experience and due consideration of that country hath taught can more perfectly open what shall in question thereof grow, and more effectually reason thereupon, than the skilfullest otherwise whatsoever.[25]

Against this background, it makes sense that the most important symbolism of a parliament was that of unity. It was part of the conventional wisdom of the seventeenth century that the king and his people, like head and body, had no true independent life: their strength was in their interdependence. Properly understood, these ideas of unity were supposed to enhance the king's position, and not to weaken it. As Henry VIII said, 'We be informed by our judges that we at no time stand so highly in our estate royal as in the time of parliament, wherein we as head and you as members are conjoined and knit together into one body politic'.[26] Disagreements between a king and his parliament were often compared to disagreements between husband and wife: there were enough married men in both houses for them to be well enough aware that such things happened. Yet matrimonial disagreements (if not taking place in the Webb household) do not normally lead to the drawing up of a constitution. They are better resolved by other methods.

It had always been a central concern of mediaeval parliaments, and of mediaeval barons before them, that the king should be well advised. In most reigns, an evil or unpopular adviser could be levered out of the king's favour without recourse to a parliament. Under Henry VIII, as Wolsey and Cromwell discovered, advisers risked being eased out of the monarch's favour by the activities of their fellow-advisers. Under Elizabeth, it had proved unnecessary to use a parliament to remove the Earl of Essex: his own behaviour ultimately offered better proof that he was a bad adviser than any parliament could do. On other occasions, monarchs persisted in hanging on to advisers whose existence constituted a grievance. In such cases, there was a tradition pre-dating parliaments, and stretching back to clause 50 of Magna Carta, that an assembly of the king's leading subjects could, in effect, make it a condition of further co-operation that the advisers in question should be removed. In the fourteenth century, this process had become partly formalised as impeachment. The process was rarely needed, and was not used between 1449 and 1621, but it existed. Only two kings before Charles I attempted to make an issue of principle out of the attempt to withstand the removal of their advisers in this manner, and it is perhaps not a coincidence that those two, Edward II and Richard II, had both ended up deposed.

### III

Sir John Fortescue, writing during the Hundred Years' War, began a myth, which has been popular ever since, that there was something especially *English* about parliaments and estates. In fact, during the fourteenth century, increasing royal needs for money (among other causes) had led to the development of similar institutions all over, or almost all over, Europe. Many of these had, in 1600, procedural and other advantages the English parliament lacked. In particular, many continental estates enjoyed a legal permanence which English parliaments did not have. The symbol of such permanence is not only recognition as enjoying the legal status of a corporation, but also the existence of permanent officials or standing committees, who could speak in the name of their estates between sessions. The Catalan Cortes chose *Diputats*, who could speak to the king on their behalf between sessions, and often did so to considerable effect. When Sully, in France, wanted to do business with the Agenais, he found the area represented by its Syndic, in whom much of the authority of the estates was vested between sessions.[27]

One of the crucial issues, as Professor Major has recently reminded us, is that of control over the *collection* of taxation. It was because many French provincial estates had control over the collecting of the taxes they voted that they were able to pay their own salaried officials, and thereby to ensure some continuous legal existence. By contrast, in the English parliament all the salaried officers, the Lord Chancellor, the Speaker, the Clerk of the parliaments, the Gentleman Usher of the Black Rod, etc., were paid by the crown. With the theoretical exception of the Speaker, they were also appointed by the crown.

English parliaments, however, enjoyed a clear advantage over most of their continental counterparts in that, at least until 1603, they were clearly *national* assemblies. In France, the estates which mattered in the seventeenth century were, as any reader of Professor Major's new book must appreciate, not Estates General, but estates particular. The heart of French representative institutions was in the provincial estates. By contrast, the crown enjoyed the advantage of being the sole guardian of the *national* interest, and the sole focus for national loyalties.[28] In Spain, it was not at all clear what 'nation' the king's subjects belonged to: was there one nation of Spaniards, or separate nations of Castilians, Aragonese, Catalans, Valencians, Portuguese, etc.?[29] In the Iberian peninsula, there was one king and many cortes, and the cortes, almost necessarily, tended to appear as champions of particularism. In Italy and Germany, estates, like most other institutions, were provincial, and even in the Netherlands, the Estates General were much limited by their labyrinthine relationship with the seven provincial estates. Perhaps only in Sweden did estates share with the king the opportunity to champion the national interest.

In England, on the other hand, it was possible to define a nation as a body which shared a common parliament. Sir Edwin Sandys, in 1607, said that 'it is not *unus grex* [one people] until the whole do join in making laws to govern the whole: for it is fit and just that every man do join in making that which shall bind and govern him; and because every man cannot be personally present, therefore a representative body is made to perform that service'.[30] Yet this conviction, like so many others, was being stated *because* in at least one significant respect, it had become out of date. For Sandys was speaking in the English parliament, on the union between England and Scotland, and the drift of his argument was that the English and the Scots could not be one nation, because they did not have one parliament. From 1603 onwards, it was a new cause of instability in relations between crown and parliament that they were relations between a king of Great Britain and a parliament of England. In particular, during the Short Parliament of 1640, the king saw a rebellion by his own Scottish subjects, which he had no choice but to put down, where the English parliament saw an unpopular foreign war, which they were not bound to encourage by any grant of money.

Ireland created similar problems for rather different reasons. The Earl of Leicester, probably about the time of his appointment as Lord Deputy of Ireland in 1641, carefully noted the constitutional position:

> the kingdom of Ireland was conquered by the kings of England, and it may be reckoned among the patrimonials appertaining to the king (of which Grotius speaks) ... because it was acquired by him out of his patrimony and not by the parliament, therefore it belongs to the king and not to the parliament.[31]

The English parliament periodically made claims to authority over Ireland, but these claims were *ultra vires*: Ireland had its own parliament, which took a very dim view of any suggestion that it was subordinate to the parliament of England.[32] Professor Koenigsberger's suggestion that relations between different parts of multiple kingdoms were a cause of instability in England, as well as on the continent, appears to be abundantly justified.[33] In a sense, then, the Union of the Crowns, in 1603, made it less true than it had been before that English parliaments were truly national assemblies. From a British point of view, they were no such thing.

With the possible exceptions of Francis Bacon and John Pym, members of parliament seem to have been remarkably little influenced by finding themselves an English parliament advising a British king: indeed, the 'British problem' might have been a less significant cause of instability if it had affected English thinking more than it did.

## IV

By contrast, members of the Commons, if not of the Lords, were much more influenced by awareness of their own impermanence. This awareness of impermanence had a profound influence on the ways in which members felt able to pursue political objectives. Members of parliament who came to Westminster normally expected to remain there for three months at most, and then to return to their normal base of operations. Moreover, a considerable proportion of the members were in a hurry to go home. In the summer of 1641, when the summer recess was most unseasonably delayed, Sir Arthur Hesilrige and Zouch Tate set off for home without leave. The Serjeant at Arms was sent after them, and summoned them to return, but they refused. Bishop Parkhurst, shortly before the parliament of 1572, was perturbed about lodging with the only person who had offered him accommodation: 'as well because there is no furniture, as because she is noted to be a great enemy to religion'. It comes as no surprise to find Parkhurst reporting that 'on the 30th [May] the session having finished, we all hastened homewards, thoroughly tired of the City'. In 1629, the Earl of Manchester was unable to provide lodgings for his brother Lord Montagu, because 'my sons, now all at home, take up all the room'.[34]

A realistic member of parliament, however seriously he regarded the service, could not help looking on it merely as a diversion from his normal duties. A permanent post, which continued to exist between parliaments, was a more important source of power than even the most regular election to parliaments. In Somerset in the 1620s, there was no doubt at all that Sir John Poulett, DL, JP (but not a member of any parliament after 1614) was a more important figure than John Pym, member of parliament in all the parliaments of the 1620s, but enjoying no permanent office of more distinction than that of receiver of crown lands. In 1604, Sir Francis

Hastings, in disgrace for petitioning against the deprivation of ministers '*in aliena republica*', in a foreign county, was dismissed from all his local posts, Deputy Lieutenant, Justice of the Peace, and captain in the militia. He remained a member of parliament, because that post was not in the king's gift, but he does not seem to have felt that remaining a member of parliament reduced the sense of exclusion of 'a poor old gentleman'. Hastings is now chiefly remembered as a member of parliament, yet his letters give the impression that his sense of his own importance was based on his position as Deputy Lieutenant and Justice of the Peace, with his parliamentary position a very poor third.[35]

For those members who did not own town houses, one of the important social dislocations involved in long sessions of parliament was the expense, and a long parliament was a financial burden for which they were unprepared. Sir Henry Slingsby spent £731 on staying in London as a member of the Long Parliament in 1640–1. Sir Thomas Barrington was more fortunate, yet his household accounts too show the dislocation and the surprise involved in the slow realisation that he was taking part in a long parliament. He began by taking lodgings in Fleet Street on a weekly basis, arriving promptly the day before the parliament opened. After seventeen weeks, these had cost him £254-18s-7d, and he decided he wanted something more permanent. He then took a thirty-one-year lease of a house in Queen Street, at an annual rent of £130. By December 1641, he had realised he was in for a long haul, and apparently began to feel the need for some of the comforts the family were used to in the country. The list of things they brought up to London in December 1641 included '3 pairs of good whole blankets' and a collection of the family's own beds. Perhaps the significant fact is that Barrington did not do these things until the Parliament had been in session more than a year.[36]

For Barrington, however unexpected such a translation might be, it was not unmanageable: he was a prosperous man, of the sort who might have acquired a town house anyway, he was accompanied by his family, and his journey from Essex was a short one. For others, the dislocation was more unwelcome. During the trial of Strafford, the Earl of Bath was one of the

Lords' reporters for many of the conferences with the Commons, and appeared to be taking the trial seriously, yet his letters indicate nothing so powerfully as his longing to leave London and return to the company of his 'wench', whom he assured that she had never been out of his thoughts for an hour except perhaps when he was asleep.[37]

We should not assume that every gentleman automatically wanted to be a member of parliament. In 1624, Sir Robert Phelips, trying to clear the ground for his own candidature, approached Sir Edward Hext to find out whether he wanted to stand, and received the reply that Hext was 'so weak and feeble as I dare not go out of my parlour from the fire, and there am so loaded with clothes as you would admire and yet cannot keep myself from taking of cold, but cough all night long'. Hext's servant encouraged Phelips to take this show of reluctance seriously: 'my master doth desire his friends and well-willers by all means possible to excuse and free him from that place at this time, for that he hath already served twice in the place, and there are many more gentlemen of worth in the county worthy of the place... P.S. My master will not hinder Sir Robert's election, nor any man's else for ought I know so that he may be freed himself'.[38] So long as most members, and even some peers, had their real roots in the country, 'parliamentary government', implying as it did more or less continual parliaments, was likely to be a social, as well as a conceptual impossibility. It is not a coincidence that the rise of parliamentary government, after 1689, comes at a time when the fashion for town houses (and the money for them) had spread sufficiently widely to be likely to include most of the people likely to be elected. So far as I know, no one has maintained that gentlemen who were elected to parliament were interested only in local issues. It is a more accurate formulation to say that whatever issue they were debating, they could not be indifferent to the local repercussions of that issue.[39] This fact is particularly relevant to grants of taxation. Members might on occasion feel that the national interest, their own interest and their political beliefs could be served by a grant of taxation, and yet feel that the hostility to such a grant in their own communities might be more than, as representatives, they could safely override. In 1604, private approaches were made on the king's behalf to Sir Francis Hastings, to suggest that the Commons might vote a subsidy. Hastings expressed doubts because

> The remainder of an whole subsidy lying still on his people to be paid, the continuing of them long in payments of late years without small intermission, and the poverty the country is generally grown into thereby causeth the Commons to be loath to hear of a subsidy yet, and fearful to grant any at this time, lest the people generally should distaste, whose feelings are not least in matters of this nature.

It is of course possible to interpret such passages cynically, and to suggest that they make a good cloak for a reluctance which was personal. Yet in this case Hastings did, in spite of his misgivings, raise the possibility of a subsidy on the floor of the Commons. Perhaps, then, his hesitations deserve to be taken at face value.[40]

It was this sort of hesitation which led Queen Elizabeth to complain, in 1593, that some members regarded the necessity of their counties more than the necessity of the state.[41] Yet, however infuriating such concern with local reactions might appear to the crown in time of war, it was part of the necessary price for the existence of anything approaching a genuinely representative assembly. One of the reasons for the summons of a representative assembly was to tell the Crown about this sort of local feeling.

Some members of the Commons were not representatives in any sense recognisable today. John Pym's constituency of Tavistock was controlled by the Earl of Bedford, and I know no evidence that he ever set foot in it. He could well afford to say, in 1640, that they should consider the present necessity and not the satisfaction of the country.[42] On the other hand, those who represented populous constituencies such as Somerset, York-shire or Kent had genuinely been chosen by a substantial electorate, and could not be indifferent to the effect of their doings on those who returned them.[43] In between these extremes, there were a variety of degrees of influence. There were many cases of boroughs returning a member recom-

mended by a powerful man, yet not many of these pressures
were absolutely irresistible. A patron's chance of returning his
nominee depended in part on his care in selecting a nominee
who would be congenial to those who were asked to return him.
There is thus no absolute antithesis between elected members
and those returned by patronage. It was the easier for
boroughs to reject patrons' nominees because there was a law
still in force which said that all members had to be resident in
their constituencies. This seems to have been a classic case of a
law being honoured in the breach: the 1571 parliament spent a
long time considering a bill to repeal it, and chose not to
because, so long as the law was on the books, it was always
possible for a borough to refuse a nominee on the ground that
he was not a resident, and therefore it would be illegal to
return him.[44] There is, then, a possibility that local sentiment
influenced even those which appear to be nomination returns.

If we concede that Professor Hirst is right that a number of
members of the Commons were representing substantial
numbers of electors, and that their political behaviour might
be influenced by pressure, instructions or other electoral
considerations, we still have to decide how this evidence ought
to be used. There are two ways it may be fitted into the general
story. One is to assume that electoral pressure confers considerable extra strength on members of parliament: to assume that,
as 'representatives of the people', they were in a position to
wrest more power from the Crown than they could have done
without it. The other way of interpreting this evidence would
be to regard it as a considerable political embarrassment to
many of the Commons. In a case like the Oxford session of
1625, electoral pressure then could open up a gap between the
minimum that would satisfy the crown and the maximum that
could be explained away in the country, leaving members in
the position of embarrassed pig-in-the-middle. In this way,
electoral pressure may have diminished members' freedom of
choice, and thereby reduced their usefulness to the king. In
1629, a Welshman was in trouble for saying that the king was
the 'pollingest' king that ever was, and he would be chased out
in favour of the Elector Palatine. He said that the king would
lose the hearts of his subjects by charging them so deep with
loan money *and subsidies*.[45] Any former member of parliament

who heard this may have felt some alarm: it may have been axiomatic in law that the consent of a parliament would be taken for the consent of the whole realm, but members could not be sure that it would always be axiomatic in fact.

## V

Indeed, this sensitivity to local pressure contributed a good deal to bringing the whole parliamentary system to the verge of extinction. This collapse, between 1625 and 1640, is the more striking for the fact that the system which was proving inadequate had been in regular use for some three hundred years. During that time, it had survived numerous crises. impeachments, power struggles, unpopular wars, and even three depositions of kings. Why, when the system had proved so tough in the face of many strains, did it prove so inadequate in the middle of the seventeenth century?[46]

It does not appear that the system by which the king relied on frequent parliaments for legislation and extraordinary supply had lost any of its hold on the emotional loyalties of Englishmen. To people like Lord Keeper Coventry or Sir Robert Phelips, parliaments symbolised the unity of the King with his people. They were thus important evidence that he was not a tyrant. For those involved in local government, it was also important that the king occasionally wanted their advice. Many of them undertook a backbreaking load of work, for reasons in which loyalty, as well as self-importance, played a part. In return for this body of work, they expected an occasional hearing. Moreover, if the principle of consent to taxation were ever formally abandoned, many believed the crown's appetite for money might prove insatiable.

On the other hand, there is very little evidence to suggest that, before November 1640, many members wanted parliaments to do more than they had. In particular, there is no sign during the 1620s of any change in the idea that parliaments were occasional and short-term assemblies. Without a change in this point, parliaments could not enjoy much more status than they already did. Charles I's continental wars offered the prospect of very frequent parliaments, but the reaction of members was not to cry out for annual parliaments: it was to cry out against annual subsidies.[47]

Nor is there much sign, early in Charles I's reign, of any conscious attachment to a programme of unparliamentary government. Those who billed Charles, in 1625, as a prince 'bred in parliaments' were making a fair point. Charles, as Prince of Wales, had been a regular attender in the House of Lords in two consecutive parliaments. The help he gave to the passage of such measures as the Monopolies Act of 1624 did not suggest that he came to the throne handicapped by any unparliamentary outlook. Even more, many of Charles's councillors, such as Manchester, Coventry or Secretary Coke, shared many of the same principles which informed a man like Sir Robert Phelips. Whatever brought the system to the verge of collapse, it does not appear to be the clash of two rival constitutional ideologies. Strongly held beliefs there certainly were, but these were not two rival bodies of beliefs. They were one shared body of beliefs, whose application was frequently in dispute. There was nothing new about this, and it was hard to see why it should have brought the system to a halt.[48]

Just as it is necessary to see what uses parliaments had for the king in order to understand why they were created, so it is necessary to understand what they were no longer offering to the king in order to see why they came so near extinction. In essence, the problem was that, from the 1590s onwards, parliaments were not offering the crown enough to live on, while at the same time insisting that the crown should take nothing but what they gave to it. For example, the parliament of 1628 voted five subsidies, amounting to approximately £275,000. This appeared to them to be an act of unparalleled generosity, and they insisted, in turn, that the king should raise no revenues but the ones he was legally entitled to. The king, then, was given £275,000 towards needs that were near a million, on condition that he did not try to get anything else. No wonder that the king, in the end, tried to wriggle out of the financial straitjacket, and raise money by means he was not entitled to. What is remarkable is not that the king did this, but that he did not do it sooner. In November 1640, Sir Benjamin Rudyerd reported a widespread opinion that parliaments would take more from the king than they gave to him.

Rudyerd's answer, that the hearts of his subjects were the greatest treasure the king could have, was good political theory, and good English constitutional convention, but set against the abolition of ship money, it was remarkably poor financial arithmetic.[49]

How did this gulf open up between the income the king derived from parliaments and the income he needed to live on? A great deal of it happened because of events in the country, not at Westminster. English parliaments did not control the assessment of the taxes they voted, and the fall in the yield per subsidy, from £130,000 in the middle of Elizabeth's reign to £55,000 in 1628, cannot be blamed on members of parliament: it must indicate a considerable resistance to taxation in the country at large. In 1628, the Privy Council was reduced to sending out circular letters asking that the yield of the subsidies should not be less than it had been in 1563, and this over a period in which the value of money had fallen substantially.[50]

Why so intense a reluctance to pay taxes? Reluctance to pay taxes is normal, but in this period, it was either exceptionally strong or exceptionally effective. Part of this is the result of inflation, and of the pressure of growing population on food resources. The war taxation of 1597–1601 had come during a period of what George Abbot called 'great cleanness of teeth', when taxpayers might reasonably feel that the purchase of food (if available) had first claim on their resources. The years c.1600–30 were, in most of Europe, the period when the population curve reached a peak, and therefore times of considerable economic hardship. It is also possible that population mobility, combined with the engrossing of land into fewer hands, had the effect of narrowing the country's taxable base. There were certainly fewer taxpayers on the subsidy books, and the decline may not have been entirely due to evasion.[51]

At the same time as the country's capacity to pay was going down, the crown's needs were going up. Inflation, in part, explains both phenomena, but it is not the whole explanation. In 1559, Lord Keeper Nicholas Bacon, opening Queen Elizabeth's first parliament, asked his hearers to

consider the huge and wonderful charge newly grown to the

crown, more than ever before hath been wont, and now of necessity to be continued – as first the maintenance of garrison in certain places on the sea coasts, as Portsmouth and others, with new munition and artillery, besides the new increased charge for the continual maintenance of the English navy to be ever in readiness against all evil haps, the strongest wall and defence that can be against the enemies of this island . . . in mine opinion, this doth exceed the ancient yearly revenues of the crown.[52]

Sixteenth- and seventeenth-century warfare was not only more expensive than that of the Hundred Years' War: it also demanded that a far greater proportion of the sinews of war be provided, on a regular basis, out of the crown's budget. In 1610, Robert Cecil, setting out the cost of garrisoning Ireland, again reminded his hearers of the novel point that much of the expense of war now went on in peacetime.[53] This was why the crown now needed what it requested in 1610: not occasional supply from parliaments when needed, but regular and permanent additions to its revenue. Such a request necessarily disturbed the whole basis for co-operation between crown and parliaments: the use of an occasional body for regular supply was likely to be an unstable system. These growing needs created a pressure for parliaments either to become much more important, or to become obsolete. Either they had to give the crown what they had never done before, or they had to let the crown raise the money without their consent. It is because such a choice went clean against everyone's inclinations that it was evaded for so long. When things cannot continue as they have been, conservatism becomes a force for instability.

What drove Charles I to do without parliaments for eleven years was his need for money. Among the things which particularly scarred Charles were the refusal of supply in time of war, in 1626, and the refusal to grant Tonnage and Poundage in 1628 and 1629. Yet taxation had never been the only thing which required general consent: new laws did also. It is striking how little the crown appears to have been handicapped during the 1630s by the lack of ability to make new and clearly binding laws. Here, the general conservatism of the early seventeenth century is relevant: the law-making power appears crucial in periods of rapid change, like the 1530s, when new laws are urgently needed. During the early seventeenth century, there appears rather to have been a feeling that there were too many laws already. Sir Edward Coke, as Speaker of the Parliament of 1593 'came to speak of laws, that were so great and so many already, that they were fit to be termed *elephantinae leges*, therefore to make more laws it might seem superfluous'. The view was often expressed that what was needed was rather a codification of laws, to make them more intelligible. James I, in 1610, even expressed the view that the laws should be in English. This, like many other utterances about laws during the early seventeenth century, shows that the law reform movement of the interregnum had a pre-history. An amateur parliament, busily legislating about any item that takes its fancy, can cause considerable legal confusion.[54]

If the crown did not want parliaments to make new laws, and get more money without them than it had done with them, it is no wonder it did not call them for some time. Neither of the reasons which had led the crown to see advantage in calling parliaments ever since the reign of Edward I appeared to be valid any longer.

Yet it soon appeared that the importance of parliaments to Englishmen could not be measured by what they did in settled times. In settled times all parliamentary authority was derivative: parliaments were the moon to the royal sun. Yet in unsettled times, many people would instinctively turn to a parliament to put the stamp of general authority, and of respectability, upon whatever emergency measures the situation demanded. The more startling the emergency character of these measures, the more important it was that as many people as possible should share the responsibility by being parties to them. There can be few better examples of this way of thought than Lord Burghley's Interregnum Bill of 1584. Burghley's draft recounts that, in the event of the Queen's assassination, there would be an 'interregnum', and the realm would want a lawful sovereign. He provided that the Privy Council, whose places would normally cease on the death of the sovereign who appointed them, should remain in office 'by authority of this parliament', 'until by a greater assembly in a

parliament of the three estates of the realm further order shall
be published'. The parliament which had last met was then to
reassemble, to reappoint the Councillors or to appoint new
ones, to try titles to the crown, and 'declare their decision in
the form of an Act of parliament'. Any who resisted this
determination were to be proclaimed traitors to the crown by
the authority of the three estates. They were to authorise *some*
members of the Council to spend public money. There is very
little this bill does not allow to a parliament, but the
arrangement is, in its essence, temporary: it is to hold the fort
until a new king can be put securely on the throne.[55] It is worth
comparing this with the argument of Serjeant Manwood, in
1571, that whoever denied the authority of a parliament to
determine the succession thereby denied the queen's title.[56] By
contrast, after 1603, when the throne was securely settled, Sir
Edward Coke vehemently denied that such a thing as an
interregnum could exist, and even so devoted a parliamentarian as Edward Alford was prepared to say that an Act of
parliament could do anything *except* alter the succession to the
crown.[57]

The two ideas most people seem to have been unwilling to
give up were the attachment to parliaments as an expression of
unity, and the belief in their necessity as an emergency remedy
in unsettled times. Beyond this, there remained a deep attachment to the principle of consent, which Charles I was too in-
articulate to answer, like Cromwell, by asking 'where shall we
find that consent?'.

## VI

Though this attachment to parliaments was intense, it was not
yet in any sense an 'opposition' creed. Indeed, in 1640, some of
the people who were expressing it most intensely were a faction
within Charles I's Privy Council. Charles, if the term had been
available to him, might have chosen to describe them as 'the
wets', but he still employed them. So long as he did, they could
continue to believe that their principles were compatible with
the crown's service. Among these people, one of those whose
views are best documented is Secretary Vane. On 30
September 1640, he wrote to his fellow-Secretary Windebank,

saying the Danish Ambassador had hoped to mediate between the king and the Scots, but this was now unnecessary, 'the king being now resolved to proceed therein with advice of his peers and kingdom, which is but high time'. In May 1641, he sent his fellow-Councillor Sir Thomas Roe a horrified report of the Army Plot, concluding: 'I hope my next will tell you that his Majesty is resolved to reconcile himself with his people, and to rely upon their counsels, there being now no other left'.[58] The Earl of Leicester, who succeeded Strafford as Lord Deputy of Ireland, made notes about 'alteration of government by settled parliaments, or sovereign courts or counsels . . . in vain is the net laid in sight of any bird, *Prov.*'[59] The Earl of Northumberland, Lord Admiral, reported during the Bishops' Wars that 'it grieves my soul to be involved in these counsels'.[60] Those who thought this way probably included Manchester, Salisbury, Holland, Leicester, Northumberland, Vane, Roe, Pembroke, Saville and, among those no longer in office, Secretary Coke and Lord Keeper Coventry. It is to be hoped that such a list can show that strongly held parliamentary convictions did not have to be opposition convictions. The parting of the ways, for this group, did not come in the 1630s: it came between the Army Plot of May 1641, which advertised Charles's growing unparliamentary convictions, and the dismissal of Secretary Vane, in December 1641, which advertised that Charles no longer wished to be served according to their convictions. After that point, every member of this group except Coventry, who was dead, became either a parliamentarian or a neutral in the Civil War.[61] This highlights the fact that in a monarchy, what drives a man into an 'opposition' stance is not his convictions, but the king's attitude to those convictions. A man is pushed into opposition not because the king disagrees with him, but because the king no longer wishes to hear him or be served by him. It was not until the very end of 1641 that it was clear to Charles's inner circle of advisers that a strong and principled attachment to parliaments was incompatible with Charles's service. Their judgement should be taken seriously, for they had more opportunities to form it than a lifetime's research can ever give us.[62]

In the country at large, it was ship money and the Bishops' Wars which seem to have turned attachment to parliaments into a controversial conviction. In Kent, Sir Roger Twysden recorded some of the conversation of the county gentry about ship money, and the issue appeared to be producing something of a polarisation. Some said that 'if a kingdom were in jeopardy, it ought not to be lost for want of money if it were within it', but others argued that 'in so high a point every man ought to be heard and the reasons of every one weighed, which could not be but in parliament'. This group turned to Chapter 35 of Fortescue, which is Fortescue's most pointed contrast between the lawful government of England and the arbitrary government of France.[63] This line of reasoning was much accentuated in 1639, when the king committed himself to a war without attempting to secure the co-operation of a parliament. It was probably the first time this had been done since 1323. It was when this reaction was reaching its height that Charles I was roundly defeated by the Scots, and his authority collapsed.

Among those unsettled times which made people reach for a parliament to put things together again, disputed successions and royal minorities were closely followed by the collapse of effective royal authority. Someone had to keep things going, and a parliament, by sharing the responsibility, seemed the best way of doing it. It is hard not to agree with Professor Hirst that in 1640, things had changed so much since the 1620s that we are in 'a new world'.[64] This fact was immediately symbolised by two highly significant novelties in the business the king laid before the long parliament. There are few more important royal powers than control of foreign policy and control of the spending of money. In 1640, Charles handed over the task of negotiating a treaty with the Scots to the Lords, and the task of paying the English and Scottish armies to the Commons, in both cases because he was unable to do the job himself. The negotiation had to be handed over, partly because, like Charles V at the Peace of Augsburg, Charles I had a repugnance for doing what he knew had to be done. It also had to be handed over because the Scots, with the power of a conquering army, insisted that they would not agree to any treaty unless it were confirmed by an English parliament.[65] The paying of the armies had to be handed over because Charles simply had no money to do it. It was thus by the king's own act that the two houses began to exercise powers that no parliament had exercised for a very long time. Yet even so, it remained the assumption of all seasoned politicians that what was going on was not a long-term shift to 'parliamentary government', but a set of emergency measures designed to put the kingdom together again. The House of Lords, in March 1641, had no idea of what it was implying when it suspended several lawsuits (which infringed the parliamentary privilege of the Prince of Wales) 'during the continuance of the present parliament'.[66] Even Pym was looking forward to a longer tenure of power, not as a member of parliament, but as Chancellor of the Exchequer. The story of the causes of the Civil War is the story of why this rescue operation was unsuccessful, and that story, mercifully, does not have to be told here.

For the purposes of this chapter, it is possible to end remarks on the changes in the nature of a parliament brought about during the first two years of the long parliament by looking at two Acts, the Triennial Act and the Act Against Dissolution. These were both made necessary by the immediate exigencies of defeat by the Scots, the Triennial Act because the Scots insisted on it as a security for the peace treaty,[67] and the Act Against Dissolution because those who were lending money to pay the armies on the credit of future subsidies insisted on security for their loans. Yet, however immediate the circumstances that gave rise to them, these two Acts are an intellectual watershed in the history of parliaments in England. They gave the parliament a permanent, institutional existence, and, for the first time, make it accurate to speak of 'parliament' and not of 'parliaments'.

These two Acts, passed within eight weeks of each other, gave Parliament the secure status it had never had before. It is permissible to leave the last word with the Earl of Leicester, writing in his commonplace book in or after 1641, and probably referring to the Act against dissolving the parliament without its own consent:

The parliaments of England heretofore were like tenants at will, depending upon the will of the lord, that is, of the king, and as the death of the lord was a determination of his will, and a cessation or determination of the parliament [cf. tenants at will, see Coke, 1 Institut. lib. 1 cap. 8]. But since the Act of parliament made in this king's time, the parliament is no more tenant at will, nor hath only *possessionem nudam et precariam*, but is as tenants for years or for life not determinable at the will of the king, and corporations never dying (as it is in the law) the parliament which is a corporation never dies, nor ceaseth at the death of the king, that is, the death of the king is no determination of it, and it is not likely that they will be weary of their immortality.[68]

# 7. National and Local Awareness in the County Communities

## ANTHONY FLETCHER

### I

STUDY of the English county communities has proved a fruitful approach to the period 1600–40. In recent work on Lincolnshire and Warwickshire, however, the notion of the county community has been sharply criticised and in a general survey of the use of the concept in Stuart historiography Clive Holmes has questioned its validity. One of the difficulties is that most writers have focused their attention upon the gentry community, that is the circle of leading members of a shire who monopolised its organs of political expression and set the tone of its administrative and religious life. But work on elections has shown that independently-minded electors sometimes held different attitudes from the gentry. We cannot, in other words, always use the term county community, assuming gentry domination of county politics and universal deference, as a synonym for the entire population of a shire. Another difficulty is that the notion of the county as a self-conscious society remains intangible and it can only be demonstrated at times of crisis when the gentry or the grand jury gave it formal expression. Critics such as Christopher Hill have pointed out the danger of sentimentalising the county communities. Another difficulty is that those who have adopted the notion as a framework of analysis have perhaps been credited with more ambitious aims than they had in mind. It was predictable that we should learn that there was much variation in the sense of identity and degree of cohesion of the county communities. 'Generalisations', declares Christopher Hill, 'have proved to be premature', but generalisations were not necessarily intended. The supposed 'disarray' of the county community historians is no more than a useful debating point.[1]

Those who are critical of the notion of the county community quite rightly stress the importance of studying other kinds of communities such as the neighbourhood or the *pays*. But it would be unfortunate if historians came to think of men's loyalties in this period in mutually exclusive terms. What we need is a more subtle approach to the overlapping loyalties and identities that men felt. Richard Cust and Peter Lake have shown in their study of Sir Richard Grosvenor that he used a range of terms which included neighbourhood, shire, county, country and commonwealth in his grand jury charges of 1625 and 1626 and his 1624 election address. The key word is 'country': sometimes Grosvenor used it in a purely local sense, meaning the County Palatine of Cheshire, but on other occasions it seems to refer to 'some concept of the common good that transcended pure localism and instead referred to the national community of which the local formed but a part'. Grosvenor both played on local consciousness and sought to awake national consciousness.[2] This chapter takes the existence of both for granted and will not attempt to quantify either. The county communities provide the framework of the argument because they were the principal unit of local government and politics. Anyone who participated in one of the gatherings of a shire – assizes, quarter sessions or a county election – is likely to have glimpsed something of what belonging to his county meant. These participants of course included numerous yeomen and townsmen, even husbandmen, craftsmen and labourers, as well as the gentry. Some sense of loyalty to the county was undoubtedly prompted and sustained by contact with the institutions of county government. Many may have felt this only dimly but the gentry, whose horizons were steadily being lifted from their own parishes and estates, surely felt it most powerfully.

Derek Hirst has demonstrated that during the 1620s there was a growing sense of parliament's importance as a forum for the remedy of grievances and as the representative body of the nation. Nevertheless parliament was still seen, in so far as initiative lay with its members from the localities, as an institution designed to deal with local and particular problems. Unsolicited advice was not expected or normally offered on matters of wider import. The Nottinghamshire JPs, to take but one example, sent up a draft bill to the knights of the shire in 1625 for reforming abuses committed by the clerk of the market, but they were hesitant about the business: they wrote 'not with any opinion to tie the wisdom of that House to any ignorant form of order but only to express what we desire'.[3]

Before 1640 conscious attempts to send a representative to participate in a national debate on national issues seem to have been rare. In 1604 Sir Edward Montagu declared that he was 'straightly enjoined by the county for which I serve' to speak up about certain specific issues including the suspension of nonconformist ministers. This wording hints at the precocity of some of the puritan gentry in Northamptonshire, who may have had an unusual awareness that they were taking up matters of concern to likeminded men in other shires. But if most men's briefings remained persistently traditional, once they were at Westminster MPs increasingly found themselves intent on remedying the same grievances as their colleagues. Many of the policies pursued by the first two Stuarts made nonsense, in the eyes of any thoughful parliament man, of the distinction between matters of national and local importance.[4]

It took time for the mass of country gentlemen to grasp that issues they were used to regarding in a local context might need to be pursued in co-operation with other men of the same status not just within their district or region but across the country as a whole. An individual with a foot both at court and in the country could help along this process. Thus Richard Cust and Peter Lake have shown how Sir Richard Grosvenor was able during the 1620s to forge 'important ideological links between the arena of national politics and local society'. The frustrations of a decade when the localities had no voice at Westminster and the coincidence during that decade of a series of outstandingly vexatious political programmes – ship money, war with Scotland, Arminianism – undoubtedly did much to inculcate the notion that the Stuarts did harbour some kind of overall political design which could be effectively resisted only by co-ordinated action. Hence the unprecedented degree of interest shown in the elections for the parliaments of 1640.[5] A nationwide debate followed, during the next two years, that was remarkable for its scope and intensity. Pamphlets and newsbooks poured from the London presses. Carriers left London loaded with correspondence, as those at the centre of things scribbled furiously to keep friends and neighbours at home abreast of developments. The principal form of collective expression among country gentlemen became the county petition, a declaration or statement of views which claimed, often dubiously, to speak in the name of a whole shire. In the months before civil war broke out both John Pym and Charles I drew much confidence from the support they received in the form of petitions. Indeed it would not be going too far to say that, by their energetic involvement in the political crisis, those who were informed and articulate in the localities made it possible for Pym and Charles to contemplate a resort to arms.[6]

What has been said so far, it may be suggested, provides a bare outline of the process with which this essay is concerned. But we are discussing a process that no two counties experienced at exactly the same pace or in quite the same way. It is not simply, as Alan Everitt has put it, that each county had 'its own distinct ethos and loyalty', though this remark points to the complexity of the problems the subject poses.[7] We must confront a set of three main variables: the structure of county society at its highest level together with the social relationships of the gentry; the extent and strength of gentry catholicism and puritanism; the impact of the whole range of early Stuart policies from Arminianism in the church to fiscal expedients and the exact militia. This chapter investigates certain patterns produced by the interaction of these variables.

## II

In the first place there were several counties where the sheer ambition and egocentricity of a single individual is immediately evident. It is instructive to compare Yorkshire, Somerset and Kent: in all three cases national awareness is apparent unusually early. A large and competitive group of gentry jostled for power and status in Yorkshire. Demand for parliamentary seats was keen and election contests were exceptionally frequent. In the West Riding the instability of the cloth trade, in the East and North Ridings the strong catholicism of some of the gentry, provided urgent local issues. In the midst of all this for some twenty-five years stood Sir Thomas Wentworth: his imperious personality and ceaseless activities were the focus of Yorkshire politics. Almost from the moment that he inherited his father's estates at Wentworth Woodhouse in 1614, Sir Thomas seems to have set his mind upon supremacy in the shire. From 1617 onwards he was engaged in a deadly feud with his neighbour the aged, hot-tempered and arrogant Sir John Savile of Howley. Savile had hoped to patronise his young and thrusting neighbour by recommending him in 1615 for the office of *custos rotulorum*, when he himself was forced to resign the post because of scandals connected with his incumbency. When, with the Duke of Buckingham's help, Savile tried to recover the post, Wentworth refused to back down. The younger man's pride is evident in the wording of his response: 'it might justly be taken as the greatest disgrace that could be done unto me'.[8]

In a recent examination of Wentworth's parliamentary career, S. P. Salt has argued that, while he often professed an obligation to serve his county, his political stance at many points can best be understood in terms of personal convictions and tactical considerations.[9] His first concern was always his own advancement: the best proof of his political skills is the success he finally achieved in 1628 when the king gave him a viscountcy and the Presidency of the Council of the North. The feud with Savile, which was given a convenient stage by the Parliaments of 1621, 1625 and 1628, had in the meanwhile done much to raise the political consciousness of the large but dispersed Yorkshire electorate, for Wentworth brought a new sophistication and prowess in management to the county contests. His preparations in 1621 for treating all his supporters, freeholders of however doubtful qualifications as well as gentry, were meticulous. His scheme for arraying his supporters at Tadcaster, so that he could arrive at the polling field with an impressive cavalcade, was carefully designed to impress floating voters.[10]

Wentworth believed he could manipulate his Yorkshire

countrymen. His celebrated speech at Rotherham in April 1621, an interim report on his service at Westminster, shows his complete if cynical understanding of the role that was expected of him and that might in the long run smooth his path to high office. Having foisted his courtier friend Sir George Calvert on the county as his running mate, he now sought to justify his failure to bring home any legislation that would please his constituents.[11] As the decade wore on Savile began to show the desperation of a man driven on to the defensive. He campaigned even more vigorously in the West Riding cloth towns, thus excessively raising expectations there of what parliament would achieve on their behalf. His lack of connections among the leading county families caused him to stoop to using a calculated catholic smear against William Mallory, his rival in the 1625 election.[12]

Until 1628 Wentworth and Savile fought on the same ground, each in his own way posing as the champion of localism. But Wentworth's 1628 appointments changed all this: his new supremacy and his immediate efforts to build his own following brought a more distinct pattern of county factionalism. Men like Christopher Wandesford, one of those who wrote to congratulate the Lord President on his change of fortune at court, were reinstated in the commission of the peace; his allies joined the Council of the North and the deputy-lieutenancy. There was a mixture of politics and spite in the quarrels of the next five years. In 1629 Wandesford urged Wentworth to cultivate the Richmondshire gentleman Sir William Gascoigne with the advice that he would be a friend against 'the near combination of all this country against you partly for malice . . . . partly for religion'. He was referring to Wentworth's rigorous levying of recusant fines on the numerous North Riding catholics.

In fact Wentworth managed to enrage and frustrate most of the leading families who did not enjoy his special favour. His ostentatious building activities at Ledstone and the King's Manor in York, his haughtiness and his delight in humbling his enemies were the blatant marks of his Presidency. He ruthlessly crushed Lord Fauconberg's conspiracy to engineer his downfall; he dragged Sir David Foulis, who was rash enough to accuse him of misappropriating the king's revenue, before Star

Chamber; he fined and imprisoned Sir John Bourchier, who had ordered the destruction of some fences in the royal park Wentworth had created in the forest of Galtres.[13] From Ireland, between 1633 and 1640, Wentworth kept up an incessant correspondence about Yorkshire affairs, caustically dismissing his enemies in splenetic letters to officials at court. Brian Stapleton, a North Riding magistrate, he told Sir John Coke soon after he had left the county, was 'as arrant a saucy Magna Charta man as in all the country'. But by 1640 the severe impact of ship money and the Scots war had created a hard and determined unanimity among the Yorkshire gentry. In October, two of Wentworth's leading opponents, Ferdinando Lord Fairfax and Henry Bellasis, won the knightships of the shire. Realising too late how serious the county's disenchantment was, he tried that month to rally the moderate gentry by playing the role of conciliator between king and county.[14] Now his enemies were ready to destroy him. The fervent political awareness which he had done so much to create in his own shire was at last turned against him. It contributed significantly to his downfall.

T. G. Barnes has shown how the personal hostility between Sir Robert Phelips and John Lord Poulett became 'indelibly impressed' upon the fabric of Somerset's political life. Their feud began during the election campaign of 1614. Both men had sat before, Phelips, through his father's patronage, at the age of only seventeen; both set their minds on this occasion on a knightship of the shire. Phelips, too rashly, ran on his own, while Poulett paired with the elderly gentleman Sir Maurice Berkeley. Instead of taking the county by storm as he expected, Phelips' tactics misfired and he lost the contest. He could never forgive Poulett for the dishonour his failure brought him. Over the next years he concentrated on winning supremacy at home: this came easily to him in the magistracy but eluded him in the lieutenancy where Poulett held sway. Only a few months after he was appointed a deputy lieutenant in 1625, Phelips found himself dismissed through Poulett's machinations. Three years elapsed before he was reappointed. The passionate hatred between the two men was predictably exacerbated in 1628 when Poulett's assiduous cultivation of contacts at court brought him the reward of a baronage.[15]

Sir Robert Phelips was a man of tremendous energy and intense application. In Barnes's account he is the indefatigable local antagonist, twisting every available administrative issue to challenge his rival. In Conrad Russell's account of the 1620s parliaments he is a man who sincerely tried to give good service both to his country, in the sense of his own shire, and to the king's government. Conrad Russell characterises him as the 'most vocally aware' of all the members of those parliaments 'of belonging to an institution whose survival was on probation'. The common feature of these studies is Phelips' ambition for fame and reputation, the driving force of his career. Not that he, any more than Wentworth, was entirely opportunistic. His speeches at Westminster on such issues as the arbitrary courses of the lieutenancy and the alehouses patent show his understanding of the importance of precedent and his concern to preserve the established constitution. He cared deeply about the question of the Palatinate and he shared the fears of many of his colleagues about the future of protestantism.[16]

Phelips' impact on Somerset politics was great because in most cases he led from conviction as well as out of malice towards Poulett. Yet even when he was being opportunistic his personality was such that he was capable of quickly raising the political temperature in the gentry community. Thus his intervention on behalf of Archbishop Laud in the matter of churchales in 1633, during a period of mildness forced upon him by the need to regain favour at court, sparked off a new controversy.[17] Comparison of the county's reaction to the forced loan in 1626 and to ship money in the 1630s gives us the measure of Phelips' role: in the former case he made a tactical retreat from Somerset and there were no outright refusals of the levy, in the latter resistance was concentrated in the neighbourhood of Phelips's estates and those of three of his closest allies. In militia affairs likewise Phelips' lead gave lesser men the confidence to question warrants and to defy those in authority. He adroitly manipulated a current of ill-will against the deputy lieutenants: his scathing criticisms of the muster-master encouraged countrymen to refuse his wages and his questioning of the obligation of JPs to assist the deputies spread consternation on the Bench. All this is not to suggest that Phelips created Somerset's opposition to Charles I's govern-

ment, but there can be no doubt that he did much to mag-
nify it.[18] Two of his particular concerns appeared in the
petition of the grand jury at the Bath assizes in 1638: the 'great
and invented taxations by new invented ways' and the abuses of
the saltpetre men. Yet this petition is also a reminder that not
even so commanding a figure as Sir Robert Phelips was likely to
have a hand in every county pie. The grand jurymen, demon-
strating their localist horizons, were bothered about the
number of horses that were commandeered by the postmasters
on the main road to the west, the abundance of vagrants in
their districts and the neglect of watch and ward. Moreover a
reference to the disorders and thefts associated with recent bull
baitings shows that the grand jury sympathised with the
magisterial attitude to popular gatherings. Phelips had
appeared as Laud's champion in the matter of churchales
because Poulett was on the other side. In this instance, unlike
most of the causes he adopted, he raised political awareness by
opposing rather than patronising the local consensus of
opinion.[19]

Geography, tradition and the county's enjoyment of a large
and able parliamentary delegation all contributed to the
exceptional political consciousness of the Kentish gentry in the
two decades before the civil war. The shire elections on
Penenden Heath near Maidstone in the 1620s were rowdy
affairs. Many of the freeholders and gentry were sensitive to
religious issues and involved in the tense court–county
relationships of the Duke of Buckingham's ascendancy. They
had a well-developed sense of an MP's accountability: thus the
fate of Sir Edwin Sandys in the 1626 election can be related to
his failure to fulfil specific undertakings on the subject of
taxation. In the 1630s, the gentry gave a personal lead to the
shire by their resistance to ship money and militia exactions.[20]
It is at this stage that Kent provides a third example of a single
individual who became the focus of county politics and exacerbated the tensions of gentry society.

Sir Edward Dering, the head of an ancient family, was vain
and impetuous, clever and mercurial. Alan Everitt has written
of the 'strain of restless ambition' in his character. Attachment
to Buckingham had brought him the lieutenancy of Dover
Castle: in the early 1630s Dering took his responsibilities

seriously, energetically executing royal fiscal demands including
the much disliked knighthood fines. But he was not simply an
obedient courtier. In fact Dering's career at this time is a useful
reminder that administrative loyalty to the Caroline regime did
not necessarily imply unquestioning acceptance of its religious
policies. Alan Everitt has shown how Dering's keen interest in
theology and his wide contacts made his manor at Surrenden
Dering 'the natural centre of the ecclesiastical opposition in the
county'. In the same period his cousin and close friend Sir
Roger Twysden was quietly assuming the political leadership of
the shire. For a good many years the potential for rivalry
between these two men was kept in check by their common
antiquarian interests. But in the excitement of the elections for
the Parliament of April 1640 Dering's searching ambition
broke loose. He felt his way towards a declaration of his
candidacy for a knightship by testing the friendships he had
cultivated over the previous years and by seeking to dissuade
Twysden from supporting Sir Henry Vane the younger, a close
neighbour of his in west Kent. At the assizes in March Dering
felt sufficiently confident to stand. From that moment he
fought Twysden, who now with Vane's backing stood against
him, indefatigably: he drew up his own poll book, canvassed
up and down the shire and eventually lost the contest.
Twysden, by contrast, did nothing to procure votes. After the
election he wrote a memorandum about it 'for posterity's sake,
because it was carried with great contestation between myself
and a near kinsman of mine'. What the exceptionally well-
documented Kentish campaign in early 1640 indicates is that a
personal rivalry which attracted strong factional support was
bound in so well-informed a community to draw national issues
into greater prominence than usual. The two smears that were
used effectively against Dering were that he had been for the
'knighting money' and that he was 'none of our church'. The
second one, according to a mild and conciliatory letter of
Twysden's, may have been based on a misinterpretation of
Dering's well-known refusal to go up to the altar rails to receive
communion.[21]

Balked in the spring, Dering was all the more determined to
sit as knight of the shire in the autumn. This time he was not
content to base his hopes on a massive canvas. He stood on an
avowedly political platform, committing himself to the cause

of reform in the church. His stance was designed to appeal to a wide spectrum of opinion for he was careful to leave his actual views somewhat ambiguous. It was probably well known that during the 1630s his interest in theology had gone hand in hand with fierce persecution of separatists in the district where he lived. Playing the reformer, Dering won support from both moderate high churchmen like George Strode of Squerryes and radical puritans of various persuasions like William Barrett, Richard Robson and Thomas Wilson. The ploy worked and Dering rode up to Westminster. In retrospect it is clear that despite his injection of the religious issue the election was in fact another personal contest between Dering and Twysden, who according to Kentish custom did not stand a second time himself but instead promoted his own candidate.[22] Dering had at last secured the centre of the Kentish stage: the sequel was two years of manoeuvring and factionalism which confirmed the county's long-standing reputation for political activism and involvement.[23]

## III

The election contests of this period are not in themselves evidence of political divisions among a county's gentry. The Short Parliament election in Somerset, David Underdown has suggested, was dominated by 'the old politics of local precedence'. Sir Robert Phelips had died in 1638: no-one carried on the torch of political campaigning on national issues. The social prestige of a knightship of the shire was such that leading families strove for it more or less competitively almost everywhere. The bitter contest in Dorset in 1626, for instance, was entirely familial and personal. There, as in several other counties, the leading families usually tried to settle the knightships in private or at worst, as happened in 1614, they drew lots to decide who should step down.[24]

A classic case of quiet negotiation, in Herefordshire in 1626, is documented in some correspondence of Sir Robert Harley and Sir Walter Pye. Harley wrote to Pye on 6 January: while signifying his own desire to stand he asked Pye to confirm his intentions. Pye assumed their partnership would not be questioned. 'I believe it will be so without any opposition', he told Harley 'and if it please the gentlemen of this county to think me worthy to serve I will not decline it'. The whole business was completed a few days later when the justices rode in to the Epiphany quarter sessions at Hereford. There was in fact some dispute when Sir John Scudamore proposed Harley and Pye to the assembled gentry, but this was merely over the question as to which man, the rising Knight of the Bath or the Knight Bachelor from an ancient county family, should be named first in the election return.[25]

In Cheshire, where there was only a single parliamentary borough, the knightships were contested in 1624, 1626 and 1628; there would have been a fight in 1625 as well had not some of the gentry insisted that the candidates should draw lots rather than go to a poll. Yet in Derbyshire, another county enjoying only a single borough, there were no contests during the 1620s. Malcolm Wanklyn's account of the social instability of Cheshire is helpful in explaining this contrast between the two counties. About twenty men jockeyed for place in the 1620s and 1630s 'with young ambitious men striking attitudes and trying to shake the tenuous hold of upstart peers and aged baronets, courtiers and time servers'. Much of the dissension was due to a row between the county's baronets and those who had recently purchased Irish peerages. This was still the overriding issue in the Short Parliament election. One observer, John Werden, attributed the bitterness in Cheshire in 1640 entirely to the ambition of the contestants, 'who all joined in their own profit where there was a bare pretense of a public good and now rend the bowels of it to advance their own interests and popularity'. Oddly this produced a complete reversal of the tendency we have observed elsewhere for personal rivalries to accentuate political polarisation. The barons put up as their candidates the bizarre combination of the conservative Sir Thomas Aston and the religious radical Sir William Brereton. They appear to have been attempting to defeat their rivals by a team that would appeal to all men. Aston and Brereton, as Peter Lake has pointed out, had been the two most prominent defenders of the county's rights over ship money and this probably had much to do with their success. But whereas Brereton's opposition to ship money had almost certainly been based on principle, Aston was using a political issue 'to establish himself at the forefront of county affairs'.[26] For the moment the potential for ideological and personal conflict between Aston and Brereton was not realised.

The Norfolk election for the Short Parliament provides another example of cut-throat competition against a background of political unanimity. John Potts, writing to his supporter Thomas Wodehouse, described the dramatised atmosphere: 'the die is cast and we come to the trial, where I expect the strongest opposition which cunning, scorn and anger can invent to disgrace myself or defeat others' freedom'. The problem was that three men were standing for two places: Potts's rivals were Sir Edmund Moundeford, who had sat for Thetford in 1628, and Sir John Holland. Some could not resist the temptation to make capital out of the known catholicism of Holland's wife: 'there are too many religions in Holland', his detractors wittily noted. But the quarrel was essentially about the best man for the crucial task at Westminster. 'You, Sir, are the man', declared Wodehouse to Potts, 'accounted one of those few we can now find to settle our hopes upon this employment.'[27] Norfolk is celebrated for the political precociousness, based on a struggle between the court and county factions, which its gentry had displayed in the reign of Elizabeth. Hassell Smith has suggested that the constitutional conflict which affected every aspect of the county's government at that time may have been 'as exceptional as it was premature'. If so it nevertheless had a legacy. Norfolk gentry were quite obviously more used than most in the early seventeenth century to regarding local politics and parliamentary business as two aspects of a continuing process. There was an exceptionally strong tradition of canvassing and of large turnouts at elections. Candidates expected to be chaired into the field and special prestige was attached to the first place in the poll. The impression is of a gentry community that was not ideologically split but that was well informed, relatively cohesive and anxious to participate fully in national affairs. It is in this context that Potts's rhetoric in 1640 must be understood.[28]

## IV

Three particular patterns of emerging national awareness in

the period 1600 to 1640 can be proposed. In the first gentry factionalism was a symptom of ideological conflict; in the second opposition to Stuart policies in both the political and religious spheres was based on the cohesion of puritan groups that might include some of the people as well as gentry; in the third political consciousness was more specifically stimulated by Caroline military and fiscal policies. No doubt there are counties that do not easily fit any of these patterns. Much more work is needed on the chronology of an emerging consciousness of political issues that transcended county and regional boundaries and on the nature and strength of that consciousness shire by shire. But this is no reason not to offer a provisional argument.

In the first place there were counties where men reared in the godly tradition which emphasised preaching, market day lectures and sabbatarianism easily found themselves at odds with others who saw their zeal as excessive or even positively objectionable. References in this chapter to puritanism must be understood as referring to this godly tradition and not to irreconcilable oppositionism, presbyterianism or sectarianism. Sussex is probably the best documented example of a distinctive ideological clash. I have shown elsewhere how a group of JPs in the eastern division, who were characterised by an opponent as 'the puritan faction', sought to use quarter sessions to challenge and overrule Archbishop Laud's ecclesiastical policies. The coalition that stood against them consisted of the Arminian cleric Edward Burton, the church papist Sir Henry Compton and several JPs of moderate religious views. By 1640 the puritan caucus had effectively captured control of the eastern Bench: its leaders, Sir Thomas Pelham and Anthony Stapley, were able to carry off the knightships, with a show of entertainment for the freeholders, in both the elections of that year. In this case a factional conflict due to religious differences contained the seeds of the civil war division between parliamentarians and royalists.[29]

There are no exact parallels to what happened in Sussex. In the other cases where religious controversy within the gentry community can be detected before and during 1640 – in Essex, Gloucestershire, Suffolk and Warwickshire – it is harder to assess how far that controversy had actually disrupted the normal tenor of social relationships before the Long Parliament met.

The Gloucestershire gentry were used to settling upon their representatives in an amicable manner. The choice at the assizes in March 1640, Sir Robert Cooke and Sir Robert Tracy, reflected the well-established convention that one of the knights should come from the Severn vale and the other from the Cotswolds. At this stage no poll was in prospect. But there was a plot, in which Cooke himself was probably an accomplice, to spring the candidature of Nathaniel Stephens at the last minute. Stephens was the most energetic opponent of the Caroline regime in the shire: he had recently been omitted from the commission of the peace because of his resistance to ship money. He was also, as a local correspondent told Laud's chaplain Peter Heylin, a man with 'an opinion of much zeal towards the zealous'. Stephens' campaign was backed by a group of silenced and deprived puritan clergy, several of whom were open advocates of the Scottish cause. It only failed because of the chicanery of Tracy's brother, who happened to be in office as sheriff. An observer's conclusion that, though Tracy would win, 'the general cry goes altogether for Stephens' indicates the strength of his party, particularly below the level of the county families.[30]

'There were perhaps few counties', Alan Everitt has written of Suffolk, 'where political and constitutional issues were more widely realised among the gentry.' Puritanism, surely founded in an Elizabethan tradition, guided many of the gentry's political consciences. The leading figure in the shire in the decades before the Civil War was Sir Nathaniel Barnardiston, a man of exceptional moral stature who in his own village of Kedington set before the community a pattern of parochial godliness. All in all Suffolk puritanism exhibited a tone of high seriousness.[31] It seems to have been too high for some of the gentry, who refused to accept in the spring of 1640 that Barnardiston's election to one of the knightships was a foregone conclusion. There were some abortive manoeuvres to hold the election at Beccles rather than Ipswich, where Sir William Playters, a conscientious deputy lieutenant who probably led the anti-Barnardiston faction, was influential. The autumn election was manifestly a political contest. It was a disordered affair lasting several days. Barnardiston and his running mate Sir Philip Parker sought re-election by rallying the puritan sailors and craftsmen of the Ipswich district. Their clerks at the poll were three Ipswich men who had been excommunicated by Bishop Wren. They were opposed by Henry North, the son of a prominent JP whose candidacy had the backing of clergymen with conservative or Arminian sympathies and moderate gentry like Sir Robert Crane. The final voting figures are indicative of the ferocity of the struggle: more than 2000 votes each for Barnardiston and Parker against 1422 for North.[32]

The cases of Essex and Warwickshire are distinct from those of Gloucestershire and Suffolk in the sense that resident nobility played an important role in the politics of these two counties on the eve of the Civil War. In each case an outstanding puritan peer was able to focus and control the loyalties of the godly from various ranks of society. The Earl of Warwick's championship of his county's interests went back many years.[33] His assertive leadership of the opposition to ship money in Essex, together with his wide territorial influence and dominating position in administration, held the promise of electoral supremacy once the Personal Rule collapsed. His triumph in 1640, when his candidates Sir Harbottle Grimston and Sir Thomas Barrington carried the knightships, may have looked predictable but the election was not in fact a walkover. Warwick won because he mounted a blatantly popular and political campaign in a county that was alert and ready to be aroused. He combined conventional canvassing of his gentry dependents, such as the trained band captains, with a campaign from the pulpit by puritan clerics. He also appealed to the townsmen in the boroughs of Chelmsford, Colchester, Harwich and Maldon.[34] Warwick's antagonist was Henry Neville, a sympathiser with Archbishop Laud and his ecclesiastical programme. In a bitter account of the outcome of the poll he contested the properness of 'mean conditioned and factious' men from the towns, who were 'no way concerned in the election', being allowed to exercise rights under the forty-shilling freehold qualification. It is probable that Neville stood with the public support of the two Essex nobles who most disliked Warwick: the aging Lord Maynard, a stalwart opponent of the Scots, and the Earl of Carlisle, whose parents had been close friends of the Earl of Strafford.[35] Maynard was overshadowed by Warwick in the lieutenancy and had much to lose in terms of local influence from his machinations. After the election Maynard wrote peevishly to Barrington: 'I shall not easily suffer myself hereafter upon the persuasions of others in any popular assemblies where fellows without shirts challenge as good a voice as myself'. He acknowledged the 'respectful conduct' at the hustings of 'men of quality' but he denounced the intervention of the vulgar, declaring that it was not fitting that the king's honour 'and the place wherein I serve him should suffer from disrespect to my person'.[36] Here is a classic exposition of the shock that popular and ideological local politics gave to conservative social sensibilities.

Warwickshire, Ann Hughes has suggested, lacked the social cohesion which was a feature of many gentry communities in this period. The 1640 elections, she argues, involved 'a struggle between two groups who were overtly and completely committed to different sides in the national struggle'. Early in the year William Combes and Sir Thomas Lucy, prominent allies of the radical puritan peer Lord Brooke, were dismissed from the Bench, probably because it was believed that they were prompting resistance to ship money. Brooke's defiant response to this court manoeuvre was to see that they were elected to the knightships. In the autumn Brooke's courtier rival the Earl of Northampton stirred himself to challenge his hegemony: he instructed his wife on 29 September to canvass 'all the gentlemen of the country in whom I have any interest' on behalf of his son Lord Compton. This was the first time that the knightships had been openly contested in Warwickshire since 1604. The struggle between the two factions was long drawn out and fierce. Brooke lost in the end because he was interested only in rallying those who shared his militant religious views and he failed to woo the major gentry families. He lacked the broad territorial influence that Warwick exercised in Essex. The autumn election roused the gentry – Compton was smeared as a recusant – and left Warwickshire on tenterhooks for the outcome of the new parliament.[37]

## V

Buckinghamshire and Northamptonshire were two counties where the godly tradition was quite as deeply rooted as in those shires that have just been discussed yet in neither case was there an ideological conflict in the 1640 elections. Buckinghamshire enjoyed a generous allocation of seats at Westminster and by and large the leading families were of one mind.[38] John Andrewes, the Arminian rector of Beaconsfield, related the virulent puritan spirit of many of the county's clergy and laity in a series of reports to his ecclesiastical superiors during the 1630s. He found men of his own outlook heavily outnumbered. Those who were well-meaning, in other words in sympathy with Laud's policies, he explained were 'overawed by the justices and lay gentry'. In a conversation with a JP whom he met on the road in 1635, the magistrate scathingly dismissed Sir Nathaniel Brent's orders at the recent metropolitical visitation: 'I dare assure you', Andrewes was told, 'neither clergymen or laymen (if they be gentlemen or men of any wealth) do keep them but laugh and jeer at them.'[39] Brent's attempt to abolish the mustering of the trained bands in churchyards, a practice he regarded as sacrilegious, came to nothing because the deputy lieutenants terrorised potential witnesses into silence. Among these deputies was John Hampden, already before the ship-money case of 1637 a man of considerable influence in the county's gentry circles. Predictably it was he and his close friend Arthur Goodwin who led the large and earnest delegation of Buckinghamshire gentlemen that sat in the 1640 Parliament.[40]

The godly tradition in Elizabethan and Jacobean Northamptonshire sprang from the commitment of certain influential families like the Knightleys of Fawsley and the activism of the Northampton townsmen.[41] By the 1630s the gentry seem to have withdrawn somewhat from the forefront of the movement: this may explain the tense relations at the election in March 1640 between the freeholders and those gentry who were identified, as sheriffs or deputy lieutenants, with enforcing government policy in the 1630s. A report by Sir Christopher Yelverton, who had been able to collect only £32 of the ship money for which he was held responsible, shows how little he was disposed to fall in with the clamorous freeholders.[42] The leadership of the oppositionist movement at this stage seems to have fallen to Northampton puritans and their allies among the minor gentry and yeomanry. Thus it was possible for a degree of social tension to emerge at the election, based not so much on real disagreement about who should go to Westminster as on divergent attitudes about how vociferously they should be expected to express the county's grievances. There was an ugly scene at the hustings: cries of 'we'll have no deputy lieutenants', we are told, greeted the gentry from 'all quarters and corners of the castle yard'. The men chosen, John Crewe and Sir Gilbert Pickering, in fact had impeccable oppositionist antecedents. The general petition about grievances that was handed to them may have been the work of the same men who had presented a petition against ship money at the Kettering quarter sessions in January. Its indictment of Charles I's ministers was comprehensive:

We have been unusually and insupportably charged, troubled and grieved in our consciences, persons and estates by innovation in religion, exactions in spiritual courts, molestations of our most godly and learned ministers, ship money, monopolies, undue impositions, army money, wagon money, horse money, conduct money and enlarging the forest beyond the ancient bounds.

It was no coincidence that the county which, with startling precociousness, had 'straightly enjoined' Sir Edward Montagu to raise the topic of suspended ministers in 1604 produced the boldest and fullest local agenda for the Parliament of April 1640.[43]

## VI

In the third distinct pattern of emerging national awareness political consciousness can be related directly to Caroline military and fiscal policies. Religious disaffection was not necessarily absent in these cases but it appears to have been secondary. Hassell Smith has made the point that even in the reign of Elizabeth the advanced political understanding and involvement of certain shires may be related to the weight and incidence of taxation.[44] This is all the more likely in the 1620s and 1630s, when militia rates, purveyance and ship money all bore most heavily on the southern and eastern counties.[45] The gentry communities of this region were not mollified by the fact that their counties were generally recognised as the wealthiest and most populous.

In Middlesex, where the experienced parliament man Sir Gilbert Gerrard overwhelmingly defeated the court candidates in the spring of 1640, there were considerable arrears on every single one of the ship-money writs issued between 1635 and 1639. The petition Gerrard agreed to present appears to have been brought into the polling field by men below the ranks of the leading gentry. The inclusion of a request for annual parliaments, which also appeared in the Northamptonshire petition, hints at the possibility of some kind of correspondence between the two shires. But there was no sign in Middlesex of the social tension which marred the Northamptonshire election.[46]

In counties like Berkshire, Hampshire and Wiltshire a decade of grumbling at inns and manor houses reached sudden fruition with the collapse of the Personal Rule in 1640. The political education of the 1630s was manifested in the elections and in open revolt that summer over administrative measures. 'The most striking feature of the resistance, and the one which above all assured its success, was the compliance of the county gentry', C. G. Durston has argued in his account of the failure of the Berkshire deputy lieutenants to collect coat and conduct money.[47] At the summer assizes in Berkshire the grand jury presented a petition of grievances that was forwarded to the king. The jurymen's motives were no doubt localist as well as national, but their agenda could equally well have come from Essex or Northamptonshire: the principal items included monopolies, the effect of impressment on the availability of labour for the harvest and the rigid execution of the forest laws.[48] Cumulative anger had produced an emerging sense of the necessity for co-operative action.

Opposition to ship money was fiercer in Wiltshire than in most southern counties. A petition to the king formulated in the late summer of 1640 and signed by many leading men employed deferential language that belied their determined mood: a new parliament was essential, it asserted, 'so your loyal people may be secured from their fears and unburdened of their pressures and your majesty assisted with faithful counsels'. The gentry expressed themselves more blatantly by their replacement of the Earl of Pembroke's candidate in the autumn election by the radical oppositionist Sir Henry Ludlow. Hampshire gentry showed their minds more quietly, simply re-electing in October the two local stalwarts who had sat in the spring. Well-supplied with parliamentary boroughs, they were able to send a strong delegation to Westminster.[49]

For much of the 1620s there had been little sense of collective involvement in national affairs among the gentry of the relatively remote counties of Devon and Cornwall. But the Cornish election contest in 1628 suggests that among some of the leading families at any rate there was by then a growing understanding of the potentialities of a parliament. The deputy lieutenants opposed the candidatures of Sir John Eliot and William Coryton for the knightships on the grounds that because they were in disfavour at court they would be unable to obtain the benefits that the county desired.[50] Defence of the coast against piracy mattered more than anything else in the maritime towns and villages of the west. Thus serious resistance to ship money came late, in Devon during 1638, in Cornwall during 1639, after news of Hampden's stand against it had at last percolated the region. It was the Scots War that finally roused Devon and Cornwall. The king's ministers, as a friend put it in a letter to Sir Richard Buller, had suddenly behaved 'like one that casts himself into the river and must needs trouble his friends to rescue him from drowning'. The failure of the Duchy of Cornwall nominees in the 1640 elections was spectacular. At the Devon assizes in August that year thirty-eight leading gentry signed a petition summarising the county's grievances.[51]

Continuity of gentry leadership could be an important aspect of the process of political alienation. Lincolnshire illustrates this particularly clearly. The shire's vocal Long Parliament delegation included four men who had set an example to their neighbours in 1627 by their default as commissioners for the forced loan and who had sat in 1628. Two of these men, Sir Anthony Irby and Sir John Wray, had also led the county's resistance to ship money. Another member in 1640, Thomas Grantham, was the son of an MP in the 1628 Parliament who had been a supporter of Sir John Eliot and had been imprisoned for his resistance to the loan. The case of Lincolnshire also shows how an outstanding local issue would drive home the general lesson of the Stuart monarchy's challenge to property rights. The fen drainage programme united and galvanised the gentry and populace. Clive Holmes has shown how at various times during the 1630s the crown used both legal chicanery and repressive force to achieve its ends. 'We stand not assured of our *terra firma*', declared Sir John Wray in the Short Parliament, 'for the fen drainers have entered our lands and not only have made waste of them but also have desiesed us of part of our soil and freehold.' The potent mixture of bitternesses which moved the Lincolnshire electorate is well summarised by a rhyme in circulation in 1640:

> Choose no ship sheriff, nor court atheist
> No fen drainer, nor church papist.[52]

In the north the Scots War was crucial to the political awakening of a region where politics still tended to be localist and personal. In Durham the eirenic policies of Bishop Morton collapsed and tension between puritans and Arminians mounted.[53] At Newcastle-upon-Tyne the trading companies formulated a statement of their grievances, which their MP Sir Henry Anderson used as the basis for a speech in parliament.[54] In Lancashire strong antagonism to the enforcement of the king's military programme emerged in the summer of 1640. Ralph Assheton and Roger Kirkby were very likely elected in October because of their reputation as men committed to reform. Although there is no definite evidence of a contest it seems unlikely that the Earl of Derby's candidates, unopposed in the spring, stood down entirely voluntarily.[55]

## VII

In broad terms it does seem to be the case that distance from the capital militated against political articulateness. News reached the remote counties more slowly and often by the time it had done so the kaleidoscope of Westminster and Whitehall affairs had changed. Southern and eastern gentry were given an enormous advantage by the uneven distribution of parliamentary boroughs. Thus in Staffordshire, Donald Pennington has suggested, 'national politics even in 1640 did not matter much'.[56] In Pembroke, Cardigan and Carmarthen, Howell Lloyd has argued, the gentry showed 'a minimal grasp of significant political principles and a dogged introspectiveness'.[57]

The first 1640 elections generally bear out a regional pattern of political awareness such as has been proposed in this chapter. In so far as there was electioneering at all in counties like Cumberland, Derbyshire, Nottinghamshire, Shropshire, Staffordshire and Westmorland, it signified personal competition, of the kind that we have encountered in Cheshire and Norfolk, rather than ideological division.[58] But the speed of the political awakening in several of the counties more remote from London between the spring and autumn of 1640 should be noted. One example, Lancashire, has been mentioned but there are also others. Sir Thomas Littleton sat as knight of the shire for Worcestershire in April but was not re-elected in October. He was seen as having failed his countrymen and he was derided at the autumn poll as a man 'fitter to break parliaments than to serve in a parliament'.[59] In Cheshire the barons abandoned their support for Sir William Brereton on the second occasion, almost certainly because they were shocked by his openly radical stance over the spring and summer. Brereton ran on his own and returned to Westminster as knight of the shire through the vociferous aid of a group of puritan clergy.[60]

In the end civil war forced men everywhere to lift their eyes from their own fields and market towns. But it is important that we take full account of the complexity of the process of political education in the preceding years. It is evident that sustained factional struggles of the kind that occurred in Somerset and Yorkshire were the exception rather than the rule in the 1620s and 1630s. By and large the issues of 1640 were not 'fused in the crucible of petty local rivalries': they were absorbed, pondered and articulated in the context of a whole range of particular local conditions.[61] In county after county concern for local interests gradually shaded into concern for the good of the nation as a whole or the 'commonwealth' as some of the gentry like to term it. Stuart policies did often impose a moral dilemma upon men: their obligation and loyalty to their own community – village, town or county – was put at variance with their obligation and loyalty to the monarchy and state. Any subsidy commissioner or deputy lieutenant knew this dilemma. Many men, to one extent or another, acted according to their localist inclinations and defied the crown, but even as they did so discussion with friends and colleagues and the political participation that necessarily accompanied such defiance could not but widen their mental horizons and broaden their general political consciousness. It is not the case that there was a dichotomy between local and national consciousness in this period: we need not suppose that the one was checked as the other burgeoned. That for a whole host of reasons national political awareness did burgeon between 1600 and 1640 seems indisputable. This does not of course explain why a civil war broke out in 1642. But it is highly relevant to the overall context of that most surprising and unintended catastrophe.

# List of Abbreviations

| | |
|---|---|
| Add. MS | Additional Manuscript |
| *AHR* | *American Historical Review* |
| AMAE | Archives du Ministère des Affaires Étrangères |
| AO | Archives Office |
| *APC* | *Acts of the Privy Council of England* |
| ARA | Algemeen Rijksarchief |
| BGSA | Bayerisches Geheimes Staatsarchiv |
| *BIHR* | *Bulletin of the Institute of Historical Research* |
| BL | British Library |
| BN | Bibliothèque Nationale |
| Bodl. Lib. | Bodleian Library |
| BUP | Bibliothèque Universitaire et Publique |
| *CJ* | *Commons Journals* |
| *CSPD* | *Calendar of State Papers, Domestic* |
| *CSP Ven* | *Calendar of State Papers, Venetian* |
| CUL | Cambridge University Library |
| D'Ewes, *Journals* | Sir Symonds D'Ewes, *Journals of All the Parliaments* (1682) |
| *DNB* | *Dictionary of National Biography* |
| *EHR* | *English Historical Review* |
| *EcHR* | *Economic History Review* |
| *Faction* | *Faction and Parliament: Essays on Early Stuart History* (ed.), Kevin Sharpe (Oxford, 1978) |
| Gardiner | S. R. Gardiner, *History of England from the Accession of James I*, 10 vols (1883–4) |
| Hartley I | T. E. Hartley (ed.) *Proceedings in the Parliaments of Elizabeth I; vol. I, 1558–81* (Leicester, 1981) |
| HA | Historical Association |
| *HJ* | *Historical Journal* |
| *HMC* | *Historical Manuscripts Commission Report* |
| *JBS* | *Journal of British Studies* |
| *JEH* | *Journal of Ecclesiastical History* |
| *JMH* | *Journal of Modern History* |
| *LJ* | *Lords' Journals* |
| NRS | W. Notestein, F. H. Relf and Hartley Simpson (eds), *Commons Debates in 1621*, 7 vols (New Haven, 1935) |
| *Origins* | *The Origins of the English Civil War* (ed.) Conrad Russell (1973) |
| PC | Privy Council |

P&P                Past and Present
PRO                Public Record Office
Proc. Hug. Soc.    Proceedings of the Huguenot Society
RO                 Record Office (County)
Rot. Parl.         Rotuli Parliamentorum
SO                 Signet Office
SP                 State Papers
TRHS               Transactions of the Royal Historical Society

# Bibliography

Note: The place of publication is London unless otherwise stated.

## 1. THE CAUSES OF WAR: A HISTORIOGRAPHICAL SURVEY

The best historiographical introduction to the period is R. C. Richardson, *The Debate on the English Revolution* (1977). This should be supplemented by J. S. Morrill's survey in *History Today* (September 1982) 51–2, and brought up to date by a reading of the current debate on the validity of the Whig interpretation in specialist journals: notably *JMH*, 49 (1977), and 50 (1978); and *P&P* 92 (1981). Lawrence Stone, *Social Change and Revolution in England, 1540–1640* (1965) puts the storm over the gentry in context and includes a selection of extracts and documents. The first part of the introduction in *Origins* is also a useful historiographical guide to the period.

## 2. THE JACOBEAN RELIGIOUS SETTLEMENT: THE HAMPTON COURT CONFERENCE

The fact that there is no adequate history of the Jacobean Church does not suggest a lack of industry or interest, since studies of facets of its religious life, and especially of puritanism, abound. The reason may lie in the absence of an agreed definition of the subject. The period lies uneasily between the well-defined themes of Elizabethan religious history and the mid-century crisis. Patrick Collinson's 1979 Ford Lectures, *The Religion of Protestants: The Church in English Society 1559–1625* (Oxford, 1982) contain studies which may contribute to a history. See also his article 'Lectures by Combination: Structures and Characteristics of Church Life in Seventeenth-Century England', *BIHR*, XLVIII (1975), 182–213. Roland Green Usher's massive work *The Reconstruction of the English Church*, 2 vols (London and New York, 1910) is written from a very different standpoint. It devotes 700 pp. to the decade 1600–10 and equates the Jacobean religious settlement with the administrative achievements of Archbishop Bancroft, to which disproportionate importance is attached. Usher prints important documents relating to Hampton Court and gives a thorough if one-sided account of the conference which should be compared with Gardiner and with more recent interpretations: Mark H. Curtis, 'Hampton Court Conference and its Aftermath', *History*, XLVI (1961), 1–16; and Frederick Shriver, 'Hampton Court Re-visited: James I and the Puritans', *JEH*, XXXIII (1982), 48–71. S.B. Babbage, *Puritanism and Richard Bancroft* (1962) provides the fullest account of the episcopal repression which followed Hampton Court. But the analysis is more acute in B.W. Quintrell's article 'The Royal Hunt and the Puritans, 1604–1605', *JEH*, XXXI (1980), 41–58.

Successive stages in the interpretation of Elizabethan puritanism are marked by M. M. Knappen, *Tudor Puritanism* (Chicago, 1939; paperback edn 1965), Patrick Collinson, *The Elizabethan Puritan Movement*, (1967 and 1982) and Peter Lake, *Moderate Puritans and the Elizabethan Church* (Cambridge, 1982). Two of Christopher Hill's finest books, written in tandem, provide a subtle and richly documented analysis of puritanism as the ideology of dynamic social groups and the solvent of traditional structures: *Economic Problems of the Church from Whitgift to the Long Parliament* (Oxford, 1956) and *Society and Puritanism in Pre-Revolutionary England*, (1964; paperback edn, 1966). William Haller's classic *The Rise of Puritanism* (New York, 1938; paperback edn 1957) views the same religious culture through different spectacles. Many other books on seventeenth-century puritanism have appeared, but most suffer from a too rigid and schematic distinction between puritanism and Anglicanism. See, for example, J. Sears McGee, *The Godly Man in Stuart England: Anglicans, Puritans, and the Two Tables, 1620–1670* (New Haven and London, 1976).

The reader of this chapter has not been told very much about the doctrinal content of English Calvinism. He should consult R. T. Kendall, *Calvin and English Calvinism to 1649* (Oxford 1979). All earlier accounts of Arminianism will be superseded by the forthcoming book by Nicholas Tyacke, based on his thesis 'Arminianism in England in Religion and Politics from 1604 to 1640' (Oxford University, D.Phil., 1969). In the meantime an essay by Dr Tyacke is essential reading: 'Puritanism, Arminianism and Counter-Revolution', in *Origins*.

There is much of relevance in an earlier 'Problems in Focus' collection: F. Heal and R. O'Day (eds) *Church and Society in England Henry VIII to James I* (1977). The judgements on the reign of James I expressed in two surveys of ecclesiastical history are mostly very sound: Claire Cross, *Church and People 1450–1660* (Glasgow, 1976); H. G. Alexander, *Religion in England 1558–1662* (1968). A useful guide to the polemics of the period is Peter Milward, *Religious Controversies of the Jacobean Age: A Survey of Printed Sources* (1978).

### 3.  THE PERSONAL RULE OF CHARLES I

Gardiner provides the indispensable narrative. His subtlety and moderation are remarkable. But he is not always read with the same care and open-mindedness with which he wrote. Nor was he concerned with many questions which historians now consider to be important. The author is engaged upon a full-length study of the Personal Rule.

On the history of Charles I's relations with parliament and the events of 1628–9, see *Faction* and the brilliant re-evaluation by Conrad Russell, *Parliament and English Politics* (1979).

There is no really satisfactory biography of Charles I, nor is one imminently expected. The latest, Pauline Gregg's *Charles I*, is a brave, at times shrewd, attempt, but draws on little new material. The king's own role in government and his responsibility for courses and policies pursued await further study. There are some sound, if not exciting, biographies of Caroline courtiers: M. Havran, *Caroline Courtier: The Life of Lord Cottington* (1973); M. Van Cleave Alexander, *Charles I's Lord Treasurer: Sir Richard Weston, Earl of Portland* (1975); G. Huxley, *Endymion Porter* (1959). But as a centre of political life, the court too has been neglected. Perez Zagorin's *The Court and the Country* (1969) provides some useful information, but the thesis is crude and oversimplified. Peter Thomas has written much more sensitively on the culture and style of the court: P. Thomas, 'Charles I of England: the tragedy of absolutism' in A. G. Dickens (ed.) *The Courts of Europe* (1977) pp. 191–212; 'Two Cultures? Court and Country under Charles I' in *Origins*, pp. 168–93. These essays argue for the emergence of two distinct cultures, which is open to question. Brilliant insight into the cultural and political milieu of the court are found in two short books: Stephen Orgel, *The Illusion of Power* (Berkeley, 1975) and Roy Strong, *Charles I on Horseback* (1970).

The central administration is authoritatively analysed in Gerald Aylmer, *The King's Servants*, a book which repays frequent reference and rereading. See too my essay on 'Honour and Retrenchment: The Court and Household of Charles I' in D. Starkey (ed.) *The English Court from the Wars of the Roses to the Civil War* (forthcoming). The Privy Council as an institution of business is studied in E. R. Turner, *The Privy Council of England in the Seventeenth and Eighteenth Centuries 1603–1784*, 2 vols (Baltimore, 1927–8). Work remains to be done on the composition and politics of the Council.

Understanding of the religious history of the decade requires careful consideration of the king's own position and his relationship with Archbishop Laud. Hugh Trevor-Roper, *Archbishop Laud, 1573–1645* is splendidly incisive and entertaining, but does not deal fully with theological issues. Nicholas Tyacke's essay, 'Puritans, Arminians and Counter-revolution', in *Origins*, pp. 119–43 offers a valuable perspective and a suggestive interpretation which has met with general acceptance. The present writer remains unconvinced.

The history of the localities is where most and some of the best work has been done. Among the very best are T. G. Barnes, *Somerset 1625–40* (Cambridge Mass., 1961); Anthony Fletcher, *A County Community in Peace and War: Sussex 1600–1660* (1975); C. Holmes, *Seventeenth Century Lincolnshire* (Lincoln, 1980); J. S. Morrill, *Cheshire 1630–60* (Oxford, 1974).

The local response to ship money and the problems caused by the Scots war are briefly but brilliantly treated in J. S. Morrill, *The Revolt of The Provinces* (1976). The events and immediate causes of the Scottish rebellion may be pursued in D. Stevenson, *The Scottish Revolution, 1637–1644* (Newton Abbot, 1973).

4.   SPAIN OR THE NETHERLANDS? THE DILEMMAS OF
EARLY STUART FOREIGN POLICY

Foreign policy having been the Cinderella subject of early seventeenth-century research, no modern detailed study exists. For a general account the reader is still dependent on the relevant sections of S. R. Gardiner's *History of England*, which has the merit of being based on French, Spanish and Dutch as well as British archives. The early chapters of the surveys of G. M. D. Howat, *Stuart and Cromwellian Foreign Policy* (1974) and J. R. Jones, *Britain and Europe in the Seventeenth Century* (1966) are also useful, particularly regarding Anglo-Dutch relations, although both works are more concerned with foreign policy after 1649. For international relations during the first half of the seventeenth century, Geoffrey Parker, *Europe in Crisis, 1598-1648* (1979) and his forthcoming *The Thirty Years War* are recommended.

In the notes to the text, reference is made to the more important items in the relatively scanty recent monographic and periodical literature, together with the most useful biographical studies. Much of the best recent research on specific areas of foreign relations remains in dissertation form or has been published on the continent. For relations between England and the protestant world in general, see S. L. Adams, 'The Protestant Cause: Religious Alliance with the West European Calvinist Communities as a Political Issue in England, 1585-1630' (Oxford University, D. Phil., 1973), for Anglo-Dutch relations see J. C. Grayson, 'From Protectorate to Partnership: Anglo-Dutch Relations, 1598-1625' (University of London, Ph.D., 1978), and for Anglo-Palatine relations, E. Weiss, *Die Unterstützung Friedrichs V von der Pfalz durch Jacob I und Karl I von England im Dreissigjährigen Krieg* (Stuttgart, 1966). Spanish policy is illuminated in E. Straub, *Pax et Imperium: Spaniens Kampf um seine Friedensordnung in Europa zwischen 1617 und 1635* (Paderborn, 1980), J. Alcalá-Zamora y Quiepo de Llano, *España, Flandes y el Mar del Norte, 1618-39* (Barcelona, 1975), and P. Brightwell, 'Spain and the Origins of the Thirty Years War' (Cambridge University, Ph. D., 1967). An excellent account of James I's attempts to mediate in the early stages of the Thirty Years War is provided by A. W. White, 'Suspension of Arms: Anglo-Spanish Mediation in the Thirty Years War, 1621-1625' (Tulane University, Ph.D., 1978). Anglo-French relations remain relatively understudied but G. Lutz, *Kardinal Giovanni Francesco Guidi di Bagno: Politik und Religion im Zeitalter Richelieus und Urbans VIII* (Tubingen, 1971) is very useful for French policy in the middle 1620s, and the Duke of Buckingham's French policy will be discussed in the forthcoming University of Washington at St Louis dissertation of T. Cogswell.

5.  FINANCIAL AND ADMINISTRATIVE DEVELOPMENTS

There is no modern general work on crown finance and administration. Apart from Gardiner, the following are useful: W. R. Scott, *The Constitution and Finance of English, Scottish and Irish Joint-Stock Companies to 1720*, 3 vols (Cambridge, 1910-12); F. C. Dietz, *English Public Finance, 1558-1641* (New York and London, 1932); Conrad Russell, 'Parliament and the King's Finances' in *Origins*, pp. 91-116; Robert Ashton, 'Deficit Finance in the Reign of James I', *EcHR*, 2nd ser., 10 (1957-8), 15-29; G. L. Harriss, 'Medieval Doctrines in the Debates on Supply,

1610-29' in *Faction*, pp. 73-103.

On the problems of rewarding crown servants, see Joel Hurstfield, *The Queen's Wards* (1958); G. E. Aylmer, *The King's Servants: The Civil Service of Charles I* (1961).

On cost cutting: Menna Prestwich, *Cranfield: Politics and Profits under the Early Stuarts* (Oxford, 1966); P. R. Seddon, 'Household Reforms in the Reign of James I', *BIHR*, 53 (1980), 44-54; and G. E. Aylmer, 'Attempts at Administrative Reform, 1625-40', *EHR*, 72 (1957), 229-59.

For particular revenues, see H. E. Bell, *An Introduction to the History and Records of the Court of Wards and Liveries* (Cambridge, 1953); H. H. Leonard, 'Distraint of Knighthood: The Last Phase, 1625-41', *History*, n.s. 63 (1978), 23-37; M. D. Gordon, 'The Collection of Ship Money in the Reign of Charles I', *TRHS*, 3rd. ser., 4 (1910), 141-62; Gordon Batho, 'Landlords in England: The Crown', in Joan Thirsk (ed.), *The Agrarian History of England and Wales, IV, 1500-1640* (Cambridge, 1967), pp. 268-73. And for the crown's borrowing and credit-worthiness: Robert Ashton, *The Crown and the Money Market, 1603-1640* (Oxford, 1960).

### 6.   THE NATURE OF A PARLIAMENT IN EARLY STUART ENGLAND

### 1.  Mediaeval Background

E.B. Fryde and Edward Miller (eds), *Historical Studies of the English Parliament*, 2 vols (Cambridge, 1970); J. S. Roskell, *The Commons and their Speakers 1376-1523* (Manchester, 1965); May McKisack, *The Fourteenth Century* (Oxford, 1959); K. B. McFarlane, *The Nobility of Later Mediaeval England* (Oxford, 1973) and *Lancastrian Kings and Lollard Knights* (Oxford, 1973); G. L. Harriss, 'Mediaeval Doctrines' and *King, Parliament and Public Finance in England to 1369* (Oxford, 1975).

### 2.  How Things Worked

J. E. Neale, *The Elizabethan House of Commons* (1949), to be read in conjunction with G. R. Elton, 'Tudor Government: Points of Contact: Parliament', *TRHS* (1974) and 'Parliament in the Sixteenth Century', *HJ* (1979), and with Sheila Lambert, 'Procedure in the House of Commons in the Early Stuart Period', *EHR* (1980), and Elizabeth Read Foster, *The House of Lords 1603-1649* (Chapel Hill, 1983). On elections, see Derek Hirst, *The Representative of the People?* (Cambridge, 1975).

### 3.  Accounts of Particular Parliaments

T.L. Moir, *The Addled Parliament of 1614* (Oxford, 1958); Robert E. Zaller, *The Parliament of 1621* (Berkeley, 1971); Robert E. Ruigh, *The Parliament of 1624* (Cambridge Mass and Oxford, 1971); Conrad Russell, *Parliaments and English Politics 1621-1629* (Oxford, 1979); Anthony Fletcher, *The Outbreak of the English Civil War* (London and New York, 1981).

### 4.  Current Controversy

(a) The Traditional Interpretation: W. Notestein, *The Winning of the Initiative by the House of Commons* (1924); D. H. Willson, *The Privy Councillors in the House of Commons 1604-1629* (Minneapolis, 1946).

(b) Revisionist works. *NB* The authors of these works have never claimed to agree further than in rejecting the traditional interpretation: G. R. Elton, 'A High Road To Civil War?', in Charles H. Carter (ed.), *From the Renaissance to the Counter-Reformation: Essays in Honour of Garrett Mattingley* (New York, 1965); Conrad Russell, 'Parliamentary History in Perspective 1604-1629', *History*, 61 (1976); Mark Kishlansky, 'The Emergence of Adversary Politics in the Long Parliament', *JMH*, 49 (1977) (readers should not rely on summaries and citations of this article: most of them are inaccurate, and some seriously misleading); Paul Christianson, 'The Peers, The People and Parliamentary Management in the First Six Months of the Long Parliament', *JMH*, 49 (1977); *Faction* (ed.) Sharpe; Conrad Russell, 'The Parliamentary Career of John Pym 1621-1629', in Peter Clark, A. G. R. Smith and N. R. N. Tyacke (eds), *The English Commonwealth 1547-1640: Essays Presented to Joel Hurstfield* (Leicester, 1979); Conrad Russell, 'Monarchies, Wars and Estates in England, France and Spain c.1580-c.1640', *Legislative Studies Quarterly*, 7 (1982).

(c) Criticisms of revision: J. H. Hexter, 'Power Struggle, Parliament and Liberty in Early Modern England', *JMH*, 50 (1978); Derek Hirst, 'Unanimity in the Commons, Aristocratic Intrigues and the Origins of the English Civil War', *JMH*, 50 (1978); 'Revisionism Revised: Two Perspectives in Early Stuart Parliamentary History', in *P&P*, 92 (1981): includes Theodore K. Rabb, 'The Role of the Commons', Derek Hirst 'The Place of Principle' and Christopher Hill, 'Parliament and People in Seventeenth-Century England'. The debate continues.

## 5. Sources

Elizabeth Read Foster, *Proceedings in Parliament 1610*, 2 vols (New Haven, 1966); W. Notestein, F. H. Relf and Hartley Simpson, *Commons' Debates in 1621*, 7 vols (New Haven, 1935); *Notes of Debates in the House of Lords 1624 and 1626* (ed. S. R. Gardiner) (Camden Series, 1879); *Debates in the House of Commons in 1625* (ed. S. R. Gardiner) (Camden Series, 1879); *Parliamentary Debates in 1628* (ed. Robert C. Johnson, Maija J. Cole, Mary Frear Keeler and William B. Bidwell) (New Haven, 1977).

## 6. Context

Parliamentary history should be studied in context, and in proportion, with non-Parliamentary political history, for which see the bibliographies to other chapters.

## 7.  NATIONAL AND LOCAL AWARENESS IN THE COUNTY COMMUNITIES

The seminal work on the county communities was A. Everitt *The Community of Kent and the Great Rebellion 1640-1660* (Leicester, 1966). Other studies followed, some of them extending or giving greater depth to the concept by paying more attention to the people as well as the gentry: P. Clark, *English Provincial Society from the Reformation to the Revolution* (Hassocks, 1977); A. J. Fletcher, *A County Community in Peace and War: Sussex, 1600-1660* (1975); J. S. Morrill, *Cheshire, 1630-1660* (Oxford, 1976); D. Underdown, *Somerset in the Civil War and Interregnum* (Newton Abbot, 1973); D. Hirst *The Representative of the People?* (Cambridge, 1975) cast much light on voting and elections. C. S. R. Russell, *Parliaments and English*

*Politics 1621–1629* (Oxford, 1979) provided a fresh view of parliamentary debate in the light of county studies.

The first sign of a backlash was a review by C. Holmes in *American Historical Review* (1978) of my book on Sussex. He developed his views in his own county study *Seventeenth Century Lincolnshire* (Lincoln, 1980) and in a general survey 'The County Community in Stuart Historiography', *JBS*, 19 (1980). D. Underdown also discussed the Everitt model and subsequent adaptations of it in an essay 'Community and Class: Theories of Local Politics in the English Revolution' in B. C. Malament (ed.), *After the Reformation* (Manchester, 1980). A thesis by A. Hughes on Warwickshire, shortly to be published, will add to the debate.

Much work on the county communities has been integrated into the general analysis of the period by authors of surveys: see, for instance, R. Ashton, *The English Civil War* (1978) and B. Coward, *The Stuart Age* (1980). But in such surveys the particular theme of this chapter has mostly been handled obliquely. J. S. Morrill, *The Revolt of the Provinces* (1976) argues that the provincial response to the political crisis, 1640–42, 'was largely conditioned by local events and local power structures'. A. J. Fletcher, *The Outbreak of the English Civil War* (1981) puts rather more emphasis on the impact of national issues at the local level. J. S. Morrill's critical bibliography *Seventeenth Century Britain* (1980) contains a list of further county and urban studies. R. Cust and P. G. Lake have shown in their outstanding article, 'Sir Richard Grosvenor and the Rhetoric of Magistracy', *BIHR*, 54 (1981), that study of individuals who were mediators between the centre and the localities is a fruitful approach to the problem of the growth of political consciousness.

# Notes and References

An abbreviated reference is given where the title has appeared in the bibliography (or has been previously cited in Notes)

## INTRODUCTION  *Howard Tomlinson*

1. See Abbreviations for full titles.
2. R. H. Parry (ed.), *The English Civil War and After, 1642–58* (1979).
3. The word may need some clarification. I apply it here and elsewhere to those historians who stress the accidental nature of the Civil War, as opposed to the 'neo-Whigs', who, to a greater or lesser degree, accept the progressive Whig interpretation.
4. Fletcher, *Outbreak, passim.*
5. Mr Peter White, of Wellington College, also suggests, in an as yet unpublished article, that *post*-1629 the theological consensus was again re-established.

## 1.  THE CAUSES OF WAR: A HISTORIOGRAPHICAL SURVEY
### *Howard Tomlinson*

For the references contained in a number of these notes, I am indebted to Richardson, *The Debate.*

1. Clarendon, *Selections*, pp. 122, 132, 221.
2. Clarendon, p. 3.
3. Clarendon, pp. 69–71, 73–8, 122–3, 135, 142–3, 157–8, 172–3, 222–3, 253.
4. Clarendon, pp. 1–2.
5. Harrington, *Political Works*, pp. 197–8.
6. David Hume, *The History of Great Britain*, vol. I, (ed.) Duncan Forbes (Penguin, 1970).
7. J. W. Burrow, *A Liberal Descent: Victorian Historians and the English Past* (Cambridge, 1981), p. 26.
8. *The Miscellaneous Writings and Speeches of Lord Macaulay*, popular edn. (1882), p. 154.
9. Burrow, *Liberal Descent*, pp. 43–5.
10. *The Works of Lord Macaulay* (8 vols, 1866) vol. I, Ch.1, *passim.*
11. Leopold von Ranke, *A History of England principally in the Seventeenth Century* English translation, 6 vols (Oxford, 1875). See particularly his remarks in the preface to vol. I.
12. Quoted in Burrow, *Liberal Descent*, p. 98.

13. Quoted in R. G. Usher, *A Critical Study of the Historical Method of Samuel Rawson Gardiner* (Washington University Studies III, part 2, no. 1, 1915), pp. 5–8.

14. J. C. Morison, *Macaulay* (1882).

15. S. R. Gardiner, *History of England 1624–28* (1875), vol. I, preface; *History of England 1603–42*, new edn (1893–6), vol. I, p. vi.

16. Usher, *Critical Study*, p. 20.

17. S. R. Gardiner, *History of England, 1693–97* (1895 edn), preface.

18. On Gardiner, I am particularly grateful to Conrad Russell and Kevin Sharpe for their helpful suggestions.

19. G. M. Trevelyan, *England Under the Stuarts* paperback edn. (1977), especially introduction, end of Ch.2 and pp. 187–9.

20. For an excellent introduction to the debate, see Stone, *Social Change*.

21. H. R. Trevor-Roper, 'The Gentry, 1549–1649', *EcHR*, Supplement I (1953), 44.

22. See below.

23. Christopher Hill, 'A Bourgeois Revolution?', in J. G. A. Pocock (ed.), *Three British Revolutions: 1641, 1688, 1776*, (Princeton, 1939), pp. 111, 112. In another recent article Hill has re-emphasised the role of the people in creating political and social tension: 'Parliament and People in Seventeenth Century England', *P&P*, 92 (August 1981), 118–24.

24. Brian Manning, *The English People and the English Revolution* (1976). Manning's book, with its acceptance of the idea that 'the middling sort of people', impelled by class hatred, made the revolution, in part documented Hill's bourgeois hypothesis. It met with a frosty reception from two young scholars in particular. See John Miller's review in the *Times Higher Educational Supplement*, 28 May 1976, p. 16 and John Morrill's review article in *HJ* 20 (1977), 229–36.

25. A. M. Everitt, *The Local Community and the Great Rebellion*, HA pamphlet (1969), pp. 3–4.

26. A. G. Wood, *Nottinghamshire in the Civil War* (Oxford, 1937), p. ix.

27. Alan Simpson, *The Wealth of the Gentry, 1540–1660: East Anglian Studies* (Cambridge, 1961); Mary Finch, *The Wealth of Five Northamptonshire Families, 1540–1640*, Northants Record Society, 19 (1956); J. T. Cliffe, *The Yorkshire Gentry from the Reformation to the Civil War* (1969); H. A. Lloyd, *The Gentry of South-West Wales, 1540–1640* (Cardiff, 1968).

28. See especially Alan Everitt, *Suffolk and the Great Rebellion, 1640–60*, Suffolk Records Society, 3 (1969); *The Community of Kent and the Great Rebellion, 1640–60* (Leicester, 1966); *Change in the Provinces; the Seventeenth Century* (Leicester, 1972); *The Local Community*.

29. See below.

30. See particularly Hirst, *Representative of the People?* although Hirst's work on the electorate owes more to J. H. Plumb's influence than to Everitt's.

31. Ronald Hutton, 'An Armistice in Civil War Studies', *HJ*, 23 (1980), 729.

32. This phrase has been used by Kevin Sharpe to open a lecture on 'Crown, Parliament and Locality, 1603–42', delivered at Wellington College in May 1979.

33. Derek Hirst, for example, has been classed as 'a revisionist', 'an unreconstructed Whig', and a 'post-revisionist'. See his article 'Unanimity in the Commons', *JMH*, 50, no. 1 (March 1978), 69; and Hill, 'Parliament and People,' (n.23 above), p. 118.

34. For a trenchant review see G. R. Elton, 'The Unexplained Revolution', in *Studies in Tudor and Stuart Politics and Government*, 2 vols (Cambridge, 1974), vol. II, pp. 183–9.

35. Lawrence Stone, *The Crisis of the Aristocracy* (Oxford, 1965), pp. 12–13.

36. See his review in *HJ*, 16 (1973), 205–8. Elton also questioned Stone's treatment of the Tudor period. Other historians have criticised Stone's presuppositions and his methodology. See, for example, Paul Christianson, *JBS* 15 (1976), 40–52; J. H. Hexter, *JMH*, 50 (1978), 12–14.

37. The title of an article originally published in *From the Renaissance to the Counter-Reformation*, pp. 325–47, and reprinted in *Studies in Tudor and Stuart Politics and Government*, vol. II, pp. 164–82.

38. In J. S. Roskell, 'Perspectives in English Parliamentary History', *Historical Studies*, vol. II, pp. 296-323; and G. L. Harriss, 'Medieval Doctrines in the Debates on Supply', *Faction*, pp. 73–104.

39. See especially J. H. Elliott, *The Revolt of the Catalans: A Study in the Decline of Spain, 1598–1640* (Cambridge 1963) and H. G. Koenigsberger, *Dominium Regale or Dominium Politicum et Regale: Monarchies and Parliaments in Early Modern Europe* (Inaugural Lecture, King's College, London, 1975). Conrad Russell's debt to Elliott, in particular, is evident from Russell, 'Monarchies, Wars and Estates in England, France and Spain, c.1580–c.1640', *Legislative Studies Quarterly*, VII, 2 (May 1982), pp. 205–20. I am grateful to the author for sending me a copy of this article.

40. Professor Russell has explained in a letter to me that his family background has been more of a help than a hindrance: 'it has enabled me to spot, very clearly, that I was dealing with a [Whig] tradition that went no further back than Exclusion'.

41. See, in particular, Conrad Russell, 'Parliamentary History in Perspective, 1604–29', *History*, 56 (1976), 1–27 and *Parliaments and English Politics*; Kevin Sharpe, 'Parliamentary History, 1603–29: In or Out of Perspective' in *Faction*, pp. 1–42; and the relevant articles in *JMH*, 49, no. 4 (1977).

42. *Origins*, p. 1.

43. Hirst, *P&P*, no. 92 (August 1981), 80.

44. See, in particular, Hexter and Hirst, *JMH*, 50, no. 1 (March 1978), 1–71; Rabb and Hirst, *P&P*, no. 92 (August 1981), 55–99.

45. *Faction*, p. v.

46. *Origins*, p. 1.

47. Antony Fletcher's new book in which he argues, on the basis of a mass of central and local sources, that civil war 'came about because of the coincidence of hopeless misunderstanding and irreconcilable distrust with fierce ideological conflict' (*Outbreak*, p. 415) is, in my view, the most satisfactory interpretation to date.

48. Elton, *Studies in Tudor Politics and Government*, vol. II, p. 165.

49. Quoted in Richardson, *The Debate*, p. 16.

## 2.   THE JACOBEAN RELIGIOUS SETTLEMENT:
### THE HAMPTON COURT CONFERENCE   *Patrick Collinson*

I am grateful to Dr Jenny Wormald who has read this chapter and from her close knowledge of James VI and I has corrected a number of errors in perspective.

1. Sir George Paule, *The Life of John Whitgift* (ed. 1699), p. 96; Lambeth Palace Library, MS 3152, ff. 4–5.

2. *A Century of Sermons ... Preached by John Hacket*, with a life of Hacket by Thomas Plume (1675), p. xii.

3. Edward Cardwell, *A History of Conferences and Other Proceedings Connected with the Revision of the Book of Common Prayer* (Oxford, 1849), p. 168.

4. Paule, *John Whitgift*, p. 78.

5. Cardwell, *History of Conferences*, p. 170.

6. David Calderwood, *The True History of the Church of Scotland*, ed. T. Thomson and D. Laing, vol. VI, Wodrow Society (Edinburgh, 1849), p. 220.

7. (Hugh Broughton), 'Articles reproving John Archbishop of Canterbury and Thomas Bishop of Winchester for errours against the hope and ground of salvation', PRO SP 52/64/2. Cf. *DNB*, art. Broughton.

8. *A supplication of the Family of Love* (Cambridge, 1606).

9. Quoted, D. H. Willson, *James VI and I* (1956), p. 149.

10. See Patrick Collinson, *The Elizabethan Puritan Movement* (1967) and M. M. Knappen, *Tudor Puritanism* (Chicago, 1939); and Patrick Collinson, *English Puritanism* (1983), which contains a bibliographical guide to other accounts and sources.

11. The petition is most accessible in J. P. Kenyon (ed.), *The Stuart Constitution* (Cambridge, 1966), pp. 132–4. A manifesto published in 1605 by thirty ministers of Lincoln diocese and known as *An abridgement* supplies details of 746 supporters which, it has been suggested, may be some indication of the number of signatures secured in May–July 1603. (R. G. Usher, *The Reconstruction of the English Church* (1910), vol. I, p. 290 n.1.) *The answere of ... the Universitie of Oxford ... to the humble petition of the ministers of the Church of England* (1603) was endorsed by the University of Cambridge.

12. BL Sloane MS 271 is a collection of petitions, letters and other papers made by Robert Smart, vicar of Preston Capes, Northants., and significantly containing both Elizabethan and (mainly) early Jacobean items. It bears some affinity to a file of the papers of an Elizabethan and Jacobean puritan MP, Sir Edward Lewkenor of Denham, Suffolk, BL Add. MS 38492. The passages quoted are taken from notes of a letter sent to Northamptonshire by the London minister Stephen Egerton (BL Sloane MS 271, f. 20$^r$); and 'Advices Tending to Reformation', BL Add. MS 38492, f. 62$^r$, which also exists in variant versions in BL Add. MS 28571, f. 199 (annotated in Cecil's

hand) and PRO SP 16/470/99, which has been misplaced in cataloguing and calendaring to September 1640. (I owe this reference to Professor Conrad Russell.) BL Sloane MS 271 f. 20$^r$ contains notes made from 'Advices'.

13. *Basilikon Doron* (ed. 1603), Sigs. A4$^v$–6$^r$.

14. Some of these reports will be found in letters and extracts from letters by E(mund) Snape, S(tephen) Egerton and perhaps others, BL Sloane MS 271, ff. 20$^v$, 21$^v$, 23–5$^r$. See also the 'speeches bruited upon and after Maister Doctor Reynolds returne to Oxon concerning the late conference before his Maiestie', Usher, *The Reconstruction of the English Church*, vol. II, pp. 340–1.

15. Jenny Wormald, *Court, Kirk and Community in Scotland 1470–1625*, The New History of Scotland (1981), p. 148.

16. Bodl. Lib. MS Rawlinson B 151, f. 95$^v$. The petitioner was Thomas Bywater, the date 20 February 1605.

17. BL Sloane MS 271, f. 20$^r$; BL Add. MS 38492, f. 62$^r$.

18. Cardwell, *History of Conferences*, p. 199.

19. Quoted, Arthur P. Kautz, 'The Selection of Jacobean Bishops', in *Early Stuart Studies: Essays in Honor of David Harris Willson*, ed. Harold S. Reinmuth (Minneapolis, 1970), p. 154.

20. Dudley Carleton to John Chamberlain, 15 January 1604; PRO SP 14/6/21. There is much evidence of Pickering's and Galloway's activities in BL Sloane MS 271.

21. Frederick Shriver, 'Hampton Court Re-visited: James I and the Puritans', *JEH*, XXXIII (1982), 52–3.

22. 'A Proclamation concerning such as seditiously seeke a reformation in Church matters', 24 October 1603; *Stuart Royal Proclamations*, vol. I, *Royal Proclamations of King James I 1603–1625*, ed. J. F. Larkin and P. L. Hughes (Oxford, 1973), pp. 60–3. The point was strengthened in the king's letter to the two archbishops which followed on 26 October (PRO SP 14/4/33). Compare the interpretation of Mark H. Curtis, 'Hampton Court Conference and its Aftermath', *History*, XLVI (1961), 5–6 with Shriver, 'Hampton Court Re-visited', pp. 53–7. For the Sussex petitions, reported to the Privy Council by Bishop Watson of Chichester on 15 October, see R. B. Manning, *Religion and Society in Elizabethan Sussex* (Leicester, 1969), pp. 207–17. The phrase 'some that are in especial credit with his Highness' echoes 'Advices Tending to Reformations'. Two of the surviving copies of this document were in the government's hands.

23. James I (to the Earl of Northampton), n.d.; Cardwell, *History of Conferences*, pp. 160–1. The recipient was identified by Gardiner, (edn 1895), vol. I, p. 159.

24. *The Diary of Baron Waldstein: A Traveller in Elizabethan England*, ed. G. W. Groos (1981), pp. 93–101; Cardwell, *History of Conferences*, p. 161.

25. Copies of an account of the Lambeth Conference, evidently composed by one of the two puritan representatives, Walter Travers, in BL Add. MS 48064, folios 49–63 and Doctor Williams's Library Morrice MSS, calendared, A. Peel (ed.) *A Seconde Parte of a Register* (Cambridge, 1915) vol. I, 275–83. The date is supplied by Paule, *John Whitgift*, pp. 40–1.

26. John Cosin, 'The Sum and Substance of the Conferences Lately Held at York House Concerning Mr Mountague's Books', in *The Works of John Cosin* (Oxford, 1845), vol. II, pp. 17–81. See Roger Lockyer, *Buckingham: The Life and Political Career of George Villiers, First Duke of Buckingham 1592–1628* (1981) pp. 306–7.

27. BL Sloane MS 271, f. 21$^v$.

28. William Barlow, *The summe and substance of the conference* (1604), repr. Cardwell, *History of Conferences*, pp. 167–212; 'Anonymous Account' entitled 'A declaration of the conference', BL Harl. MS 828, f. 32, printed, Usher, *The Reconstruction of the English Church*, vol. II, pp. 341–54; a further account in BL Add. MS 38492, f. 81 (copy, Cambridge University Library MS Mm.1.45, folios 155–7, printed, Usher, vol. II, pp. 335–8); a very short puritan account printed by Usher from Barlow, Usher, vol. II, pp. 338–41; letters from the king (Cardwell, *History of Conferences*, pp. 160–1), Bishop Tobie Matthew (ibid., pp. 161–6), Patrick Galloway (ibid., pp. 212–17), James Montague (Ralph Winwood, *Memorials of Affairs of State* (1725), vol. II, pp. 13–14; Dudley Carleton (PRO SP 14/6/21).

29. *HMC MSS Lord Montagu of Beaulieu*, pp. 32–40; Josias Nicholls, *The plea of the innocent* (1602); Patrick Collinson, 'John Field and Elizabethan Puritanism', in *Elizabethan Government and Society*, ed. S. T. Bindoff, J. Hurstfield and C. H. Williams (1961), pp. 127–62.

30. Henry Jacobs, *A christian and modest offer of a most indifferent conference or disputation* (Middelburg, 1606), p. 29. Expectations about the puritan representation were adjusted from time to time in the months preceding the conference. On 23 August 1603 it was thought in puritan circles that the spokesmen would be Reynolds, Chaderton, (Walter) Travers, Sparke, (Francis) Marbury, Knewstub, (John) Ireton and (Arthur) Hildersham. (BL Sloane MS 271, f. 21$^v$; PRO SP 14/3/48.) On 8 December 1603 it was reported that Humfrey Fen of Coventry had been substituted for Ireton. (Sloane MS 271, f. 23$^r$, confirmed by PRO SP 14/6/15, which also names (Thomas) Cartwright and (Richard) Field.)

31. The only surviving example occurs in the life of Richard Field by his son, Nathaniel Field, *Some Short Memorials Concerning the Life of R. Field*, ed. J. le Neve (1717), p. 9. I owe this reference to Dr Nicholas Tyacke.

32. Thomas Sparke, *A brotherly perswasion to unitie* (1607), Sig. A4$^r$ and *passim*; Jacobs, *A Christian and modest offer*, p. 29; Shriver, 'Hampton Court Re-visited', 57–8; C. M. Dent, 'Protestants in Elizabethan Oxford' (Oxford University D.Phil. thesis, 1980) pp. 388–97.

33. As plausibly reported by Stephen Egerton, 30 November 1603; BL Sloane MS 271, f. 23$^v$.

34. Usher, *The Reconstruction of the English Church*, vol. II, p. 338. Field is named, apparently as a puritan spokesman, in three documents: BL Add. MS 38492, f. 81$^v$; PRO SP 14/6/15; *HMC MSS Montagu of Beaulieu*, p. 34. Dr Nicholas Tyacke has helped me with the 'cross-benchers', and especially with James Montague, who with a certain puritan self-consciousness wrote 'Emmanuel' at the head of letters written at this time. (*HMC Salisbury MSS*, XVII, pp. 28–9.)

35. *HMC* ibid., p. 271; Usher, *The Reconstruction of the English Church*, vol. II, pp. 338, 342.

36. Cardwell, *History of Conferences*, p. 161.

37. Gardiner, vol. I, pp. 146–59; Usher, *The Reconstruction of the English Church*, vol. I, pp. 310–33; Curtis, 'Hampton Court Conference' pp. 1–16; Shriver, 'Hampton Court Re-visited', pp. 48–71. For 'that unkoth motto', see London University Library, MS 610.

38. N. R. N. Tyacke, 'Arminianism in England'; H. C. Porter, *Reformation and Reaction in Tudor Cambridge* (Cambridge, 1958); Lake, *Moderate Puritans*.

39. According to Bishop Matthew's account; Cardwell, *History of Conferences*, p. 164.

40. Stuart Clark, 'Inversion, Misrule and the Meaning of Witchcraft', *P&P*, no. 87, pp. 98–127; Stuart Clark, 'King James's *Daemonologie*: Witchcraft and Kingship', in S. Anglo (ed.), *The Damned Art: Essays in the Literature of Witchcraft* (1977), pp. 156–81.

41. Gardiner, vol. I, p. 198.

42. Babbage, *Puritanism and Bancroft*. For the 1584 subscription campaign, see Collinson, *Elizabethan Puritan Movement*, part 5.

43. Quintrell, 'The Royal Hunt and the Puritans', pp. 58, 44.

44. *HMC Salisbury MSS*, XVI, p. 363. For the petition of the Northamptonshire gentry, see W. J. Sheils, *The Puritans in the Diocese of Peterborough 1558–1610*, Pubns of the Northants. Record Socy, XXX (Northampton, 1979) pp. 110–12.

45. The decisions made at the conference and entrusted to the bishops for implementation are contained in a list of 15 items in PRO SP 14/6/16 (copy, BL Lansdowne MS 89, no. 17, f. 29), and a related memorandum in SP 14/6/18. A list sent by Patrick Galloway to the Edinburgh presbytery, which generally tallies, is said to have been a copy corrected in the king's own hand. (Cardwell, *History of Conferences*, pp. 212–17.)

46. *Constitutions and Canons Ecclesiasticall* (1604), Sigs. H2, T–T2.

47. *Stuart Royal Proclamations*, vol. I, p. 61.

48. Robert Baillie, *A dissuasive from the errours of the time* (1646) p. 7.

49. Shriver, 'Hampton Court Revisited', p. 63.

50. Ibid., pp. 62–3. See Christopher Hill, *Economic Problems of the Church from Whitgift to the Long Parliament* (Oxford, 1956).

51. Gardiner, vol. I, p. 158.

52. But see my *The Religion of Protestants: the Church in English Society 1559–1625* (Oxford, 1982).

53. All Souls College Oxford MS 155, ff. 49–52.

54. Nicholas Tyacke, 'Puritanism, Arminianism and Counter-Revolution', in *Origins*, pp. 119–43.

55. Collinson, *The Religion of Protestants*, pp. 45–52.

56. Thomas Morton, *A defence of the innocencie of the three ceremonies of the Church of England* (1618).

57. Rosemary O'Day, *The English Clergy: The Emergence and Consolidation of a Profession 1558–1642* (Leicester, 1979).

58. *A Century of Sermons . . . by John Hacket*, p. xii.

59. John Hacket, *Scrinia Reserata: A Memoriall Offer'd to the Great Deservings of John Williams, D.D.* (1693), I. pp. 63–4.

### 3. THE PERSONAL RULE OF CHARLES I   *Kevin Sharpe*

A draft of this chapter was read at the Institute for Advanced Study, Princeton. I am grateful to John Elliott and the participants of the seminar for their helpful comments. I would also like to thank Gerald Aylmer, John Morrill, Conrad Russell and Lawrence Stone for their valuable advice and criticism.

1. See Gardiner. His account is not always read with the same balance and subtlety with which it was written.

2. See, for example, Lawrence Stone, *Causes of the English Revolution* (1972), pp. 117–35; T. K. Rabb, 'The Role of the Commons', *P&P*, 92 (1981), 65.

3. Above, p. 9.

4. Russell, *Parliaments and English Politics*, p. 212.

5. *CSPD 1628–9*, p. 531; cf. ibid., p. 482; G. L. Harriss, 'Medieval Doctrines', in *Faction*, pp. 73–104.

6. For a favourable view of Buckingham's military leadership which bears out Charles's confidence, see Lockyer, *Buckingham*.

7. Russell, *Parliaments and English Politics*, Ch. 6; *CSPD 1627–8*, p. 473, Sir James Bagg to Buckingham, 20 December 1628.

8. Compare the views of Sir John Coke and George Wither: *CSPD 1625–49*, p. 244; *Britain's Remembrancer* (1628), STC 25, 899, p. 236ᵛ; W. Knowler (ed.), *The Earl of Strafford's Letters and Despatches* 2 vols (1739), II, p. 53; cf. Gardiner, VII, pp. 26–7.

9. Sir Rob. Aiton to Carlisle, 18 July 1628, *CSPD 1628–9*, p. 218; Edward Hyde, Earl of Clarendon, *The History of the Rebellion*, ed. W. D. Macray (6 vols, 1888), I, p. 51; Gardiner, VI, p. 346; Dorchester to Queen of Bohemia, 27 August 1628, *CSPD 1628–9*, p. 270; *CSPD 1628–9*, pp. 177, 178–9, 218, 239, 247.

10. *History of the Rebellion*, I, 56; *CSPD 1625–49*, pp. 291–3; K. Sharpe, 'The Earl of Arundel, His Circle and the Opposition to the Duke of Buckingham, 1618–28', *Faction* p. 237; *CSPD 1628–9*, p. 268, Nethersole to [Carlisle] 24 August 1628.

11. *CSPD 1628–9*, p. 339, Dorchester to Carlisle, 30 September 1628; ibid., p. 340.

12. *Britain's Remembrancer*; cf. *CSPD 1628–9*, pp. 258, 268, 340, 388.

13. PRO SO 1/1/173ᵛ, Charles I to Conway, 21 September 1628; PRO SO 1/2/108, Charles I to Pembroke; J. P. Kenyon (ed.), *The Stuart Constitution* (1966), p. 18.

14. E.g. PRO SO 1/1/173ᵛ; SO 1/2/108.

15. BL Lansdowne MS 620 f. 74; cf. PRO SO 1/2/128 and *CSPD 1629–31*, p. 40.

16. *CSPD 1628–9*, p. 339.

17. C. Thompson, 'The Divided Leadership of the House of Commons in 1629', in *Faction*, pp. 245–84; T. Rymer, *Feodera*, XIX, 62, Heath to

Carlisle, 7 March, 1629; PRO SP 16/138/45; cf. Coke, *CSPD 1628-9*, p. 516.

18.  B. Donogan, 'A Courtier's Progress: Greed and Consistency in the Life of the Earl of Holland', *HJ*, 19 (1976), 317-53; G. E. Aylmer, *The King's Servants*, p. 62; *CSPD 1628-9*, p. 339, Dorchester to Carlisle, 30 September 1628; *History of the Rebellion* I, p. 61.

19.  Chateauneuf reported to Richelieu that with respect to the queen Charles 'vit en grande amitié, familiarité et privauté, mais il ne lui donne ni lui laisse prendre aucune part dans les affaires'. PRO (Baschet Transcripts) 31/3/66 f. 121. He also described the queen as 'timide et craintifre', ibid., f. 213.

20.  Philip Warwick, *Memoires of the Reigne of Charles I* (1701), p. 70; *CSPD 1631-3*, p. 427. Note the way in which the decision concerning ship money was made, *CSPD 1634-5*, pp. 161-3.

21.  'The King's personal commands and his private letters were sealed with the signet only'. G. E. Aylmer, 'Studies in the Institutions and Personnel of English Central Administration 1625-1642' (Oxford University D.Phil. 1954), p. 370. Signet Office letters from 1628 are in PRO SO 1/1-3. They are somewhat misleadingly catalogued as 'Irish Letter Books'.

22.  R. Ollard, *Image of the King*, p. 30; Pauline Gregg, *King Charles I*.

23.  Lucy Hutchinson, *Memoirs of the Life of Colonel Hutchinson*, ed. C. H. Firth, 2 vols (New York, 1885) vol. I, p. 119; Philip Warwick, *Memoires*, pp. 64-5, 113.

24.  *HMC Cowper*, I, p. 382; *CSPD 1629-31*, p. 478; T. Birch (ed.), *The Court and Times of Charles I*, 2 vols (1848) vol. II, p. 91; (Pory to Puckering, 13 January 1631;) Warwick, *Memoires*, p. 66.

25.  G. E. Aylmer, 'Attempts at Administrative Reform, 1625-1640', *EHR*, 72 (1957), 229-59; *Court and Times of Charles I*, vol. II, pp. 36, 40; *HMC De Lisle and Dudley*, VI, pp. 88, 139; Aylmer, D.Phil. thesis, p. 286; *The Poems of Thomas Carew* (1870), pp. 197-235, especially pp. 204-6.

26.  The work of the commission of buildings is an example.

27.  Buchanan Sharp, *In Contempt of All Authority: Rural Artisans and Riot in the West of England 1586-1640* (Berkeley, 1980), pp. 78-80; *HMC Buccleuch-Whitehall*, I, pp. 270-1.

28.  Stone, *Crisis of the Aristocracy*, Ch. III. Conrad Russell has pointed out to me that the sale of titles, revived in 1642, may have been a feature of war finance; Stone, *Causes of the English Revolution*, p. 125; *CSPD 1628-9*, p. 379.

29.  *HMC Cowper*, I, 373; *HMC Gawdy*, p. 136; Stone, *Causes of the English Revolution*, pp. 125-6; *Crisis of the Aristocracy*, pp. 94-6, 117, 351.

30.  Rymer XIX, 374; PRO PC 2/42/242; 2/42/290; 2/43/65; 2/44/161; PRO C115 M36 8439; M36 8437. Bundles of returns of those living in London are in Bodl. Lib. Bankes MSS 14, 62.

31.  Bodl. Lib. Bankes MSS. 49/8; 50/48, 49; PRO PC 2/42/263; 2/43/157; PRO SO 1/2/4ᵛ; *CSPD 1631-3*, p. 185; D. Coke, *The Last Elizabethan: Sir John Coke 1563-1644* (1937), pp. 211-12.

32.  PRO SO 1/2/187; cf. BL MS. Add 11, 674; PRO PC 2/43/81; 2/43/311; 2/44/99, 336; 2/45/320; 2/48/59; SO 1/2/187-7ᵛ.

33.  Gardiner, VII, pp. 125.

34. J. Rushworth, *Historical Collections*, 8 vols (1680–1701) II, p. 7; *CSPD 1628–9*, p. 547; *CSPD 1629–31*, p. 118. *Articles Agreed Upon by the Archbishops and Bishops of Both Provinces and the Whole Clergie, reprinted by His Majesties Commandment with his Royal Declaration prefixed thereunto* STC 10, 051. *Bibliotheca Regia or The Royal Library* (1659) p. 224; P. Heylyn, *Cyprianus Anglicus* (1671), pp. 188–90.

35. *CSPD 1633–4*, p. 212; *CSPD 1634–5*, p. 88. PRO PC 2/43/304; W. Scott and J. Bliss (eds), *The Works of William Laud*, 7 vols (1847–60), VI, pp. 350, 479.

36. E.g. PRO SO 1/2/55$^v$, 73, 112$^v$, 134$^v$, 141, 152, 177$^v$.

37. PRO PC 2/49/293.

38. See *Faction*, pp. 37–42; ibid., pp. 236–7.

39. When Charles went on progress to Scotland, the Council met twice weekly and also reported to the queen on Sundays, PRO C115/M.31/8152; Manchester reported to Montagu in December 1635, 'The King every Sunday afternoon sits to see what returns every sheriff makes...', Northants Record Office Montagu MSS 33, box B2, f. 21.

40. Berks. RO, Trumbull MSS., Trumbull Add. MSS 54, 55, 56.

41. PRO PC 2/41; PRO PC 2/41/354; 2/42/142.

42. PRO PC 2/41/514; *CSPD 1633–4*, p. 266; PRO PC 2/44, at end.

43. G. R. Elton, 'Tudor Government: The Points of Contact: I. Parliament; II, The Council; III, The Court', *TRHS*, 24–6 (1974–6).

44. BL MS. Harleian 6988 f. 74. PRO C115/M32/8348. *CSPD 1635*, p. 128. *CSPD 1633–4*, p. 352.

45. *CSPD 1628–9*, p. 542.

46. J. C. Sainty, *Lieutenants of Counties, 1585–1642*, *BIHR* Supplement 8 (1970); PRO PC 2/50/208.

47. Bodl. Lib. Ms. Tanner 148 f. 67; See, for example, Bodl. Lib. Ms. Tanner 68, visitation of the diocese of Norwich, 1635–8.

48. Gardiner, VII, p. 167. PRO SO 1/2/26, Charles I to commissioners.

49. PRO SP 12/206/25.

50. Montagu MS I f. 60.

51. Kent AO, Dering Mss., U.1311 02 compositions for knighthood.

52. Leonard, 'Distraint of Knighthood', *History*, 63, 1978, 23–37.

53. *CSPD 1631–3*, p. 278.

54. See Wentworth's remarks on the problems caused by this, *Strafford Letters* II, 411; PRO SO 1/3/109.

55. *CSPD 1625–49*, p. 493; Hants RO, Herriard Collection, Jervoise MSS., boxes 012, 013 militia Papers. I am grateful to Mr J. L. Jervoise for permission to see and cite papers in his collection.

56. *CSPD 1629–31*, pp. 15, 20; PRO SO 1/3/109.

57. Bodl. Lib. Bankes MS 42/55, Northamptonshire election 1640.

58. Bodl. Lib. Tanner MS 177 f. 19$^v$.

59. L. Boynton, *The Elizabethan Militia* (1967), Ch. 8.

60. *State Papers Collected by Edward, Earl of Clarendon*, 3 vols (Oxford, 1767) vol. I, p. 80, Hopton to Windebank, 7 Apr. 1634.

61. PRO C115/M31/8215.

62. See Chapter 5; Morrill, *Revolt of the Provinces*, p. 24.

63. Rushworth, II, pp. 258–9; *CSPD 1634–5*, pp. 295–6.

64. Rushworth, II, pp. 259–61.

65. They dominate the Council registers and state papers for 1635.

66. Kent AO, Twysden MSS., U47/47/Z1, p. 234.

67. For a classic example, see C. Holmes, *Seventeenth Century Lincoln-shire*, p. 132.

68. Bristol was assessed at £250 for ship money in 1638, £640 in 1639. Coat and conduct money cost the town £700: *CSPD 1640*, p. 121.

69. CUL Buxton MSS. box 96. I am grateful to Clive Holmes for drawing my attention to this collection. Morrill, *Revolt of the Provinces* p. 28; ibid., p. 29; PRO SP 16/459/21.

70. Garrard told Cottington that he would rather pay 'ten subsidies in parliament than ten shillings this new old way of dead Noye's'. But significantly he did not question the legality, *Strafford Letters*, I, p. 357. Cf. Saye and Sele's objections in 1635, Gardiner, VIII, p. 93.

71. P. Lake, 'The Collection of Ship Money in Cheshire during the 1630s: A Case Study in the Relation between Central and Local Government', *Northern History*, 1981. I am grateful to Peter Lake for his kindness in sending me a typescript of this article.

72. I am grateful to Conrad Russell for this observation.

73. BL Harleian MS 3796 f. 70. I owe this reference to Dr Patricia Haskell.

74. *CSPD 1635*, p. 470.

75. The king himself had first submitted ship money to the opinion of the judges, Gardiner, VII, pp. 206–10.

76. There was a full discussion of the question at Maidstone: Kent AO, Twysden MS U47/47 Z1, 2, pp. 102–10.

77. CUL Buxton MSS box 96; *Court and Times of Charles I*, vol. II, p. 275; *HMC De Lisle and Dudley*, VI, p. 138, 21 December 1637; *History of the Rebellion*, I, p. 87; PRO C115/N4/8619, John Burghe to Viscount Scudamore, December 1637.

78. See the comments of the French ambassador, PRO 31/3/66 pp. 131–8; Rymer, XIX, 62; *Strafford Letters*, I, p. 419.

79. *History of the Rebellion*, I, p. 84.

80. PRO C115/N3/8152.

81. *History of the Rebellion*, I, p. 84; T. G. Barnes, *Somerset 1625–40: A County's Government during the 'Personal Rule'* (Cambridge, Mass., 1961), Ch. VII; *CSPD 1633–4*, pp. 61, 94.

82. *History of the Rebellion*, I, p. 96.

83. I owe this phrase to Conrad Russell.

84. PRO C115/N4/8617. The hundreds of letters in the Scudamore collection have never been used systematically. I am preparing a short report on these papers.

85. Gardiner, VIII, p. 302.

86. PRO C115/N8/8814, 8815.

87. *Strafford Letters*, II, p. 189; Bodl. Lib. MS Clarendon 14, no. 1321.

88. Hants. RO, Jervoise MSS.; *CSPD 1640*, p. 458; *CSPD 1640*, pp. 314, 315; Morrill, *Revolt of the Provinces*, p. 29.

89. *CSPD 1639–40*, p. 420; *CSPD 1640*, pp. 123, 152. I am grateful to Caroline Bartlett for these references; *CSPD 1639–40*, pp. 588–9; *CSPD*

*1639–40*, p. 564; *CSPD 1640–1*, pp. 148–9.
  90. Aylmer, D.Phil thesis, p. 324.

4. SPAIN OR THE NETHERLANDS? THE DILEMMAS OF EARLY STUART
   FOREIGN POLICY  *Simon Adams*

The archival research upon which this essay is based was made possible by
generous grants from the British Academy, the Carnegie Trust for the
Universities of Scotland and the University of Strathclyde. The editor of this
volume, Christopher Hill, Peter Lake, John Morrill, Geoffrey Parker,
Christopher Thompson and Jenny Wormald read earlier drafts; for their
comments I am extremely grateful.

  1. Russell, *Parliaments and English Politics*, p. 64.
  2. G. Parker, 'The "Military Revolution", 1560–1660 – A Myth?', *Spain
and the Netherlands, 1559–1659: Ten Studies* (1979), pp. 94–103.
C. Russell, 'Parliament and the King's Finances', in *Origins*, p. 96.
  3. H. C. Scott (ed.), 'The Journal of Sir Roger Wilbraham ...
1593–1616', *Camden Society*, 3rd ser., IV (1902), p. 49; G. Parker, 'The
Dutch Revolt and the Polarization of International Politics', *Spain and the
Netherlands*, pp. 77–8; Frederick V to James I, 25 April 1622, quoted in
A. W. White, 'Suspension of Arms: Anglo-Spanish Mediation in the Thirty
Years War, 1621–1625' (Tulane University, Ph.D., 1978), p. 336. L.-M.
Avenel (ed.), *Lettres, Instructions Diplomatiques et Papiers d'Etat du
Cardinal Richelieu*, vol. I (Paris, 1863), p. 91, instructions for M. de La Ville
aux Clercs 22–3 May 1625.
  4. Adams, 'The Protestant Cause', pp. 59–60, 118, 360. Russell,
'Parliament and the King's Finances', p. 113.
  5. [R. Scrope and T. Monkhouse (eds.)], *State Papers Collected by
Edward Earl of Clarendon*, vol. I (Oxford, 1767), p. 509, Sir Francis
Windebank to Lord Aston, 11 April 1636. J. Alcalá-Zamora y Quiepo de
Llano, *España, Flandes y el Mar del Norte (1618–39)*, (Barcelona, 1975),
p. 346. For further discussions of the impact of neutrality upon English
commerce in the 1630s, see J. S. Kepler, *The Exchange of Christendom: The
International Entrepot at Dover, 1621–1641* (Leicester, 1976) pp. 42ff., and
H. Taylor, 'Trade, Neutrality and the "English Road", 1630–1648', *EcHR*,
25 (1972), 236–60.
  6. W. T. MacCaffrey, *Queen Elizabeth and the Making of Policy,
1572–1588* (Princeton, NJ, 1981), pp. 481–91; J. E. Neale, *Queen Elizabeth
and her Parliaments, 1584–1601* (1957), pp. 166–83; Adams, 'Protestant
Cause', p. 59.
  7. Peck, 'The Earl of Northampton', *HJ*, XXIV (1981), 537–41.
  8. E. R. Foster (ed.), *The Proceedings in Parliament: 1610* (New Haven,
1966), vol. II, pp. 136–7.
  9. S. L. Adams, 'Foreign Policy and the Parliaments of 1621 and 1624', in
*Faction*, pp. 162, 164. For a different interpretation, see C. Russell, 'The
Foreign Policy Debate in the House of Commons in 1621', *HJ*, XX (1977),
289–309.
  10. M. L. Schwarz, 'Lord Saye and Sele's Objections to the Palatine

Benevolence of 1622: Some New Evidence and its Significance', *Albion*, IV (1972), pp. 18.

11. R.B. Wernham, *The Making of Elizabethan Foreign Policy, 1558–1603* (Berkeley, Calif., 1980), pp. 64–5.

12. Adams, 'Foreign Policy', p. 151; W. Notestein *et al.* (eds), *The Commons Debates for 1621* (New Haven, Conn., 1935), vol. III, p. 458, vol. IV, p. 443; *CJ*, vol. I (1803), p. 740.

13. Parker, 'Dutch Revolt and Polarization', pp. 77–80; Alcalá-Zamora, *España y el Mar del Norte*, esp. pp. 178ff; M. Roberts, *Gustavus Adolphus*, vol. I (1953), p. 224. R. J. Bonney, *Political Change in France under Richelieu and Mazarin, 1624–1666* (Oxford, 1978), p. 259.

14. *Clarendon State Papers*, I, p. 75, Windebank to Sir A. Hopton, 16 February 1634; p. 510, Windebank to Aston, 11 April 1636.

15. R. W. Kenny, *Elizabeth's Admiral: The Political Career of Charles Howard, Earl of Nottingham, 1536–1624* (Baltimore, Maryland, 1970), pp. 292ff. Lockyer, *Buckingham*, pp. 76, 91; A. P. McGowan (ed.), *The Jacobean Commissions of Enquiry, 1608 and 1618*, Navy Records Society, vol. 116 (1971).

16. *Clarendon State Papers*, I, pp. 76, 106–7, 109, 112–13; Alcalá-Zamora, *España y el Mar del Norte*, p. 350.

17. PRO SP 84/104/189–90; The Hague, ARA, Eerste Afdeling, Staten-Generaal 8048, Staten van Oorlog, 1621; G. Parker, *The Army of Flanders and the Spanish Road, 1567–1659* (Cambridge, 1975), p. 53–3.

18. For the Danish regiment, see E. A. Beller, 'The Military Expedition of Sir Charles Morgan to Germany, 1627–1629', *EHR*, 43 (1928), 528–39.

19. S. J. Stearns, 'Conscription and English Society in the 1620s', *JBS*, 11 (1972) 1–24. H. L. Rubenstein, *Captain Luckless: James, First Duke of Hamilton* (Edinburgh, 1975), p. 31. PRO SP 81/31/173, Sir F. Nethersole to J. Woodford, 27 November 1624.

20. PRO SP 84/95/247, Vere to Sir D. Carleton, 14 June 1620; The Hague, ARA, Eerste Afdeling, Staten-Generaal, Lias Engeland 5887, A. von Dohna to States-General, 6 June 1620.

21. *CSP Ven* vol. XX 1915, pp. 306; *Clarendon State Papers*, II (Oxford, 1773), p. 23, instructions for Col. H. Gage, 5 February 1639; pp. 31–2, Hopton to Windebank, 30 March 1639.

22. *HMC Report on the MSS of the Marquess of Salisbury*, vol. XXI (1970), Winwood to James I, 7 April 1612.

23. L. P. Smith, *The Life and Letters of Sir Henry Wotton* (Oxford, 1907), vol. II, pp. 157–9, to Carleton, 1 October 1618.

24. S. R. Gardiner (ed.), *Letters and Documents Illustrating the Relations between England and Germany . . . 1618–1620*, vol. II, *Camden Society*, XCVIII (1868), pp. 12–13, to Sir R. Naunton, 9 September 1619.

25. Bodl. Lib., Tanner Ms. 74, fos. 221–2, Abbot to Naunton, 12 September 1619.

26. PRO SP 14/176/34, to Carleton, 9 December 1624.

27. Munich, BGSA, Kasten Schwarz 16741, fos. 225-v, James I to Frederick V, 29 June 1620; J. Rushworth, *Historical Collections*, vol. I (1659), p. 140, James I to Sir E. Conway, 3 April 1624; W. B. Patterson,

'King James I's Call for an Ecumenical Council', in J. G. Cuming and D. Baker (eds), *Studies in Church History*, vol. VII: *Councils and Assemblies* (Cambridge, 1971), pp. 267–75.

28. *CSP Ven*, vol. XII (1905), pp. 369–70. PRO SP 84/68/293, Viscount Rochester to Winwood, 19 July 1612.

29. PRO SP 94/23/68–9, 74, Francis Cottington to Naunton, 17 September, 8 October 1618; Munich, BGSA, Kasten Schwarz 16738, f. 155, James I to Frederick V, 2 December 1618.

30. *HMC Report on the MSS of the Duke of Buccleuch and Queensbury at Montagu House*, vol. I (1899), p. 192, to Winwood, 3 April 1617; A. Ballesteros y Baretta (ed.), *Correspondencia Oficial de Don Diego Sarmiento de Acuña, Conde de Gondomar, Documentos Inéditos para la Historia de España*, vol. I (Madrid, 1936), pp. 106–7, Gondomar to Philip III, 12 October 1617.

31. Lockyer, *Buckingham*, pp. 144, 232.

32. E. C. Williams, *Anne of Denmark* (1970), p. 146.

33. White, 'Suspension of Arms', pp. 112, 184–5, 551–2; P. Brightwell, 'Spain and the Origins of the Thirty Years War' (Cambridge University, Ph.D., 1967), p. 123; E. Straub, *Pax et Imperium: Spaniens Kampf um seine Friedensordnung in Europa zwischen 1617 und 1635* (Paderborn, 1980) pp. 164, 170, 173, 184–5; Adams, 'Protestant Cause', p. 256; *Correspondencia Oficial de Gondomar*, vol. III (Madrid, 1944), p. 216, Sarmiento to Philip III, 15 January 1614; W. Ramirez de Villa-Urrita, *La Embajada del Conde de Gondomar á Inglaterra en 1613* (Madrid, 1913), pp. 27, 63.

34. Alcalá-Zamora, *España y el Mar del Norte*, pp. 143, 180–81, 217–18; R. Ródenas Vilar, *La Política Europea de España durante la Guerra de Treinta Años (1624–30)* (Madrid, 1967), pp. 8, 60; *Correspondencia Official de Gondomar*, I, p. 112, Gondomar to Philip III, 12, October 1617. PRO SP 94/23/141, Cottington to Sir Thomas Lake, 7 January 1619.

35. *Clarendon State Papers*, I, appendix, p. x.

36. Quoted in Gardiner, VIII, p. 100.

37. *Clarendon State Papers*, I, p. 356, instructions for Capt. Arthur Brett, 28 October 1635.

38. Adams, 'Protestant Cause', pp. 359–60; Paris, BN, MS Cinq Cents Colbert 467, f. 258, J. Beaulieu to J. Hotman, 16 April 1625.

39. A. B. Grosart (ed.), *The Letterbook of Sir John Eliot, 1625–1632* (1882), pp. 23–5, to Sir John Eliot, 4 November 1628; Adams, 'Protestant Cause', pp. 419–20.

40. The two recent biographies of Elizabeth – J. Ross, *The Winter Queen* (1979) and J. Gorst-Williams, *Elizabeth the Winter Queen* (1977) – are inadequate.

41. Williams, *Anne of Denmark*, p. 154.

42. R. M. Smuts, 'The Puritan Followers of Henrietta Maria in the 1630s', *EHR*, 93 (1978), 26–45.

43. V. F. Snow, *Essex the Rebel* (Lincoln, Nebraska, 1970), pp. 91–123 *passim; Clarendon State Papers*, II, p. 94.

44. Adams, 'Protestant Cause', pp. 297–300; 'Foreign Policy', pp. 144–5.

45. PRO SP 105/95/15v, to Carleton, 12 December 1617; Adams, 'Foreign Policy', p. 143.

46. Geneva, BUP Ms. Tronchin 145, f. 46v, Relation of Sr. Gregoire.

47. Morrill, *Revolt of the Provinces*, pp. 16–18; Russell, 'Parliament and the King's Finances', *Origins*, pp. 110–13.

48. Adams, 'Foreign Policy', pp. 145–6; B. Worden, 'Classical Republicans and the Puritan Revolution', in H. Lloyd Jones, V. Pearl, B. Worden (eds), *History and Imagination: Essays in Honour of H. R. Trevor-Roper* (1981), pp. 186–7.

49. Adams, 'Protestant Cause', p. 379.

50. 'Wilbraham Journal', pp. 49–50.

51. K. R. Andrews, 'Caribbean Rivalry and the Anglo-Spanish Peace of 1604', *History*, 54 (1974), 1–17.

52. Lee, *James I and Henri IV*, pp. 69ff; E. Sawyer (ed.), *Memorials of Affairs of State in the Reigns of Queen Elizabeth and King James I* (1725), vol. II, p. 148, Salisbury to Sir Charles Cornwallis, 24 October 1605; Paris, AMAE, Correspondence Politique, Hollande, IV, f. 237v, M. de Villeroy to President Jeannin, 13 November 1607.

53. *CSP Ven* vol. X (1900), pp. 471–4, 474–5.

54. C. Grayson, 'James I and the Religious Crisis in the United Provinces, 1613–1619', D. Baker (ed.), *Reform and Reformation: England and the Continent, c1500–1700* (Oxford, 1979), pp. 195–219; F. J. Shriver, 'Orthodoxy and Diplomacy: James I and the Vorstius Affair', *EHR*, 85 (1970), 449–74.

55. Berks. RO, Trumbull Mss, Alphabetical Series, I, art. 38, Abbot to W. Trumbull, 27 March 1619; Munich, BGSA, Kasten Schwarz 16734, f. 437, Frederick V to Winwood, 8 December 1615.

56. Adams, 'Protestant Cause', pp. 230–47 *passim*; CUL Ms. Dd. 3. 63, f. 50v, Northampton to Earl of Somerset, ? November 1613; f. 52v, Northampton to Somerset, n.d. (? 1613).

57. R. E. Schreiber, *The Political Career of Sir Robert Naunton, 1589–1635* (1981), pp. 36–8.

58. Adams, 'Protestant Cause', pp. 278–9, 281.

59. Lockyer, *Buckingham*, p. 143; Straub, *Pax et Imperium*, p. 182; J. H. Elliott and J. F. de La Peña (eds), *Memoriales y Cartas del Conde Duque de Olivares*, vol. I (Madrid, 1978), p. 144, Olivares to Gondomar, 23 May 1625.

60. White, 'Suspension of Arms', p. 595; Straub, *Pax et Imperium*, pp. 173, 178; A. Egler, *Die Spanier in der Linksrheinischen Pfalz, 1620–32* (Mainz, 1971), p. 76.

61. T. Christiansen, *Die Stellung König Christians IV von Danemark zu den Kriegsereignissen im Deutschen Reich und zu den Plänen einer Evangelischen Allianz, 1618–1625* (Kiel, 1937), pp. 42–52 *passim*; Roberts, *Gustavus Adolphus*, I, pp. 198–9; J. C. Grayson, 'From Protectorate to Partnership: Anglo-Dutch Relations, 1598–1625' (London University, Ph.D., 1978), pp. 282–5; R. E. Zaller, '"Interest of State": James I and the Palatinate', *Albion*, 6 (1974), 157.

62. BL Add. MS 34,324, f. 119, Notes by Sir J. Caesar of Privy Council meeting, 29 September 1620.

63. Adams, 'Foreign Policy', pp. 161, 164.

64. Lockyer, *Buckingham*, pp. 109–11; Russell, *Parliaments*, pp. 133–5.

65. Ruigh, *The Parliament of 1624*, pp. 384–7.

66. Adams, 'Protestant Cause', p. 356.

67. Adams, 'Foreign Policy', pp. 157–8; *Clarendon State Papers*, II, appendix, p. ii, Kensington to Charles, 23 March 1624.

68. P. Grillon (ed.), *Les Papiers de Richelieu*, vol. I (Paris, 1975), p. 183, memoire pour le roi (May) 1625. Paris, AMAE, Correspondence Politique, Angleterre, 32 f. 68v, La Ville aux Clercs to Marquis of Effiat, 26 October 1624.

69. Adams, 'The Road to La Rochelle: English Foreign Policy and the Huguenots, 1610 to 1629', *Proc. Hug. Soc. of London*, 22 pt. 5 (1975), 427–8; Lockyer, *Buckingham*, pp. 369–71.

70. Adams, 'Protestant Cause', pp. 349, 366; 'Foreign Policy', p. 170–1.

71. Munich, BGSA, Kasten Blau 89/3c, f. 26, Frederick V to Dorchester, 8 October 1629.

72. *Clarendon State Papers*, I, p. 35, treaty of 2 January, pp. 779–81, Windebank to Aston, 24 June 1637; Gardiner, VII, pp. 176–7; A. J. Loomie, 'Olivares, the English Catholics and the Peace of 1630', *Revue Belge de Philologie et Histoire*, XLVII (1969), 1154–66; Alcalá-Zamora, *España y el Mar del Norte*, pp. 266–7.

73. Alcalá-Zamora, *España y el Mar del Norte*, pp. 346–7, 350.

74. *Clarendon State Papers*, I, p. 629, J. Taylor to Windebank, 2 September, Arundel to Windebank, 8 September, 1636.

75. J. H. Elliott, 'The Year of the Three Ambassadors', *History and Imagination*, pp. 165–81.

76. S. R. Gardiner (ed.), *Constitutional Documents of the Puritan Revolution, 1625–1660* (Oxford, 1906), pp. 108–9, 253, 284.

77. N. Tyacke, 'Puritanism, Arminianism and Counter-Revolution', *Origins*, p. 129.

5. FINANCIAL AND ADMINISTRATIVE DEVELOPMENTS

## David Thomas

I should like to thank Norah Fuidge, David Hebb, Ann Hughes and Peter Lake for criticising drafts of this essay.

1. BL Lansdowne MS 165 f. 139.

2. F. C. Dietz, *English Public Finance, 1558–1641* (1932), p. 113.

3. D. L. Thomas, 'The Administration of the Crown Lands in Lincolnshire under Elizabeth I' (University of London Ph.D thesis, 1979), ff. 379–84; Eric Kerridge, 'The Movement of Rent, 1540–1640', *EcHR*, 2nd. ser., 6 (1953), 30–1.

4. E. R. Foster (ed.), *Proceedings in Parliament, 1610* (1966), I, p. 6.

5. P. R. Seddon, 'Household Reforms in the Reign of James I', *BIHR*, 53 (1980), 49; Gardiner, II, p. 200.

6. Foster, *Proceedings* I, p. 9.

7. Dietz, *Public Finance*, pp. 104–5, n.10, 411; Seddon, 'Household Reforms', pp. 50 n.29, 55; BL Lansdowne MS 165 ff. 158, 203.

8. R. Ashton, 'Deficit Finance in the Reign of James I', *EcHR*, 2nd ser., 10 (1957–8), 21–3.

9. PRO SP 14/35/51 and 37/105; BL Add. MS 36767 f. 196; G. Batho, 'Landlords in England: The Crown', in J. Thirsk (ed.), *The Agrarian History*

*of England and Wales, IV, 1500–1640* (1967), pp. 268–73.

10. H. E. Bell, *An Introduction to the History and Records of the Court of Wards and Liveries* (1953), p. 49 and Table A.

11. Gardiner, I, p. 296, II, p. 15; Dietz, *Public Finance*, pp. 105–7; S. R. Gardiner (ed.), *Parliamentary Debates in 1610*, Camden Society, 81 (1862), p. 166.

12. Prestwich, *Cranfield*, pp. 206–10, 227–31, 272, 341, 360, 370–1; Seddon, 'Household Reforms', pp. 48–52.

13. Prestwich, *Cranfield*, p. 371.

14. R. C. Braddock, 'The Rewards of Office-holding in Tudor England', *JBS*, 14 (1975), 32–6; Hurstfield, *The Queen's Wards*, p. 277.

15. PRO E 215/3/253.

16. Aylmer, *The King's Servants*, p. 162.

17. Stone, *Family and Fortune*, p. 14; Dietz, *Public Finance*, p. 339.

18. Aylmer, *King's Servants*, p. 163.

19. Stone, *Family*, pp. 118, 135.

20. Aylmer, *King's Servants*, pp. 106–25, 143; Prestwich, *Cranfield*, pp. 246–7.

21. PRO SP 16/408/130; Stone, *Family*, p. 118.

22. Stone, *Family*, pp. 7–10; Gardiner, III, p. 209; PRO SP 14/5/41, SP 12/283A/80 f. 167; BL Cottonian MS, Titus B iv, f. 324v.

23. Stone, *Family*, pp. 14–15, 26–7; Prestwich, *Cranfield*, p. 260.

24. Zaller, *The Parliament of 1621*, p. 32.

25. *CSPD 1598–1601*, p. 110; N. Tyacke, 'Wroth, Cecil and the Parliamentary Session of 1604', *BIHR*, 50 (1977), 120–4; Bell, *Introduction*, pp. 138–9.

26. PRO SP 16/24/48; Russell, *Parliament and English Politics*, pp. 282–4.

27. Foster, *Proceedings*, I, p. 36; Gardiner, *Debates in 1610*, pp. 163–79; Russell, *Parliament and English Politics*, pp. 282–3.

28. Foster, *Proceedings*, I, p. 142; S. R. Gardiner (ed.), *Debates in the House of Commons in 1625*, Camden Society, new series VI (1873), pp. 85, 111.

29. C. Russell, 'Parliament and the King's Finances', in *Origins*, pp. 111–14.

30. *CSP Ven 1632–6*, p. 366.

31. Gardiner, IV, p. 31; V, pp. 197, 200, 336; Scott, *Constitution and Finance*, vol. III, pp. 503, 505.

32. Foster, *Proceedings*, II, 310; Dietz, 'Public Finance', pp. 389–93; Gardiner, *Debates in 1610*, p. 165; Fletcher, *Sussex*, pp. 202–5; *APC*, 43, *1627–8*, pp. 516–17; I am grateful to Conrad Russell for this reference.

33. R. J. W. Swales, 'The Ship Money Levy of 1628', *BIHR*, 50 (1977), 166–70; Dietz, 'Public Finance', 271; Gardiner, VI, pp. 165, 220; *CSP Ven 1632–6*, p. 368.

34. *CSP Ven 1632–6*, pp. 366–7; *CSPD 1638–9*, p. 540; Gardiner, VIII, pp. 87–8; M. Whinney and (Sir) Oliver Millar, *English Art, 1625–1714* (1957), pp. 1–3.

35. G. E. Aylmer, 'Attempts at Administrative Reform, 1625–40', *EHR*, 72 (1957), 246–59; Seddon, 'Household Reforms', p. 55.

36. *CSP Ven 1629–32*, p. 298.

37. Bell, *Introduction*, pp. 49–50; Dietz, *Public Finance*, pp. 283, 375–6; *CSP Ven 1636–9*, pp. 387–8.

38. W. Hyde Price, *The English Patents of Monopoly* (1906), pp. 35–46, 113–26; Scott, *Constitution and Finance*, I, pp. 208–23; M. W. Beresford, 'The Beginning of Retail Tobacco Licences, 1632–41', *Yorkshire Bulletin of Economic and Social Research*, VII (1955), 128–36; *CSPD 1636*, pp. 7–8.

39. M.D. Gordon, 'The Collection of Ship Money in the Reign of Charles I', *TRHS*, 3rd ser., 4 (1910) 143–4.

40. Scott, *Constitution and Finance*, I, pp. 205, 233; Ashton, *The Crown and the Money Market*, pp. 173–78; PRO SP 16/410/108.

6.   THE NATURE OF A PARLIAMENT IN EARLY STUART ENGLAND

### Conrad Russell

I would like to thank the Central Research Fund of the University of London, the Twenty-Seven Foundation, the A. Whitney Griswold Fund of Yale University, and the Concilium on International and Area Studies of Yale University for grants towards the cost of reading the MSS used in this essay.

1. NRS, II, p. 3.

2. D'Ewes, *Journals*, p. 465. The fact that Coke supposed that the preamble of Ine's laws, describing how he took counsel of his notables, was evidence that he had called a parliament, should help to shed light on what Coke meant by a parliament.

3. See *LJ* III, p. 156 for a successful claim of privilege by an outlawed Beefeater called Original Bellamy, on the ground that he was the king's servant.

4. Esther S. Cope, *The Life of a Public Man: Edward, First Baron Montague of Brighton* (Philadelphia, 1981) p. 191. *HMC Buccleuch*, III, pp. 414–15.

5. *CJ*, I, 95.

6. For example, Derek Hirst in *HJ*, 23, no. 2 (1980), 455. Even if these are all printers' errors, they remain significant: printers have habits of thought too.

7. BL Loan MS 29/173, ff. 239–40. I am grateful to Ms Jacqueline Levy for this reference.

8. This point seems to have been truer in the 1620s than it was in a period of rapid change like the 1530s. Some people held to a Cromwellian notion of legislative sovereignty, while others stressed a notion of fundamental law which was closer to Sir Thomas More than to Thomas Cromwell. For the Cromwellian view see Sir Richard Grosvenor, Cheshire RO Grosvenor MSS 2 February 1624 and Robert Cecil in Elizabeth Read Foster (ed.), *Proceedings in Parliament 1610*, II p. 66. For the other view, see the Earl of Leicester: 'there are some things, resolved upon by the common and universal consent of the nation, which are immutable, and cannot be altered by the sovereign power of either king or parliament, or of both together, but must still remain as long as the nation continueth to be a nation, that is until this civil society so united be dissolved'. This is followed

by a classic statement of the doctrine of the 'ancient constitution', based on Coke and Lambarde. Kent AO De L'Isle and Dudley MSS, Z 47, unfoliated and undated, ? c. 1641. I am grateful to Viscount De L'Isle and Dudley, VC, KG for permission to quote from his family papers, and to Blair Worden for drawing my attention to this uncalendared portion of the De L'Isle and Dudley collection.

9. On the question of the crown's right or otherwise to withhold a Lord's writ of summons, see Russell, *Parliaments and English Politics*, p. 16 and references there cited.

10. John Hooker, *The Order and Usage How to Keep a Parlement in England*, in Vernon F. Snow, (ed.), *Parliament in Elizabethan England* (New Haven, 1977), pp. 145–6.

11. NRS, IV, p. 2.

12. J. G. Edwards, 'The *Plena Potestas* of English Parliamentary Representatives', in Fryde and Miller (eds.), *Historical Studies of the English Parliament*, vol. I, pp. 136–49.

13. For an example of how much discomfort this might cause, see Sir Thomas Wentworth's Rotherham speech in 1621, J. P. Cooper (ed.), *The Wentworth Papers*, Camden Society, 4th ser., 12 (1973), pp. 152–7. For an example of how far a sense of wartime emergency might be built up in order to justify a grant, see Hants. RO Jervoise MSS 0 21 (?1601). It is remarkable how few people seem to have kept the speeches they made on these occasions: the only other example known to me is Bodl. Lib. MS Rawlinson D723, ff. 29–30 (anonymous and undated, ?1621).

14. Hartley I, pp. 49, 190; *CJ*, I, p. 145.

15. Quoted by F. W. Maitland in Fryde and Miller, *Historical Studies*, p. 128.

16. PRO C218/1. For an earlier and very similar wording, see S. B. Chrimes and A. L. Brown, *Selected Documents of English Constitutional History 1307–1485* (1961), p. 362.

17. I am grateful to Dr Michael Prestwich and Dr J. R. L. Highfield for advice on this question. *Rot. Parl.* III, pp. 427–8. I am grateful to Dr Highfield for this reference. See also E. B. Fryde, 'Parliament and the French War' in Fryde and Miller, *Historical Studies*, pp. 242–61.

18. J. S. Roskell, *The Commons and their Speakers 1376–1523* (Manchester, 1965), p. 51.

19. D'Ewes, *Journals* p. 466: NRS, II p. 4. Queen Elizabeth was drawing a contrast between the members who were only counsellors during the parliament and the Privy Councillors, who were counsellors all the time.

20. Bedford Estate Office, vol. 25 (unfoliated): Fourth Earl, miscellaneous papers. I am grateful to the trustees of the Bedford Settled Estates for permission to quote from these papers.

21. *CJ*, I, pp. 226–7. An asterisk indicates those bills which reached the statute book. The proportion is far higher than it would have been later in the century.

22. G. R. Elton, 'Tudor Government: Points of Contact: Parliament', *TRHS* (1974), 183–200.

23. See, for example, the case of Martham parsonage, A. Hassell Smith, *County and Court: Government and Politics in Elizabethan Norfolk*,

(Oxford, 1974), pp. 265–76, 335–6. The story which begins here ends with the Concealments Act of 1624. See also Ashton, *English Civil War*, pp. 44, 69 and other refs.

24. R. A. Houlbrooke (ed.), *The Letter Book of John Parkhurst*, Norfolk Record Soc., 43 (1975), pp. 142–3, 163–4, 29.

25. Hartley I, p. 227. I am grateful to Mr David Brentnall for drawing my attention to this reference.

26. James Daly, *Cosmic Harmony and Political Thinking in Early Stuart England*, American Philosophical Society, vol. 69, pt. 7, (Philadelphia, 1979), p. 18; G. R. Elton, *The Tudor Constitution* (Cambridge, 1960), p. 270.

27. Elliott, *Revolt of the Catalans*, p. 7 and *passim*; J. Russell Major, *Representative Government in Early Modern France*, (New Haven, 1980), pp. 165–6, 198, 239, 383–8 and other refs. On the significance of control over collection of taxation, see also Charles Jago, 'Habsburg Absolutism and the Cortes of Castile', *AHR*, 86, no. 2 (April 1981) 307–26, especially p. 310.

28. Richard Bonney, 'The English and French Civil Wars', *History*, 65, no. 215 (October 1980), 380–1.

29. For Olivares' views on this subject, see Elliott, *Revolt of the Catalans*, pp. 204, 400–1.

30. *The Parliamentary Diary of Robert Bowyer*, ed. D. H. Willson (Minneapolis, 1931), pp. 258–9, 256n.

31. Kent AO, De L'Isle and Dudley MSS Z 47 (unfoliated). The fact that Leicester's office as Lord Deputy of Ireland was held of the king, but could not be held of the parliament may help to explain his half-hearted excursion into royalism during the Civil War. See also Roland Hutton, 'The Structure of the Royalist Party 1642–1646', *HJ*, 24 no. 3 (September 1981), 561.

32. NRS, IV, pp. 258–60, 278–81, V, 127–8; *HMC De L'Isle and Dudley*, VI, p. 407. *LJ*, IV, p. 339.

33. Koenigsberger, *Dominium Regale*.

34. PRO SP 16/483/54; *CJ*, II, p. 263; *Letter Book of John Parkhurst*, ed. R. A. Houlbrooke, Norfolk Record Society, 43 (1975), pp. 171, 69; *HMC Buccleuch*, I, p. 268.

35. M. Claire Cross (ed.), *Letters of Sir Francis Hastings*, Somerset Record Society, 69 (Frome, 1969), pp. 90, 107 and *passim*.

36. J. T. Cliffe, *The Yorkshire Gentry* (1969), pp. 125–6; Essex RO Barrington MSS DD/Ba A 14. In the references to 'good' blankets and beds, it is tempting to place weight on the adjective.

37. Kent AO U 269/C267 (Sackville MSS). The *Lords' Journals* show Bath as one of the most conscientious members.

38. Somerset RO Phelips MSS 224/12 and 219/32. Hext's remarks about the cold are the more credible for being dated 19 January.

39. Clive Holmes, 'The County Community', *JBS*, 19 (1980), 54–73, has done a useful service by pointing to the limits beyond which revisionist stress on localism should not be allowed to go. It is, however, a moot point who, if anyone, holds the ideas he is attacking. I am grateful to him for not suggesting that I do so.

40. M. Claire Cross, *Hastings' Letters*, pp. 85–6; *CJ*, pp. 242, 994–5. Hastings appears to have predicted with painful accuracy the arguments

employed by Hoskins and Sir Richard Spencer against his proposal.

41. D'Ewes, *Journals*, 466.

42. A. H. A. Hamilton, (ed.), (1877), *Notebook of Sir John Northcote*, p. 107.

43. Hirst, *The Representative of the People?*

44. Hartley I, pp. 225–31.

45. *CSPD 1628–9*, vol. 146, no. 27.

46. G. L. Harriss, 'Mediaeval Doctrines in the Debates on Supply 1610–1629', in *Faction*, pp. 73–103.

47. Russell, *Parliaments and English Politics*, pp. 251, 283n, 284, 426–7.

48. See G. L. Harriss in *Faction*, p. 98: 'it would be difficult to claim that any of the disputes over supply during these twenty years (1610–29) either raised new constitutional principles or resulted in more politically damaging conflicts than those of earlier centuries'.

49. PRO SP 16/471/38.

50. Hants. RO Jervoise MSS 0.21: I am grateful to Dr Kevin Sharpe for this reference. *APC 1628–9*, pp. 516–17. See D'Ewes, *Journals*, 458, for Lord Keeper Puckering, in 1593, quoting the queen to the effect that the problem was largely caused by the wealthy turning the tax on the weaker. This problem was in large measure a legacy of the Elizabethan war with Spain.

51. A. B. Appleby, *Famine in Tudor and Stuart England* (Stanford, 1978), p. 141. See Keith Wrightson and David Levine, *Poverty and Piety in an Essex Village Terling 1525–1700* (1979), pp. 29–36. If other parishes, like Terling, 'filled up at the bottom', the number of taxpayers would not have risen in proportion to population. I am grateful to Dr Wrightson for some helpful correspondence about this very tentative suggestion, for which he should not be held responsible.

52. Hartley, I, p. 37.

53. Foster, *Proceedings*, II, pp. 14–21.

54. D'Ewes, *Journals*, p. 459; Foster, *Proceedings*, II p. 60. I am indebted for this paragraph to David Lie'erman, 'The Province of Legislation Determined', (University of London, Ph.D., 1980). The questions he has asked about the eighteenth century should also be asked about the seventeenth.

55. Sir John Neale, *Elizabeth I and Her Parliaments*, vol. II (1957), pp. 45–6; PRO SP 12/176/22 and 30. It is to be hoped that Burghley may be allowed to have had parliamentary principles (which differed from the queen's) without being a member of an 'opposition'.

56. Hartley, I pp. 217–18. As a gloss on Henry VIII's Succession Acts, Manwood's view was surely correct.

57. Hawarde, *Les Reportes del Cases in Camera Stellata*, p. 164; NRS, V, p. 20.

58. PRO SP 16/468/116; SP 16/480/20. Roe's reply to Vane suggests that he shared the same political outlook. He said that if he did not find Vane better than he left him: 'I shall envy those that perish with honour than they that outlive the honour and peace of their country'. SP 16/480/26. Roe was writing with some of the Army plotters aboard his ship. I hope this note may show that 'the place of principle' might still be in the king's service.

59. Kent AO De L'Isle and Dudley MSS Z 47. His source, *Proverbs* 1:17, is worth reading in context.

60. Kent AO U1475 C 2/42, 7 May 1640.

61. On Leicester's flirtation with royalism, see n.31 above. For Saville see *CSPD 1641–3*, vol. CCCCXCII no. 107 and vol. CCCCXCVII no. 32.

62. Dr Hutton is undoubtedly right that the royalist party of 1642 were not 'long-established servants of the crown'. Hutton, 'The Structure of the Royalist Party', *HJ*, 24, no. 3 (September 1981), p. 554. When Charles, in 1642, set out to portray himself as the champion of the rule of law, he did so with new servants: among those old Councillors to whom this cause should have most appealed, only Lord Keeper Littleton came to join him at York.

63. Kent AO Twysden MSS U 47/47/22, fragmentary commonplace book of Sir Roger Twysden. I am grateful to Mr Kenneth Fincham for this reference. See Kenneth Fincham, 'The Judges' Decision on Ship Money in 1637: the Reaction of Kent', *BIHR*, forthcoming.

64. Hirst, *The Representative of the People?*, p. 147.

65. PRO SP 16/467/5 and 471/22.

66. *LJ*, IV p. 187.

67. PRO SP 16/471/22: the Scots' formulation, at this stage, was 'once every two years or three years at farthest', and they hoped to refer all disputes between the kingdoms to the two parliaments.

68. Kent AO De L'Isle and Dudley MSS Z 47.

7. NATIONAL AND LOCAL AWARENESS IN THE COUNTY COMMUNITIES
*Anthony Fletcher*

I am grateful to Professor Conrad Russell for his comments on a draft of this essay.

1. Holmes, *Seventeenth-Century Lincolnshire*, p. 3; A. L. Hughes, 'Politics, Society and Civil War in Warwickshire 1620–1650', (University of Liverpool Ph.D., 1980); Holmes, 'The County Community in Stuart Historiography', *JBS*, 19 (1980), 54–73; A. Everitt, 'Country, County and Town: Patterns of Regional Evolution in England', *TRHS*, 5th ser., 29 (1979), 80, 88–9; C. Hill, 'Parliament and People', *P&P*, 92 (1981), 101–3.

2. Cust and Lake, 'Sir Richard Grosvenor', *BIHR*, 54 (1981), 48–50.

3. Hirst, *The Representative of the People?*, p. 163.

4. Cope, *Life of a Public Man*, p. 34; Ashton, *English Civil War*, pp. 43–70; C. S. R. Russell, *The Crisis of Parliaments* (Oxford, 1971), pp. 266–329; Coward, *The Stuart Age*, pp. 102–55.

5. Cust and Lake, *BIHR*, 54 (1981), 52; J. P. Gruenfelder, 'The Elections to the Short Parliament 1640', in H. S. Reinmuth, *Early Stuart Studies*, pp. 180–230; M. F. Keeler, *The Long Parliament* (Philadelphia, 1954), pp. 4–80.

6. For all this see my *Outbreak*, pp. xxv–xxix, 191–227.

7. Everitt, *Community of Kent*, p. 13.

8. Cliffe, *Yorkshire Gentry*, p. 282; C. V. Wedgwood, *Thomas Wentworth, First Earl of Strafford* (1961), pp. 30–1.

9. S. P. Salt, 'Sir Thomas Wentworth and the Parliamentary Representation of Yorkshire 1614–1628', *Northern History*, 16 (1980), 130–68.

10. Hirst, *Representative of the People?*, pp. 117–18, 121.

11. Cooper, (ed.), *Wentworth Papers*, pp. 152–7.

12. A. W. Johnson, (ed.), *The Fairfax Correspondence*, vol. I, p. 7.

13. Cliffe, *Yorkshire Gentry*, pp. 295–303; Wedgwood, *Wentworth*, pp. 103–15.

14. Cliffe, *Yorkshire Gentry*, pp. 303–28.

15. T. G. Barnes, *Somerset 1625–1640* (1961), pp. 36–8, 282–7; E. Farnham, 'The Somerset Election of 1614', *EHR*, 46 (1931), 579–99; Hirst, *Representative of the People?*, p. 259.

16. Russell, *Parliaments and English Politics*, pp. 6, 20, 55, 102, 169–70, 325, 359, 407.

17. T. G. Barnes, 'County Politics and a Puritan Cause Célèbre: Somerset Churchales 1633', *TRHS*, 5th ser., 9 (1959), 103–22.

18. Barnes, *Somerset 1625–1640*, pp. 165–7, 216–43, 261–9; D. Underdown, *Somerset in the Civil War and Interregnum* (Newton Abbot, 1973), p. 19.

19. T. G. Barnes, (ed.), *Somerset Assize Orders 1629–1680*, Somerset Record Society, 95 (1959), pp. 60–1; *TRHS*, 5th ser., 9 (1959) 120.

20. P. Clark, *English Provincial Society from the Reformation to the Revolution* (1977), pp. 328–47, 357–61, 373–82; P. Clark, 'Thomas Scot and the Growth of Urban Opposition to the Early Stuart Regime', *HJ*, 21 (1978), 1–26.

21. Everitt, *Community of Kent*, pp. 56–74; F. W. Jessup, *Sir Roger Twysden* (1965), pp. 137–42.

22. D. Hirst, 'The Defection of Sir Edward Dering 1640–1641', *HJ*, 15 (1972), 198–200; W. M. Lamont, *Godly Rule* (1969), pp. 83–91; Clark, *English Provincial Society*, pp. 384–6.

23. For this period see my *Outbreak*, pp. 255–6, 307–8.

24. Underdown, *Somerset in the Civil War*, p. 241; Hirst, *Representative of the People?*, pp. 16, 115, 217; J. K. Gruenfelder, 'Dorsetshire Elections 1604–1640', *Albion*, 10 (1978), 2–3, 5, 13.

25. BL Loan MS 29/202. I am grateful to Ms Myra Rifkin for drawing my attention to these letters.

26. M. D. G. Wanklyn, Landed Society and Allegiance in Cheshire and Shropshire in the First Civil War (Manchester Ph.D. 1976), p. 71; P. Lake, 'The Collection of Ship Money in Cheshire during the 1630s: A Case Study of Relations between Central and Local Government', *Northern History*, 17 (1981), 44–71. See also J. S. Morrill, *Cheshire 1630–1660*, pp. 16, 32–3; J. S. Morrill, 'The Northern Gentry and the Great Rebellion', *Northern History*, 15 (1979), 73n.

27. R. W. Ketton-Cremér, *Norfolk in the Civil War* (1969), pp. 107–13; C. Holmes, *The Eastern Association in the English Civil War* (1974), pp. 24–5.

28. Hirst, *Representative of the People?*, pp. 121, 180, 219, 224, 259n; Hassell Smith, *County and Court*, pp. 333–6.

29. See my *Sussex*, pp. 241–3, 248.

30. *CSPD 1639–40*, pp. 580–2; Reinmuth, *Early Stuart Studies*, pp. 209, 211, 227–8; Keeler, *The Long Parliament*, pp. 350–1.

31. Everitt, *Suffolk*, pp. 12–20, 37; P. Seaver, 'Community Control and Puritan Politics in Elizabethan Suffolk' *Albion*, 9 (1977), 297–315.

32. Holmes, *Eastern Association*, pp. 18, 22–3; T. Carlyle, *Critical and Miscellaneous Essays* (1899) vol. IV, p. 332; Hirst, *Representative of the People?*, p. 148.

33. See for instance Kent RO, Sackville MS ON 139: Warwick to Earl of Middlesex, 22 April 1622. I am grateful to Professor Conrad Russell for this reference.

34. Holmes, *Eastern Association*, pp. 20–2; V. A. Rowe, 'Robert, Second Earl of Warwick and the Payment of Ship Money in Essex', *Transactions of the Essex Archaeological Society*, I (1962), 160–3; B. Donagan, 'The Clerical Patronage of Robert Rich, Second Earl of Warwick 1619–42', *Proceedings of the American Philosophical Society*, 120 (1976), 411.

35. *CSPD 1639–40*, pp. 608–9; J. B. Crumett, The Lay Peers in Parliament 1640–1644 (University of Manchester Ph.D. 1970), pp. 145–7.

36. *HMC 7th Report*, Appendix (Lowndes MSS), p. 549.

37. *CSPD 1640–1*, p. 113; Hughes, 'Politics, Society and Civil War', pp. 196–220.

38. Hirst, *Representative of the People?*, p. 217.

39. W. H. Summers, 'Some Documents in the State Papers relating to Beaconsfield', *Records of Bucks*, 7 (1892–6), 97–112.

40. Keeler, *Long Parliament*, p. 35; L. O. J. Boynton, *The Elizabethan Militia* (1967) pp. 111–15; A. M. Johnson, 'Buckinghamshire 1640–1660: A Study in County Politics', (University of Wales, M.A. 1963), pp. 35–44.

41. W. J. Sheils, *The Puritans in the Diocese of Peterborough 1558–1610*, Northamptonshire Record Society, 30 (1979).

42. *CSPD 1639–40*, p. 587.

43. *CSPD 1637–8*, pp. 535–6; *CSPD 1640*, p. 7; Keeler, *Long Parliament*, p. 57; Hirst, *Representative of the People?*, pp. 151–2, 183; Reinmuth, *Early Stuart Studies*, p. 226; Cope, *Life of a Public Man*, p. 171.

44. Hassell Smith, *County and Court*, pp. 337–8.

45. Gordon, 'Collection of Ship Money', *TRHS*, 3rd. ser., 4 (1910), 158.

46. *CSPD 1640*, pp. 7, 164; Hirst, *Representative of the People?*, p. 183; Gordon, 'Collection of Ship Money', *TRHS*, 3rd. ser., 4 (1910), 159; Keeler, *Long Parliament*, p. 186.

47. C. G. Durston, 'Berkshire and its County Gentry 1625–1649' (University of Reading Ph.D. 1977), pp. 88–124.

48. *CSPD 1640*, pp. 466–7.

49. Wiltshire Archaeological Society Museum, Devizes, Hungerford MSS, II, 281; Keeler, *Long Parliament*, pp. 48–50, 69–71; Gordon, 'Collection of Ship Money', *TRHS*, 3rd. ser., 4 (1910), 161.

50. Russell, *Parliaments and English Politics*, pp. 17–18.

51. Coate, *Cornwall* pp. 20–5; E. A. Andriette, *Devon and Exeter in the Civil War* (1971), pp. 24–42.

52. Holmes, *Seventeenth-Century Lincolnshire*, pp. 103–38; E. S. Cope, (ed.), *Proceedings of the Short Parliament of 1640*, Camden Society, 4th ser., 19 (1977), p. 228.

53. M. James, *Family, Lineage and Civil Society* (1974), pp. 168–75.

54. R. Howell, *Newcastle-upon-Tyne and the Puritan Revolution* (1967), pp. 124–5.

55. D.P. Carter, The Exact Militia in Lancashire 1625–1640', *Northern*

*History*, 11 (1976 for 1975), 102, 105–6.

56. D. H. Pennington, 'County and Country: Staffordshire in Civil War Politics', *North Staffordshire Journal of Field Studies*, 6 (1966), p. 14; J. E. Neale, *The Elizabethan House of Commons* (1963), pp. 16–17.

57. Lloyd, *Gentry of South West Wales* (1968), pp. 120, 211.

58. Keeler, *Long Parliament*, pp. 40–1, 59–60, 62–3, 69; T. T. Lewis, (ed.), *Letters of Lady Brilliana Harley*, Camden Society, 51 (1853), p. 86; *HMC Coke MSS*, III, pp. 138–41.

59. Hirst, *Representative of the People?*, pp. 147–8.

60. Morrill, *Cheshire*, pp. 34–5.

61. Barnes in *TRHS*, 5th ser., 9 (1959), p. 122.

# Notes on Contributors

HOWARD TOMLINSON is Head of History at Wellington College, Berkshire. He was formerly a student at Bedford College, University of London, and at Reading University, and won the Julian S. Corbett prize in naval history and the Alexander Prize. He is the author of *Guns and Government: the Ordnance Office Under the Later Stuarts* and is at present working on a calendar of Pepys's Admiralty letters for the Navy Records Society.

SIMON ADAMS is a lecturer in History at the University of Strathclyde. He was educated at Trinity School (New York), Haverford College, Harvard and Oxford, and during 1973–5 he held a research fellowship at the University College of North Wales. He has published several articles on aspects of Elizabethan and early Stuart politics and foreign policy and is now completing a book on *The Protestant Cause: Puritanism, Foreign Policy and English Politics, 1585–1630*.

PATRICK COLLINSON is Professor of History at the University of Kent at Canterbury. He was formerly Professor of History at the University of Sydney, Ford's Lecturer at Oxford, 1979, and Birkbeck Lecturer at Cambridge, 1981 and was Elected Fellow of the British Academy, 1982. He is the author of *The Elizabethan Puritan Movement; Archbishop Grindal;* and *The Religion of Protestants: The Church in English Society, 1559–1625*.

ANTHONY FLETCHER is Senior Lecturer in History at the University of Sheffield. He is the author of *Tudor Rebellions; A County Community in Peace and War: Sussex 1600–1660* and *The Outbreak of the English Civil War*. At present he is working on a study of the enforcement of policy and local government 1603–1714 and on the Protectorate of Oliver Cromwell.

CONRAD RUSSELL is Professor of History at Yale University, USA. He was formerly Domus Senior Scholar at Merton College, Oxford and Assistant Lecturer, Lecturer and Reader at Bedford College, University of London. His publications include: *The Crisis of Parliaments: English History 1509–1660; The Origins of the English Civil War* (ed.); and *Parliaments and English Politics 1621–1629*. He is at present working on a biography of John Pym; Parliaments and English Politics 1640–2, and on a volume in the New Oxford *History of England*, to cover 1603–43.

KEVIN SHARPE is a lecturer in History at the University of Southampton. He was formerly an undergraduate at St Catherine's College, Oxford, Hayward Research Fellow at Oriel College, Oxford, and Fellow at the Institute of Advanced Studies, Princeton, USA. His publications include *Sir Robert Cotton, 1586–1631: History and Politics in Early Modern England* and *Faction and Parliament: Essays on Early Stuart History* (ed.). At present he is working on a study of the Personal Rule of Charles I.

DAVID THOMAS is Assistant Keeper of Public Records at the PRO, in charge of the Conservation Department. He was formerly an undergraduate and postgraduate at Bedford College, University of London. He has in preparation a book on crown finance, 1603–41.

# Index

## DATE DUE

| | | | |
|---|---|---|---|
| | | | |
| | | | |
| | | | |
| | | | |
| | | | |
| | | | |
| | | | |
| | | | |
| | | | |
| | | | |
| | | | |
| | | | |
| | | | |
| | | | |
| | | | |
| | | | |
| | | | |
| | | | |
| | | | |

HIGHSMITH #45230

Printed
in USA